MW00615064

The Living Pulpit

The Living Pulpit

Sermons
That Illustrate Preaching in the
Stone-Campbell Movement
1968-2018

Mary Alice Mulligan
General Editor

Ronald Allen   Tim Sensing
Dave Bland   Bruce Shields
David Fleer   Casey Sigmon
Joseph Grana II   Richard Voelz
Contributing Editors

CBP®
ST. LOUIS, MISSOURI

Copyright ©2018 by Mary Alice Mulligan and Ronald Allen.
All rights reserved. For permission to reuse content, please contact Copyright Clearance Center, 222 Rosewood Drive, Danvers, MA 01923, (978) 750-8400, www.copyright.com.

Scripture quotations marked NRSV are from are from the *New Revised Standard Version Bible,* copyright 1989, Division of Christian Education of the National Council of the Churches of Christ in the United States of America. Used by permission. All rights reserved.

Quotations marked GN are from *Good News Bible (Today's English Version,* Second Edition). Copyright © 1992 American Bible Society. All rights reserved.

Quotations marked ASV are from the *American Standard Version,* which is in the public domain.

Those quotations marked RSV are from the *Revised Standard Version of the Bible,* copyright 1952, [2nd edition, 1971] by the Division of Christian Education of the National Council of the Churches of Christ in the United States of America. Used by permission. All rights reserved.

Quotations marked KJV are from the *King James Version.*

Scripture quotations marked AMP are taken from the Amplified® Bible (AMP), Copyright © 2015 by The Lockman Foundation. Used by permission. www. Lockman.org.

Quotations marked ESV are from *The ESV*® *Bible* (The Holy Bible, English Standard Version®). ESV® Text Edition: 2016. Copyright © 2001 by Crossway, a publishing ministry of Good News Publishers.

Quotations marked NIRV are from the *New International Reader's Version,* copyright © 1995, 1996, 1998, 2014 by Biblica, Inc.®. Used by permission. All rights reserved worldwide.

Scripture quotations marked NLT are taken from the *Holy Bible,* New Living Translation, copyright © 1996. Used by permission of Tyndale House Publishers, Inc., Wheaton, Illinois 60189, U.S.A. All rights reserved.

Scripture quotations marked NIV are taken from the HOLY BIBLE, NEW INTERNATIONAL VERSION®. NIV®. Copyright © 1973, 1978, 1984 by International Bible Society. Used by permission of Zondervan Publishing House. All rights reserved.

Scripture quotations marked NKJV are taken from the *New King James Version.* Copyright © 1979, 1980, 1982 by Thomas Nelson, Inc. Used by permission. All rights reserved.

Biblical quotations marked REB are from *The Revised English Bible* copyright © Oxford University Press and Cambridge University Press 1989.

Quotations marked TNIV are from Today's New International Version Bible, published in 2005 by Zondervan. Copyright @2005 Biblica, no longer in print.

Cover art and design: Jesse Turri

ChalicePress.com

Paperback: 9780827221857   EPUB: 9780827221864   EPDF: 9780827221871
Hardcover: 9780827221888

Printed in the United States of America.

Contents

Section Three: Christian Church (Disciples of Christ)

Preface

For much of the twentieth century, the churches in the three streams of the Stone-Campbell movement often kept their distance from each other, relating warily or even with hostility. However, over the past generation a spirit of rediscovery and reconciliation has taken root. This volume comes from that spirit as it brings together sermons from the three streams of the Stone-Campbell movement–the Churches of Christ, the Christian Churches/Churches of Christ, and the Christian Church (Disciples of Christ). Bruce Shields explains the nature and purpose of this book in relationship to our common heritage and to the three streams in the "Introduction to the Volume: Preaching in the Stone-Campbell Movement 1968–2018" (below).

The sermons in this volume are not considered "best" sermons. The editors view them as "typical" of the preaching that takes place in various preaching venues in the three streams–congregations, lectureships, meetings, conventions, and assemblies.

The sermons from preachers in each stream are presented in the approximate chronological order in which they were preached. Thus, sermons from early in the era appear first, from the middle of the second half of the twentieth century in the middle of the sermons, and the sermons from the latter part of the period at the ends of each section.

Many preachers today make use of electronic media in preaching, such as projections on a big screen. We indicate the presence of such media in this book by the use of brackets and the term "Project," and include a short description of the projection, as in [Project: Ephesians 2:9]. When ellipses occur in the sermons, they indicate notations in the preacher's manuscript and not deleted material, unless otherwise noted in the sermon introductory piece.

Where the preacher has given a specific biblical passage or passages as basic to the sermon, we cite that biblical material under the title of the sermon. While all the sermons deal with the Bible, not all preachers list a biblical text or texts at the outset of the sermon as the basis or bases for the message. In the latter cases, we simply give the title to the sermons with the preachers referring to biblical passages within the messages. In the introduction to each sermon, the editors indicate the primary Bible translation the preacher quotes. Other translations used within the sermon are indicated in parentheses. Places where preachers paraphrase Scripture are also noted in parentheses.

Joseph R. Jeter Jr., Granville T. Walker and Earline Walker Professor of Preaching Emeritus at Brite Divinity School conceived this project.

Several Stone-Campbell scholars of preaching who meet at the Academy of Homiletics informally became the contributing editors listed on the title page. The scholars in each stream selected 13 sermons typical of their stream and wrote the interpretive essays orienting readers to their stream. Bruce Shields prepared the Introduction to the book. Mary Alice Mulligan served as General Editor.

The editors express gratitude to the Oreon E. Scott Foundation for a generous grant that made possible the publication of this book, and to Matthew Myer Boulton and Verity Jones of Christian Theological Seminary–President and Executive Vice-President, respectively–for supporting this project. Several of the editors also helped underwrite publication.

The Living Pulpit 2018 is dedicated to Professor Joseph R. Jeter Jr., who embodies the core emphases of our movement in his own preaching, scholarship, and person–salvation by grace, restoring the vitality of the church with the spirit of the Gospels and Letters, and witnessing to the ecumenical unity of the church.

We send this volume into the churches with the prayer that it will contribute to the mutual respect, cooperation, and reconciliation at work across our movement.

Introduction to the Volume: Preaching in the Stone-Campbell Movement 1968–2018

by Bruce Shields

The book before you is the fourth in a series of collections of representative sermons preached among congregations related to the Stone-Campbell Movement. The first was published in 1868, about 60 years after Thomas Campbell's *Declaration and Address* was printed, so it surveys the earliest preaching of the reformation begun by Barton Stone and Thomas and Alexander Campbell. William Thomas Moore edited that collection and also the second one in 1918.[1] The third was edited by Hunter Beckelhymer and published in 1969 under the title, *The Vital Pulpit of the Christian Church*.[2] Since each of these collections surveys about 50 years of preaching, it is time for another. Our decision to include the three streams of the movement necessitated a broad-based editorial committee. You can find our names elsewhere in the book.

In any endeavor such as this, readers will think of preachers who are not represented here. To present a balanced picture, we had to limit each of the three streams of the movement to 13 preachers. Some preachers we contacted turned down our invitation for one reason or another, but we are convinced that those we feature on these pages present a good representation of the movement and the half-century that we are studying.

When the editorial committee commissioned me to write this essay, I began to think of the changes I have lived through. Born when my parents and grandparents were just getting over World War I and the Great Depression that followed it, I was introduced to a society preparing to fight a second world war. Lightweight airplanes had been used in the first war for reconnaissance, but now big ones were bombing cities and eventually carrying an atomic bomb to Hiroshima and then, on my eighth birthday, to Nagasaki. As I grew toward adulthood, the war was in Korea, then in early adulthood in Vietnam. As I write this, war is being waged by drones controlled from thousands of miles distant from the battlefield. Computers have developed in sophistication as they have become ever smaller. I recall wooden telephones screwed to walls that we cranked before giving a number to an operator. Now I carry a computerized phone in my pocket. The upcoming generation of preachers never knew a society without the ubiquitous computer and smartphone, yet preaching continues. It might be at a drive-in church or in a warehouse-type building, or even in a Gothic cathedral, but it is still somebody talking to somebody else, as it has been for two millennia and more.

Our book listens to preaching in the Stone-Campbell Movement—the Christian Church (Disciples of Christ), Churches of Christ, and Christian Churches/Churches of Christ—in the period beginning about 1968 and ending around 2018. This period saw some rather radical changes in the world, including the world of homiletics, both as preaching was taught in colleges and seminaries and as it was practiced in local congregations. This was especially the case in North America. The 1960s were years of ferment in many areas of our society. This was a decade of anti-war demonstrations, racial unrest, and general questioning of authority. The generation of people born soon after the close of World War II was not satisfied with the status quo, and they were generally suspicious of authorities. For these so-called "Baby Boomers," the action was in the streets, with young people marching, sitting in, or otherwise demonstrating for one cause or another. Professors of preaching were driven to offer courses on the relevance of preaching, because many students saw sermons as totally out of touch with where the real action was.

Yes, many people questioned whether or not preaching would survive the century. Into this quagmire came a book by Fred Craddock (who was a lifelong member of the Stone-Campbell Movement) titled *As One Without Authority*.[3] Craddock had prepared to teach New Testament, but when called to teach both New Testament *and* preaching at the Graduate Seminary of Phillips University, he had to do some hard thinking about preaching. Until that time, preaching had followed the template of developing a proposition with three or four points of analysis and argument and a conclusion to apply the proposition to life. Illustrations and poems seasoned the presentation, but the basic form was argumentation. Preachers were often educated to think and present in the same way lawyers were. They were "preaching for a verdict."[4] This meant that they were passing on information from a position of authority—what Dr. Paul Scherer liked to characterize as "eight feet above criticism."

Craddock's education in New Testament and his personal ability to tell stories (he credits his father for this[5]) led him in a different direction. He was already familiar with the so-called "new hermeneutic" that was flowering in Europe and reaching the shores of North America. It appeared to be time for a matching "new homiletic." He recognized that seminary students were now spending time in the relatively new disciplines of pastoral psychology and congregational management or leadership.[6] These fledgling specialties were emphasizing dialogue and conversation as tools in the minister's workshop. Preaching, on the other hand, was still seen as a monologue, with a few exceptions in which preachers were experimenting with staged dialogue. Newly minted preachers were feeling the tension. The practice of preaching was in search of new ways to practice.

Therefore, when *As One Without Authority* was published in 1971, its intended readership was ready. The response from reviewers was not unanimously positive, but it was soon the talk of the homiletics community. It was a plea for appreciation of the spoken word as not just a neutral conveyance of information, but rather as a communion of persons, including the person of God. It insisted that the preacher take seriously the Scriptures as speaking first to the preacher and then to the congregation. And it reminded the preacher that the divine word is primarily speech, and must be spoken to accomplish its purpose.[7]

Craddock urged a switch from deductive presentation of statements of general truth with an application at the end to inductive description from start to finish, permitting the hearer, who is now involved in the discovery of truth, to make application to her or his life. This paragraph represents his thinking:

> The plain fact of the matter is that we are seeking to communicate with people whose experiences are concrete. Everyone lives inductively, not deductively. No farmer deals with the problem of calfhood, only with the calf. The woman in the kitchen is not occupied with the culinary arts in general but with a particular roast or cake. The wood craftsman is hardly able to discuss intelligently the topic of "chairness," but is a master with a chair. We will speak of the sun rising and setting long after everyone knows better. The minister says, "All people are mortal," and meets drowsy agreement; he announces that "Mr. Brown's son is dying," and the church becomes the church.[8]

This emphasis on pragmatics instead of generalities Craddock sees as the way the Christian Scriptures come to us. His insistence that each sermon should be based on a careful study of one or more biblical texts is the foundation of his homiletic. Whether the preacher follows the guidance of a lectionary or chooses his or her own texts to study, the sermon should find its foundation and often its form in the text. Quite often Craddock invited the congregation to join him in an investigation of a text, asking questions and dealing with puzzling issues. Overall, Craddock called for inductive preparatory study and inductive presentation, which led to mutual discovery of biblical meaning for life. His influence on preaching is so deep and broad that we have elected to feature one of his sermons to stand alone in this collection.

Craddock's book was followed by a flood of books on preaching, after several decades of drought. Homiletics was interesting once more.

Churches' involvement in social issues was growing. Meanwhile preachers saw again that the sermon could instruct, motivate, and inspire action on the street. European American churches were learning what African American churches had known for decades: that preaching is an important influence in the congregation. Consider the influence of the preaching of Dr. Martin Luther King Jr. during the civil rights struggle. Following Craddock's model, when the congregation is encouraged to participate in the unfolding of the sermon and sometimes even to draw their own conclusions, the preacher catches their interest and sends them back into the world with an important discovery.

As you read the sermons in this volume, you will note the change of the shape of sermons between preachers educated before 1975 and those educated more recently. Listen to the increase in narrative content and the decrease in analysis and argument. Watch how the sermon moves ever forward toward a destination without making the roadmap obvious. Note how younger preachers invite the listener to participate in the sermonic process instead of just sitting passively taking in information. Listen also to an increase in the amount of Scripture quoted and referred to in the sermons.[9] Perhaps most important, watch how you are positioned in relation to the sermon. By that, I mean, Are you in it as a participant as it unfolds, or are you outside it as a receiver of information?

This newer way, which is very similar to how Jesus used parables in his preaching, we should not see as demeaning the older way. Communication styles change as listeners change. In the 19th century people were accustomed to listening intently to orations that often lasted an hour or more. Many people who heard Lincoln's address at Gettysburg went away disappointed. They considered it a flop because it was so different from other speeches of the time—even others of that day. It was over before most people were ready to listen. Yet today we look at it as a masterpiece of human communication. In the same way, people who listened to sermons in the first half of the twentieth century were accustomed to proposition, analysis, and proofs, with an application tacked on at the end. However, the effect of having television sets in our living rooms changed our patterns of receiving communication. Eugene Lowry recognized this connection, and in his book, *The Homiletical Plot,* he lays out a pattern for sermons that follows the format of the TV mystery show.[10]

The template of the Sunday morning sermon changed ever so slowly, but change it did. Not only did the form change, but also even the length of sermons. In contrast to the 20-minute sermon many of us professors insisted on in preaching classes, some congregations are now willing to pay attention for 45 minutes or more. I recall listening to Garrison Keillor's "A Prairie Home Companion" for the first time and realizing that my bemoaning the ever-briefer attention spans of late–twentieth-century people was overblown. People would sit for two hours listening to a man spin yarns over the radio about the fictional town of Lake Wobegone, and that meant a preacher should be able to hold their attention for 45 minutes if what the sermon communicated was real life, and not vacuous metaphysics.

So preaching has changed during these 50 years, just as it has in other time spans. It adjusts as the way people hear changes, and if it doesn't, it won't be heard. You will note also transformations in the preachers. Perhaps the most momentous difference is the inclusion in this volume of a number of female preachers. Their contributions mark another important shift in the Stone-Campbell Movement. We recognize that there remains resistance in some quarters to women in congregational leadership, but that resistance appears to continue to weaken as we go to print.

Momentous changes in the world and in the church, accompanied by important renovations in preaching during these last 50 years, are all reflected in this collection of sermons. We offer them to the movement and to the church in general as instruction in how communication changes and as a challenge to the upcoming generation of preachers to let the word go forth boldly. Preaching styles have varied and changed many times over the centuries, and they will again. Preachers should keep in mind the advice of Fred Craddock: "The goal is not to get something said, but to get something heard."[11]

A Sermon Acknowledging the Importance of Fred B. Craddock to Preaching in the Stone-Campbell Movement

In the Introduction, Bruce Shields sets out the importance of the work of Fred B. Craddock to the larger world of preaching. In addition, Craddock probably traveled in the three streams of the Stone-Campbell Movement more than any other ecclesial leader from 1968 to 2018. He was a white man who spoke comfortably in congregations of diverse racial ethnicities. His ecumenicity of spirit was especially unusual in the early years of our period, and that contributed to the growing rapprochement among the streams. In many ways, he embodied the best of our movement's commitment to the Scriptures and the vision of Christian unity. It seems appropriate to include his sermon in the broad flow of our movement rather than within one stream. Craddock paraphrases Scripture throughout the sermon.

"Attending a Baptism"[1]
Matthew 3:13–17

Our Scripture text for today invites us to attend a baptism. I do not have to tell this group how important baptism is. In the Gospel of Matthew, from which our text comes, the story begins with baptism, John baptizing in the river Jordan, and ends with baptism. The final words of Jesus at the end of Matthew are, "Go into all the world and make disciples, baptizing them in the name of the Father and the Son and the Holy Spirit, teaching them to observe everything I have commanded you. And, lo, I will be with you always, to the end of the age."

As important as baptism is, I do not have any instructions for how you are to behave during one, probably because every significant occasion tends to create its own atmosphere and itself modifies the behavior of people in appropriate ways. If you attend a funeral, say, even though it may be the first funeral you have ever attended, you need no instruction. Beforehand, people are standing around talking about everything under the sun.

"Did you have any pipes that burst?"

"Yeah, yeah. My kitchen floor was all wet and everything."

"Has Lucille had her baby?"

"Yeah, yeah, she had it Thursday."

"Really? What is it, a boy or a girl?"

"A girl."

"How many does that make now? Is that five?"

"No, that's her sixth."

"Why do they keep having them? They can't feed the ones they have. Why is it people that are poor seem to have the most kids?"

"Did your husband go deer hunting?"

"Yeah, yeah, didn't get anything–never does–but he still thinks he's the big hunter."

"Been awfully cold. Did it kill the rest of your collards, or did you bring them in?

"Well, I have about two messes in the refrigerator, but…"

And then everything stops when the widow comes in–this woman who now must face life without her husband–and the children, who overnight must grow up and help their mother without a father. You do not need instruction on how to behave. The occasion modifies and sweetens your disposition appropriate to the occasion.

The same thing is true at a wedding. Before a wedding begins, people are laughing and talking, exchanging bad jokes and stale talk and this and that. What are they discussing? Shaving cream all over the windshield and tying tin cans to the bumper and all that kind of stuff. But then the bride comes down the aisle and the nervous groom looks up the aisle hoping he will not faint, trying to keep his eye on her, and then they fold themselves together before the minister and the words begin: "Will you, in sickness and in health, poverty and wealth, forsaking everybody else, keep yourself only unto her as long as you both shall live?" You do not need instructions. The occasion modifies the behavior.

It is like children when great-grandmother comes. She is so old and has suffered so much. The children come in laughing from playing outside, and suddenly they see her and they grow quiet. They are in awe. They want to touch her; they want to hear her. She is so old, has experienced so much, and you do not have to say, "Now children, this is the way you behave around your great-grandmother…' They know.

It is the same way with a baptism. I know before a baptism that some people are kind of silly, laughing and talking and doing this and that. It is nervousness, really, but then when the minister says, "I baptize you in the name of the Father and the Son and the Holy Spirit," anyone who is not hushed into the sacredness of that moment is shallow.

So I have no instruction on how to behave as we attend a baptism. The baptism we will attend is the baptism of Jesus of Nazareth. That is a bit surprising, because of all people the one who should be exempt from baptism is Jesus. Why should he not stand high on the bank and watch the others? Why should he not let all the others come for baptism, those who need a second chance, those who messed it up, those who have waded out so deep into trouble that going across and going back is all the same? Let the people who have drifted so far from mother's prayers and father's instruction that nobody can help them, let them come. Let the people whose lives are just a tangle of bad relationships, who have messed everything up and out of ambition and greed think they are going everywhere when they are actually just circling the parking lot going nowhere, the people who are rich in things and poor in soul, let them come. But Jesus? Why is Jesus here? That is what John says: "Jesus, you should baptize *me*. I should not be baptizing you."

And Jesus replies, "Leave it alone, John. It is appropriate to do God's will. Let us do it."

So Jesus presents himself for baptism. He is 30 years old. Why is he coming now? We can speculate. In Israel, anyone entering public life did so at age 30. Maybe that's reason enough; I do not know. Maybe in the synagogue, listening to the rabbi read the Scripture while others are dozing off, something strikes him and says, "That's it–now!" Maybe in the afternoons after work in the carpenter shop, Jesus goes for long walks and communes with God and there is this stirring within him. Maybe he remembers something he saw when he was a teenager south of Nazareth. The Romans came in and gathered up some of the men of the town and strung them up on poles just to warn the people that they did not want any trouble, and there is this burning desire for justice and fairness. Maybe that is it. I do not know. Maybe it was his mother's prayers. Or, maybe he still remembers when he was twelve years old in the temple, saying, "I have to be in my Father's house."

Why now? That's a good question. I do not have an answer, but it is a good question. It is a good question if somebody 60 years old comes. Why now? It is a good question if someone 12 years old comes, stays after church, wants to say something, awkwardly stands on one foot and then the other, and finally asks, "Uh, can I be baptized?"

"You want to be baptized?"

"I want to be baptized."

"Have you been thinking about this very long?"

"Ever since I was little."

"Well, how old are you now?"

"12."

"And you have been thinking about this since you were little?"

"Yes"

"Have you talked to your folks about it?"

"Well, I mentioned it once to my mother. I don't talk to Dad much about this sort of thing."

"Well, what did your mother say?"

"She said to talk to you."

"Okay, let's talk about it. Why do you want to be baptized? Why now, why you, now?"

"I don't know."

You do not know the stirring of the Spirit of God. John says you do not know whence it comes or whither it goes; you hear the sound of it and you say, "Whew!" The wind. You did not see the wind. There is a tree standing straight and tall and proud, and then you see that tree go over, bending and touching its top to the ground, and you say, "What in the world?" It is the wind. You did not see the wind, but you saw the tree bend. And I saw a person proud and independent and arrogant, bent. What did that? The Spirit of God. I saw a ship, a sailing boat out on the lake, just hanging out there, derelict, rocking, rocking, with its sails hanging limp like they were dead. Suddenly the sails filled and the boat began to knife its way through the water, and I say, "What was that?" You say it was the wind. Did you see the wind? I didn't see the wind. How do you know? Well, look at it.

Just so, you have seen it in life. A person works six months here, six months there, moves somewhere else and does a little of this and a little of that. Then, suddenly, a transformation. Now this person has a purpose, a goal in life, and what was that? You do not know. You do not really know why now, or why this, or what happened.

All I know is this: One day, Jesus folded his carpenter's apron, having shaken the shavings from it, put it on the bench, left the shop, and went to the house and told his mother and brothers and sisters goodbye. He made his way through the grain fields of Ezdralon, down through the dark valley of the gap of Jezreel, and presented himself to John for baptism. This was God's will.

On that occasion, we learned a great deal about Jesus. A voice said, "This is my son." No question about it. *This is my son.* What does that mean? The line is a quotation from Psalm 2. It was spoken on the occasion of the crowning of the king of Israel, and now it is quoted at Jesus' baptism. He is now king. What does it mean that he is God's Son? Does he go around now in a chariot with silk cushions and wear a crown and say kingly things and elevate himself above the common folk, saying "Don't touch me—I am the Son of God. I am the king and I say kingly things and make pronouncements? Now I am going to the palace and have a nap and a banquet"?

The last part of the quotation—"My Son, my beloved, in whom my soul takes pleasure"—do you know what that is? It is a phrase from Isaiah 42. It is a line from the description of the suffering servant of God, the one who gives his life. It means touching, loving, going, doing, caring for people. *Here is my Son, the servant.* And so it was. Still wet from his baptism, Jesus left the Jordan and went about God's business. Every crying person, every brokenhearted person, every hungry person, every diseased person, every alienated person, every suffering person was his business. I am the king? I am the Son of God? Oh, no, no, no, no. What this means is, God's business is my business. And what is God's business? To serve the needs of every human being. He is a servant. Did you know that? Well, of course you knew. He actually knelt down and washed people's feet. The Son of God washed feet.

Luther said, " 'Remember your baptism?" How can people do that? In Luther's church, most of the baptisms were of infants. They were brought by their mothers and fathers and they were baptized. So how could they remember their baptisms? Luther knew that when they became 12 and 13 they would be confirmed in the church and they would claim their baptisms. "Yes," they would say, "I accept my baptism. I remember my baptism." So Luther wanted to know, "Do you remember your baptism?" Why did Luther say that? To make you feel guilty? "Aha! You've strayed from your baptism." No, no. Every one of us strays from our baptism, forgets our baptism, denies our baptism. Every one of us. Show me a bird who can say, "I look like my song." None of us can do that. But what Luther had in mind was this: Remember your baptism by claiming yourself to be a child of God and by going about God's business—serving other people.

In southwest Oklahoma, near the Washita Creek where Black Kettle and most of the women and children of his little tribe were massacred by General Custer's army when they swept down in the early morning hours on those poor people, a little community is named for the general: Custer City. My wife, Nettie, and I ministered there for three years. The population was about 450 on a good day. There were four churches: a Methodist church, a Baptist church, a Nazarene church, and a Christian church. Each had its share of the population, and on Wednesday nights and Sundays, each church had a small collection of young people. The attendance rose and fell according to the weather and whether it was time to harvest the wheat.

The best and most consistent attendance in town, however, was at the little cafe where all the pickup trucks were parked and all the men were inside discussing the weather and the cattle and the wheat bugs and the hail and the wind and whether we were going to have a crop, while their wives and sons and daughters were in one of those four churches. The churches had good attendance and poor attendance, but that cafe had consistently good attendance—better attendance than some of the churches. Men were always there.

Once in a while they would lose a member there at the cafe because his wife finally got to him, or maybe his kids did. So you would see him go off sheepishly to one of the churches. But the men at the cafe still felt that they were the biggest and strongest group in town, and so they met on Wednesdays and Sundays and every other day to discuss the weather and such. They were not bad men. Indeed, they were good men, family men, hardworking men. The patron saint of the group at the cafe was Frank.

Frank was 77 years old when I met him. He was a good man, a strong man, a pioneer, a rancher, a farmer, and a cattleman. He had been born in a sod house, and he had prospered. He had his credentials, and all the men there at the cafe considered him their patron saint. "Ha ha," they said. "Old Frank will never go to church."

One day I met Frank on the street, and he knew I was a preacher. It has never been my custom to accost people in the name of Jesus, so I just shook hands and visited with Frank. Then he took the offensive. He said, "I work hard and I take care of my family and I mind my own business." He said that as far as he was concerned, everything else is fluff. He was telling me, "Leave me alone; I'm not a prospect."

So I did not bother Frank. That is why I was surprised, indeed the church was surprised and the whole town was surprised and the men at the cafe church were absolutely bumfuzzled, when old Frank, 77 years old, presented himself before me one Sunday morning for baptism. I baptized Frank. Some in the community said that Frank must be sick, said he must be scared to meet his maker. Some said, "He's got heart trouble, going up to be baptized. I never thought old Frank would do that, but I guess when you get scared..." There were all kinds of stories. But this is the way Frank told it to me. We were talking the day after his baptism and I said, "Frank, do you remember that little saying you used to give me so much? 'I work hard, I take care of my family, and I mind my own business'?"

He said, "Yeah, I remember. I said that a lot."

"Do you still say that?" I asked.

"Yes," he said.

"Then what's the difference?"

He said, "I didn't know then what my business was."

Frank discovered what his business was. It was to serve human need. So I baptized Frank. I raised my hand and said in the presence of those who gathered, "Upon your confession of faith in Jesus Christ and in obedience to his command, I baptize you in the name of the Father, the Son, and the Holy Spirit. Amen."

Do you remember that? Do you remember that?

SECTION ONE

CHURCHES OF CHRIST

Orientation to Preaching in the Churches of Christ 1968-2018

by Tim Sensing

According to Flavil Yeakley, among the 13,000 congregations of the Churches of Christ in the United States, 45 percent have fewer than 50 members, and more than 70 percent have fewer than 100 members.[1] Most churches are concentrated in the South. Of the 30 largest churches, the northernmost is in Hendersonville, Tennessee, and the westernmost is in Lubbock, Texas.[2]

Lynn Anderson notes that "prior to the 1960s preaching among Churches of Christ drew heavily from Acts and the Epistles, and tended toward the topical and doctrinal. The 60s brought 'the Jesus movement' to the national religious scene, and with it, a renewed focus on preaching the Gospels among many in Churches of Christ. This was also followed by an upsurge in expository preaching."[3] Whether topical, doctrinal, or expository, biblical studies governed preaching trends in Churches of Christ. An emphasis on an exact historical-exegetical tradition in our churches and seminaries stressed getting the text correct by stating plainly what the text meant. All a preacher needed was to replicate the exegesis of the text found during the course of study and translate it in the pulpit. If the preacher got the text "right," then the sermon would take care of itself.

Not only was biblical studies a significant influence on the pulpit, but so was the field of speech communication. Michael Casey notes, "Speech departments have historically been a part of most of the curricula of the colleges. Batsell Barrett Baxter was the first person in Churches of Christ to receive a PhD in speech communication, from the University of Southern California in 1944... Baxter trained hundreds of preachers in such a distinctive way that at one time many could readily tell if a preacher had trained at Lipscomb College."[4] It took time for people trained in homiletics to teach in universities connected to Churches of Christ. The trend at Lipscomb was part of the larger abdication of the discipline of practical theology to the social sciences. As homiletics developed its own theological domain in the academy, Churches of Christ lagged behind.[5] The first person formally trained in homiletics to teach at a Christian college was Jerry Jones at Harding University (1966–1983). Jerry graduated (ThD) from New Orleans Baptist Seminary in 1974. Koller's *Expository Preaching Without Notes*[6] represented his preaching instruction. His teaching emphasized preaching thematic-deductive sermons from whole pericopes more so than the more common styles of verse-by-verse exposition or topical sermons supported by multiple texts.

Another example of how Christian colleges influenced preaching is seen in the rise of lectureships. "As Churches of Christ rejected General Conventions and Missionary Societies, lectureships provided the same functions–fellowship, networking, and examination of doctrinal issues."[7] Their first college lectureship was at Abilene Christian University in 1918.[8] Similarly, other churches and institutions began their own lectureships for various reasons, but often as a correction to university-sponsored lectureships. The most notable other lectureship is the Tulsa Soul Winning Workshop that began in 1976, and is sponsored by the Garnett Road Church of Christ. Craig Churchill quotes William Banowsky, who summarized, "The Lectureship has been the most vital pulpit of a pulpit-sparked movement."[9] The preaching at lectureships, it was assumed, modeled "best practices." Since preaching was so highly prized by churches, preachers desired to imitate the "stars" who were routinely asked to be keynote speakers.

While lectureships provided opportunities for preachers to hear examples, more formal continuing education opportunities have emerged. Austin Graduate School of Theology is offering its 37th annual sermon seminar in 2018. The primary focus of the seminar is to offer exegetical insights. The organizers are "committed to encouraging preaching and teaching which are: Drawn from responsible biblical interpretation; Based on faithful theological inquiry; In keeping with the Restorationist vision; Challenging and helpful to the church; Appropriate for the contemporary cultural setting."[10] The seminar is designed to provide the working preacher a combination of exegetical insights, healthy content, and preaching tips.

While other sermon seminars have appeared, another influential offering occurred at Rochester College from 1999–2009. David Fleer and Dave Bland initiated the Rochester seminar to provide insights into texts relating to the rhetorical and literary form, theological perspectives, and example sermons. The seminar relied heavily on principal New Homiletic thought leaders (e.g., Willimon, Craddock, Brueggemann, Long, Campbell, and others). Respondents and sermons likewise represented the influence of the New Homiletic. Either Chalice Press or ACU Press published all but the first of the annual lectures and sermons through the years. Subsequently, Fleer also started a preaching seminar at Lipscomb University. This venue focused on personal crafting of sermons, with feedback from experts in homiletics.

Changes in preaching style and form in Churches of Christ emerged more from a change in hermeneutics than any identifiable influence from the homiletical field. Richard Hughes notes these shifts by highlighting the influence of one man:

> As a professor of Bible and biblical theology for 19 years at Abilene
> Christian University (1967–1986) and for ten years at Pepperdine

University (1986–1996), Thomas H. Olbricht (1929–) exerted a significant impact on the content of preaching in Churches of Christ in the closing years of the twentieth century. Olbricht argued that Churches of Christ should focus their restorationist lens on a recovery of biblical theology centered in the "core message" of Scripture and in "the mighty acts of God." He claimed that the starting point for a proper understanding of the Bible "is God, Christ, and the Holy Spirit, rather than commands, examples, and necessary inferences."[11]

The hermeneutical shift fostered by Olbricht influenced a new wave of preaching in the 1990s and into the 21st century. Olbricht's more narratival theology inspired many preachers to adopt more narrative styles in the pulpit.

Olbricht influenced the recovery of homiletics at several seminaries affiliated with Churches of Christ. Faculty who were trained in homiletics and rhetoric replaced speech professors. Jack Reese at Abilene Christian University (beginning in 1988), David Fleer at both Rochester College (1995–2007) and Lipscomb University (2007–present), and Dave Bland at Harding School of Theology (1993–present) all pioneered the formal teaching of homiletics at their respective schools. Reese, Fleer, and Bland introduced new approaches to preaching influenced by the New Homiletic and post–New Homiletic.[12] All other colleges and universities affiliated with Churches of Christ that offer preaching courses today are taught by either biblical texts people, adjuncts who occasionally have homiletical training, or prominent local preachers.

The journal *Wineskins* exemplified the hermeneutical shift that defined an ever-growing preaching population. In 1992, Rubel Shelly, Phillip Morrison, and Mike Cope began editing and publishing *Wineskins,* marketed as "devoted to communicating the gospel in the language of contemporary culture."[13] The journal intended to be a "catalyst for reform" through a Christocentric lens.

Additionally, Max Lucado (1955–), pulpit preacher for the Oak Hills Church of Christ in San Antonio, Texas, since 1987, is representative of the hermeneutical changes affecting churches. Lucado's preaching is representative of Ron Allen's first category of narrative preaching, described as "sermons that are actual stories containing little if any explanatory material… The preacher may simply retell a tale from the Bible or Christian history. Sometimes such story-sermons are created from the preacher's imagination; at other times, a pastor will tell stories from movies, novels, or short stories, from the lives of the congregation or from the preacher's own life."[14] Lynn Anderson (see sermon below) is credited with influencing Lucado's narrative style. Anderson was the preaching minister for the

Highland Church of Christ, where Lucado attended while pursuing his degrees at Abilene Christian University.

The hermeneutical shift created a rift in Churches of Christ. The rift is clearly seen when examining the content of sermons. Discursive topical and expository sermons dominate the scene for many churches.[15] Haddon Robinson's *Biblical Preaching*[16] is the primary textbook used in these circles. For churches that have an affinity for a more narrative biblical theology, a variety of homiletical forms influenced by Long, Craddock, Lowry, Buttrick, and others are often seen. The collection of sermons for Churches of Christ does not include women. While the scene in pulpits is changing, inclusion of female voices is yet to be representative of the movement.[17]

Persuasion through the character of the speaker corresponds with one of the most recognizable definitions of preaching in the modern era. In the spirit of Aristotle and Augustine, Phillips Brooks, 1877, stated, "Preaching is the communication of truth by man to men,"[18] or, as we often prefer to quote, "Truth through Personality is our description of real preaching."[19] Analyzing sermons on paper is a useful exercise. However, what is lost in such analysis are the grand performances of the larger-than-life personalities of the preachers represented here. These sermons were selected not because they represented the best in homiletical theory, but because of the *ethos* and *pathos* of the proclaimer. When reading the words, those who have heard their voices can hear their cadence, style, and emotion. The influence of these practitioners on preaching in Churches of Christ is not only in the form of the sermon, but in the force of their personalities. Also, the traditional ecclesiology of Churches of Christ included a rejection of language related to clergy titles, opting for no title at all. To honor that tradition, the reader will see no prefatory title assigned to any of the preachers mentioned in this section.

Batsell Barrett Baxter

Batsell Barrett Baxter (1916–1982) received his BS degree from Abilene Christian University (1938), MA and PhD in Speech Communications from University of Southern California (1938, 1944), and BD from Vanderbilt (1957). He became president of the Southern Speech Association in 1952. He taught speech at Pepperdine College from 1938–1945. Baxter moved to Nashville to become the Chair of the Speech Department at David Lipscomb College from 1945–1956. He was chair of Lipscomb's Bible Department from 1956–1982, often teaching homiletics. He also preached for the Hillsboro Church of Christ in Nashville, 1951–1980.

Baxter authored or coedited 20 books. The most influential book connected to homiletics was *The Heart of the Yale Lectures*,[1] in which he summarizes the first 66 volumes of the Lyman Beecher lectures, and asks, "What is the secret of real influence in the pulpit?" Baxter, a European American, is best known as the principle speaker on the *Herald of Truth* radio (1966–1976) and television ministry (1960–1982).

A movement towards a "more therapeutic gospel" characterized his preaching.[2] "Pulpit preachers throughout the Churches of Christ quickly followed suit. By the late 1970s, one could listen to preachers in Churches of Christ for weeks and never hear anything approaching the traditional sectarian message that had defined the tradition for a century and a half."[3]

This sermon was first preached at Hillsboro Church of Christ, Nashville, and heard over radio station WLAC, on August 16, 1970. Baxter uses the ASV, except as noted.

"The Beautiful People"

Over the past few years there has been considerable comment regarding "the beautiful people." The designation has to do with certain affluent, knowledgeable, often highly placed, successful, attractive, and intelligent men and women. But what is true beauty and who are the beautiful people in the sight of God? In this connection we remember a statement from Solomon, who wrote of God who "hath made everything beautiful in its time" and who "hath set eternity in their heart" (Eccl. 3:11). At least in its origin and design God has made everything beautiful.

The Bible often mentions beautiful people. Sarah, for example, heard her husband Abraham's appraisal, "Behold now, I know that thou art a fair woman to look upon" (Gen. 12:11). "Rachel was beautiful and well-favored" (Gen. 29:17). "Joseph was comely, and well-favored" (Gen. 39:6). Of David it was said, 'Now he was ruddy, and withal of a beautiful countenance,

and goodly to look upon'" (1 Sam. 16:12). Bathsheba was described, "…
the woman was very beautiful to look upon" (2 Sam. 11:2). Concerning
Esther, we read, "And he brought up Hadassah, that is, Esther, his uncle's
daughter: for she had neither father nor mother, and the maiden was fair
and beautiful; and when her father and mother were dead, Mordecai took
her for his own daughter" (Esth. 2:7).

However, the Scriptures are far more concerned with spiritual beauty
than with mere physical attractiveness. We feel this in passage after passage
of the Scriptures. As an example, we might read David's statement, "Give
unto the LORD the glory due unto his name: bring an offering, and come
before him: worship the LORD in the beauty of holiness" (1 Chr. 16:29
KJV). The expression "beauty of holiness" is especially appealing. We
would do well to give this expression time and thought.

In the 27th Psalm, David added, "One thing have I asked of Jehovah,
that will I seek after: That I may dwell in the house of Jehovah all the days
of my life, To behold the beauty of Jehovah, And to inquire in his temple"
(Ps. 27:4). In the 90th Psalm, generally attributed to Moses, there are the
words, "And let the beauty of the LORD thy God be upon us: and establish
thou the work of our hands upon us; yea, the work of our hands establish
thou it" (Ps. 90:17, KJV). The inner-spiritual beauty, which God appreciates,
is referred to in Paul's statement, "…though our outward man is decaying,
yet our inward man is renewed day by day" (2 Cor. 4:16).

Examples of Beautiful People

Not only are there many passages in the Scriptures, which refer to the
inner spiritual beauty, which God appreciates, but there are numbers of
people whose lives possess this inner, spiritual beauty, which God desires
for all. Among them was Enoch, who lived almost at the dawn of history.
After telling his age, after recording the fact that he had many sons and
daughters, the record tells us "…and Enoch walked with God: and he was
not; for God took him" (Gen. 5:24). What a beautiful, intimate relationship
this suggests. Enoch was a man who lived so close to God that he can be
described as one who walked with God and one who was miraculously
taken by the Lord.

Joseph, whom we mentioned a moment ago as "comely and well-
favored," must have been outstanding in his beauty. The noted biblical
commentator, Adam Clarke, in his discussion of Genesis 39:6, said of
Joseph,

> He was beautiful in his person, and beautiful in his countenance…
> The beauty of Joseph is celebrated over all the East, and the
> Persian poets vie with each other in descriptions of his comeliness.
> Mohammed spends the twelfth chapter of the Koran entirely on

Joseph, and represents him as a perfect beauty, and the most accomplished of mortals. From his account the passion of Zuleekha (traditionally the name for Potiphar's wife) being known to the ladies of the court, they cast the severest reflections upon her... When she invited forty of these ladies to dine in her house and suddenly brought Joseph in, they are supposed to have cried out, 'This is not a human being, this is none other than a glorious angel.'"[4]

Whether this traditional story is true or not, as recorded by Adam Clarke, it does indicate the long, solid tradition which adds some meaning to the brief statement in the Scriptures about Joseph's beauty.

Leslie G. Thomas, an outstanding writer and preacher, has a book about Ruth, which he titled *The Beautiful Gleaner*. In this book he says:

Ruth is the kind of woman that draws the world after her...by the lasting qualities of her unselfish devotion, of lowly serviceableness, of...modesty. She is one of the characters that humanity takes delight in remembering. Men enjoy studying this story because it touches them with the mystery and charm of early love. Women delight in reading it because in it they recognize the best and loveliest type of womanhood.[5]

Outside the Scriptures

Turning from examples of beauty which one finds in the Scriptures, we mention several outside the Scriptures, which have a quality that can only be described as the beautiful. Martin Luther, when called upon to renounce his convictions before the Diet of Worms, had the courage to say, even though his life seemed to depend upon his renunciation of his own writings, "It is neither safe nor wise to do anything against conscience... here I stand; I cannot do otherwise; God help me—Amen!" Many a lesser person would have bowed down to the pressure. There is a rugged beauty in those who stand for their convictions at whatever cost.

Another example of this same kind of deep conviction is found in the life of Hugh Latimer, the great reformer of 16th-century England. Those who know his story recognize in him a kind of inner strength that is indeed beautiful.[6]

One of our friends, Wendell Winkler, a fellow-preacher, some months ago asked his teen-age class, "What would you like to be doing if Jesus came today?" The answers are quite interesting. One young person wrote, "If Christ came today I would like to be in a worship service praising God, or teaching someone about him." Another said, "If Christ came today I would like to be praying for the souls that rejected Christ and for those who have never heard his word." Still another wrote, "If Christ came today I'd like to be in church praising God or by my grandmother's grave so I could see her as quickly as possible." Still another young person wrote, "If Christ came today I would like for him to find me doing something nice for someone else." Yet another said, "If Christ came today I would like to be in prayer and know that my last moments were spent in contact with God." Still another wrote, "If Christ came today I would like to be sacrificially serving Christ as a teacher, or leading someone to Christ." Finally, I will quote one other, who said, "If Christ came today I would love to be at Brookhaven Rest Home, sitting next to Helen Ford. All her suffering would end then."

To me, there is something beautiful about these genuine, intimate glimpses into the feelings of these teen-age young people. Their thoughts are so unselfishly centered upon others. I think that we can certainly see that there are yet many fine Christian young people in the world. We can also see that they have received some very fine instruction, which has developed into meaningful faith. We believe that young people like these give promise for the future of the church and of Christ's way.

Transformation

Our deepest concern is for the transformation of sinful men and women, such as all of us, into spiritually beautiful people. The great tragedy of our world is that after a perfect creation with beauty on every hand, sin and degradation came into this idyllic scene and brought ugliness and tragedy. Our greatest concern is that we might be transformed again into the purity and the beauty of God's original creation. All of us have read perhaps of the alchemists of the Dark Ages who tried to transmute the baser metals into gold. In every case they failed, for such transformation is simply not possible. It is possible, however, for a far more significant transformation to take place—the transformation of sinful humans into the beautiful persons that God would have them become. Of course, this is the essence of why Christ came to earth, why he lived his sinless life as an example, and why he left his teachings for all people of all time to appropriate. The redemption or reforming of humanity is the heart of the story of the Bible.

The method by which this transformation can take place is also set forth in the Scriptures. It was Solomon who wrote, "For as [a man] thinketh in his heart, so is he." (Prov. 23:7, KJV). By determining what goes into our minds, or hearts, it can be determined what we will believe and ultimately what we will be. The same emphasis is found in the New Testament book of Philippians, where the apostle Paul said, "Finally, brethren, whatsoever things are true, whatsoever things are honorable, whatsoever things are just, whatsoever things are pure, whatsoever things are lovely, whatsoever things are of good report: if there be any virtue, and if there be any praise, think on these things. The things which ye both learned and received and heard and saw in me, these things do: and the God of peace shall be with you"

(Phil. 4:8–9). If our minds can be centered upon these positive, uplifting themes, there will inevitably be a transformation of life.

Yet another passage in which this basic concept is presented is 2 Corinthians 3:18, where we read, "But we all, with unveiled face, beholding as in a mirror the glory of the Lord, are transformed into the same image from glory to glory, even as from the Lord of the Spirit." In his Roman letter Paul further said, "And be not fashioned according to this world: but be ye transformed by the renewing of your mind, that ye may prove what is the good and acceptable and perfect will of God." (Rom. 12:2). In the prologue of John's Gospel are the words, "But as many as received him, to them gave he power to become the sons of God, even to them that believe on his name" (Jn. 1:12 KJV).

Conclusion

Most of all, however, if we would make our lives beautiful, we must follow Christ. He will lead us to perfection. He will never lead us astray. The beauty of his own life is assurance that if we will follow in his steps to the best of our ability, our lives will be beautiful, too...

The Lord's invitation is for all people of all time. If you would make your life beautiful both within and without, follow Christ and live by his teachings. It all begins when one learns of the Lord and comes to believe that Jesus is the Son of God. When this faith is strong enough, it leads one to obey the Lord's commands to repent of all past sin, to confess the Lord before others, and to be buried with him in the beautifully symbolic act of baptism. Then one is raised from the grave of water to live a new kind of life, wearing the name of Christ, and living by a different standard. Happiness, peace, beauty, along with faith and hope and love, are the qualities that the new Christian life displays. Surely this is appealing to all.

J. S. Winston

John Steve Winston (1906–2001) began his preaching career in Sherman, Texas, in 1938.[1] His strong preaching and emphasis on leadership development enhanced Winston's reputation for establishing and building churches throughout Texas. In 1945, J. S. Winston and others began the first Annual National Lectureship in Oklahoma City.[2] In 1948, he helped open the Southern Bible Institute (on the campus of the Lake Como Church of Christ in Fort Worth, Texas). Initially there were 41 students and Winston served as president. The school moved to Terrell, Texas, and became Southwestern Christian College in 1950.[3]

Winston was one of four African American men to carry the mantle of leadership for black congregations in the Churches of Christ in the second half of the twentieth century. In 1952 Winston and his family relocated to Cleveland, Ohio.

Many of Winston's sermons were reprinted under the regular column heading "Hindering Causes" in *The Christian Echo.* "Beware Covetousness of Authority: A Sin" was published there in May 1978. Although Winston was known for expositional and textual preaching, this sermon represents his topical approach. He uses the KJV.

"Beware Covetousness of Authority: A Sin"

Covetousness: A greedy avaricious sin with a miserly desire grasping for that which belongs to another. God from the beginning of time warned against covetousness. It is a sin that began with Satan's encounter with Adam and Eve in the Garden of Eden (Gen. 3). The account of covetousness is recorded in the Bible from the book of Genesis through Revelation. In just about every scriptural context where sin is catalogued, covetousness is included; it is associated with the evil works of Satan. God warns and condemns covetousness (Ex. 20:17; Deut. 5:21; Rom. 1:28, 29; 1 Cor. 6:10). "But fornication, and all uncleanness, or covetousness, let it not be once named among you as becoming saints; Neither filthiness, nor foolish talking, nor jesting, which are not convenient: but rather giving of thanks. For this you know, that no whoremongers, nor unclean person, nor covetous man, who is an idolater, hath any inheritance in the kingdom of Christ and of God" (Eph. 5:3–5).

Covetousness of Authority

Covetousness of Authority is a most dangerously evil sin. It is a lustful, voracious greed for power to rule and control. Humans desire authority because it gives them a grandiose feeling of superiority, and fills their ego.

"Their hearts goeth after their covetousness" (Ezek. 33:31). Covetousness for authoritative power is responsible for wars and destruction of whole nations. Covetousness for "Authority" causes conspiracy and undermining secret caucus meetings in order to gain power. Its works are evil.

Covetousness of Authority in the Local Church

The desire for authority, to be the leader, has always caused dissension and disputing among sisters and brothers in the Churches of Christ. Members desire to be leaders in the church because it will give them "authority" over the church. Actually, their desire for "authority" is to have power to rule over the church. They covet "Leadership Authority" because it fills their desire for power. It also fills their ego of "grandioseness"–like the Pharisees and scribes whom Jesus condemned because they sought the chief seats in the synagogues (Mk. 12:39–40; Mt. 23:2–7).

Covetousness of Authority between Elders and Preachers

Since the Restoration Movement began, there has been struggle, warring over "authority" between local congregations' elders and preachers. The local eldership concept is responsible for creating this eldership and preacher conflict. Their misconception of the local congregation's eldership "authority" has created a "power structure" that dominates the Gospel preacher, giving the local eldership complete authority over the evangelist: to rule and relegate the preacher's ministry. It makes the Gospel preacher wholly and solely responsible to their rulership. Such an eldership makes the Gospel preacher a servant to them (a puppet, so to say). Therefore, a preacher who attempts to act, or do anything in the church without this eldership's approval, can be reprimanded and fired. This has caused many preachers with families to become drifters from congregation to congregation. The complete authority of the eldership over the evangelist is definitely spelled out in most books written by members on "The Government of the Church."

I maintain this kind of eldership "authority" over the evangelist is unscriptural. If members will take a serious and unbiased look at the scriptural elder rule over the local church, they will find the eldership "authority" is a "work," a most serious work to be desired (1 Tim. 3:1). It is not an official office of high position, but of "work." The only scriptural "authority" elders have is the delegated authority to administer Christ's authority (1 Pet. 5:1–3). If they will recognize Christ's authority, they will recognize and respect evangelists and their God-ordained work in the ministry of the church and will love and honor them for their work's sake, because the evangelist labors in the ministry more than any other worker (1 Tim. 5:17, 18; 1 Thess. 5:12, 13).

Evangelist-Responsible

Because of the unpleasant experiences some ministers have suffered from the dominating rule of some local church eldership authority over the evangelist, they have been provoked, resulting in viciously attacking local congregational eldership. They have learned through study of the Scripture that such eldership is unscriptural. However wrong such an eldership may be, the evangelist must also recognize that God ordained elders to be appointed in the local church, too. Therefore, for the preacher to viciously make war on elders as a whole is just as wrong and unscriptural as it is for unscriptural eldership domination. Just because the Bible sets forth that evangelists are delegated with authority to preach, teach, set in order, ordain, and discipline in the local church, they must also recognize that their authority is also a "work" in administering the "authority" of Christ (Titus 1; 2; 2 Tim. 4:1–6). For Gospel preachers to have a desire for authority over the local church, to rule as they please, makes them guilty of the sin of covetousness. This thing of warring over authority between preacher and elders has been a great hindrance to the unity and peace of the Lord's Church (3 Jn. 9, 10).

If the evangelist does not have the ability to correct the unscriptural eldership in the church, it is far better to leave that church to another evangelist who has the ability and the know-how to deal with them, and go elsewhere to preach. Churches have been disturbed, divided, and split because of warring between the local eldership and preacher fighting for authority over the church. "But if ye have bitter envying and strife in your hearts, glory not, and lie not against the truth. This wisdom descendeth not from above, but is earthly, sensual, devilish. For where envying and strife is, there is confusion and every evil work" (Jas. 3:14–16).

If the elders and evangelists will come to recognize that the Church belongs to Christ, that he purchased it with his own precious blood, and all "authority" is vested in him, and "all glory and praise be unto Him in the Church, amen." they will respect Christ and stop fighting over "authority" (Col. 1:18; Eph. 1:22; Eph. 3:21).

They need to recognize that Christ ordained both evangelist and elders in the church "for the perfecting of the saints, for the work of the ministry, for the edifying of the body of Christ" (Eph. 4:11–12).

Instead of warring over "authority," they should think about their responsibility of being living examples of love, peace, and unity before the church (1 Pet. 5:1–3; 1 Tim. 4:12; Titus 2:6). They then will respect each other's God-ordained responsibility in the church; then the church will abound more and more in good works.

Church Quorum Leadership

I am becoming more and more disturbed over "Church Quorum Leadership" in so many congregations today. This "Church Quorum Leadership" is always made up of those who do not qualify, and some who cannot qualify, to be elders or deacons. Many of them are not considered as being faithful. They do not work; the congregation sees them mostly on Lord's Day when they are up officiating in the services. Some of them are contentious-minded; even some have more than one living spouse and children, some one child, and some no children at all. Some of them do not meet the qualifications of the committee appointed in Acts 6:3.

Their desire to be leaders is for "authority" over the church and to watch over the preacher, to see that the preacher doesn't have too much "authority" over the church, and especially the church's money. They covet "authority." Usually there is bickering and fighting going on between such leadership and the evangelist. There are more church splits among churches with the "quorum" committee trustee leadership than there are among churches with elders and deacons. Those who make up the church leadership quorum have never preached a sermon, established a congregation, or defended the doctrine or the church, yet they are "CHURCH EFFICIENCY EXPERTS." There are some quorum leaders who claim to know more about how the church ought to be run than the evangelist who has given years of studying and preaching and laboring. They claim to show that they even know better than the apostles and Jesus himself. I maintain the only scriptural "authority" to be administered in the church is the "authority of Christ" delegated to the evangelist (Titus 1; 2; 1 Tim. 1:1–6; 2 Tim. 4:1–6) and elders (Acts 20:28; 1 Thess. 5:13, 14; Heb. 13:17).

Covetousness Is Deceptive

It breeds jealousy, hatred, envy, malice, and evilness. The average person who is covetous doesn't realize it. One never thinks of oneself as being covetous. Out of all my 60-year membership, and nearly half century in the ministry in the church, I have never experienced a member of the church making a confession for the sin of covetousness. I have never heard of anyone else experiencing such a confession for the sin of covetousness. Covetousness causes one to feel that whatever belongs to another rightly belongs to oneself, regardless of what it takes to get it.

That was the feeling of the robbers who robbed, beat, and stripped the man on the Jericho road (Lk. 10:30). Covetousness caused King Ahab and his wife Jezebel to conspire to kill Naboth to get his land (1 Kings 21). Covetousness caused Judas to betray and sell the life of Jesus to his enemies for 30 pieces of silver. Covetousness for authority in the Kingdom of Christ caused strife and dissension among Christ's apostles. Jesus had to teach them that they had the Gentile concept of "authority," but "authority" in His Kingdom means: a humble work of serving, and not to be served (Lk. 22:24–27; 9:46–48). He taught them a lesson of humility by washing their feet (Jn. 13:1–17).

My Solemn Commitment

Every day I pray to my God to help me to live by the most excellent counsel the Apostle Paul gave to the saints, elders, and deacons in the Church at Philippi:

> If there be therefore any consolation in Christ, if any comfort of love, if any fellowship of the Spirit, if any bowels and mercies,
>
> Fulfil ye my joy, that ye be likeminded, having the same love, being of one accord, of one mind.
>
> Let nothing be done through strife or vainglory; but in lowliness of mind let each esteem others better than themselves.
>
> Look not every man on his own things, but every man also on the things of others.
>
> Let this mind be in you, [that] was also in Christ Jesus:
>
> Who, being in the form of God, thought it not robbery to be equal with God:
>
> But made himself of no reputation, and took upon him the form of a servant, and was made in the likeness of men:
>
> And being found in fashion as a man, he humbled himself, and became obedient unto death, even death on the cross.
>
> Wherefore God…hath highly exalted him, and given him a name which is above every name:
>
> That at the name of Jesus every knee shall bow, of things in heaven, and things in earth, and things under the earth;
>
> And that every tongue should confess that Jesus Christ is Lord, to the glory of…the Father. (Phil. 2:1–11)

Jimmy Allen

Jimmy Allen (1930–) was born in Little Rock, Arkansas. In December of 1948 he enrolled at Harding College. The teaching and influence of Harding led him to become a Christian. In the fall of 1949 he preached his first sermon. Jimmy earned his MRE degree at the Harding Graduate School in Memphis. He began teaching in the Bible Department on Harding's Searcy campus in the fall of 1959. Richard Hughes credits him for stirring a revival on campus due to his teachings from Romans on grace.[1]

Perhaps Jimmy Allen is best known for preaching in 40 area-wide multi-congregational campaigns. Some of the better-known campaigns were held in Dallas, Memphis, Seattle, Denver, Detroit, St. Louis, Indianapolis, and Philadelphia. From 1964 through 1970, almost 13,000 people responded to his preaching. More than 3,600 of them were baptized. He published *Fire in My Bones* as a self-published autobiography in 2004. Allen is Caucasian.

"The Great Meeting All Will Attend" was self-published in 1965 in a collection of his sermons *What Is Hell Like? And Other Sermons.* He uses the "Great Meeting" as a controlling metaphor for his topical message about the Day of Judgment. This sermon was first preached on Saturday, August 8, 1964, in Dallas. He preached it other times through the years covered by this volume at similar campaigns. We use it here because it is such a classic and so representative. Allen uses the KJV.

"The Great Meeting All Will Attend"

We have about 8,000 this evening, a pretty good Saturday night audience. If we have as many tomorrow evening as we had last Sunday night, in the course of this 15-day meeting we will have had 125,000 in attendance. That is good by anybody's standards. We have had a great meeting because you worked, invited others, prayed, and attended yourself. If the good Lord will extend to me the grace and strength I need to properly present this lesson, there ought to be scores of people come to the front and do the Lord's will this evening.

Gospel Meetings

This sermon is entitled "The Great Meeting All Will Attend." By way of introduction, let me say that it is customary for Churches of Christ to have gospel meetings. By gospel meetings, I mean concentrated efforts to reach the lost. I am of the opinion that if a church maintains its evangelistic edge, it ought to have at least two or three evangelistic campaigns a year. One of the greatest meetings ever held in Texas was conducted by Brother

T.B. Larimore at Sherman. That meeting was six months long. Another Texas church had a 365-night meeting. Perhaps many of the faithful workers were worn out as a result of such an extended effort, but at the end of the meeting that congregation had quadrupled its membership...[2]

There are thousands of people in this community who ought to be at this meeting. They have not come. They need to hear a gospel sermon. They need to accept Christ as their Savior. But they are watching television or reading newspapers. Go to their front yards, erect a sign 20 feet long and 10 feet high, print an announcement of our meeting in blood-red letters, but still they would not come. I hate to say it, but there are some people who simply do not appreciate our efforts to impede their progress on the road to Hell. Some people are determined to be lost and they will be lost in spite of everything we can do. The very people who ought to be here tonight, the very ones who need this message so desperately, are not here. This evening I am talking about the great meeting all will attend. The people who for some reason or another couldn't get here tonight are going to be present for that one. You and I will be there, and all the multitudes who have lived or will live are going to be present on this day of all days.

No Postponement

A number of years ago I went to the little rural community where I was reared to conduct a meeting. One night, while driving toward the church building, I noticed black clouds hanging low in the heavens. The ominous rumblings of thunder could be heard and zig-zag streaks of lightning filled the air. When I arrived at the church building, there was just a handful of the faithful present. After a hasty consultation with the leaders, it was decided to postpone the meeting until the next night.

In reply to that, someone might say, "You people didn't have much faith." I said all of that to say this: We postponed the meeting, but the great meeting all will attend isn't going to be postponed. There isn't going to be one day's delay regardless of what you or I have in mind. You may be planning to enlarge your business. Perhaps you intend to add to your home. Maybe you are going to take an extended vacation. Maybe you are about to launch a new profession. However, this meeting will occur on schedule. It's not going to be postponed.

All of us are concerned about the situation in Laos and South Vietnam... We wonder who is going to get to the moon first... We are confronted with the fall election. Who is going to be the next president of the United States?... Regardless of who wins the arms race, regardless of what happens in Southeast Asia, regardless of who is elected next November, the meeting under consideration is going to occur as planned by the God of Heaven.

It Has Been Advertised

Before our meeting started, we advertised it. We spent a great deal of money so the people in this vicinity would know about the Dallas Memorial Auditorium meeting. The meeting that all will attend has been advertised too. In Hebrews 9:27–28...in Acts 24:24–25... What was Paul doing? Among other things, he was advertising the fact that there is going to be a judgment. When he told Felix about the coming judgment, Felix was terrified. He shook in his boots. He shook like a leaf in a windstorm. He was a grown man, but he was scared at the thought of standing before God and giving an account of the deeds done in the body. Paul, according to Acts 17, spoke to the wisest people of the first-century world. Paul was on Mars Hill... Paul didn't talk about Roman tragedy. He didn't spend his time discussing Greek culture. He discussed the subject of judgment. He wanted those philosophers, educators, and poets to know about standing before God on the Day of Judgment. He was advertising.

No One Knows the Time

In advertising this gospel endeavor, we announced when it would start and when it would conclude. We also announced the time of the service each evening. However, the time of the meeting all will attend has not been announced. We don't know when it will occur. In Mark 13:32 Jesus said, "But of that day and that hour knoweth no man, no, not the angels which are in heaven, neither the Son, but the Father." Nobody knows when the judgment is going to occur. I have a book in which the author cited Mark 13:32. Following the quotation he had about a half page of comments. At the bottom of the page, upon the basis of Mark 13:32, the author said he knew when Christ was coming again. I thought, "Maybe I have misread the passage." So I went back and read it again. Once more it said that no one knows the day or the hour. Then, I read his comments again. Without too much difficulty, I concluded that he was a false teacher. When someone tries to tell you when the day of judgment will occur, you don't have to be as wise as Solomon to know that teaching is not the truth of God. The Bible says no one knows the day or the hour. Because we don't know, many of us are going to get caught unprepared...

If we read 1 Thessalonians 5:1–6, Paul says the day will come as a thief in the night. Many people will have found security in worldly affairs. They will be saying, "peace and safety." But all at once, time and timely things will come to an end. It will be like labor pains striking a woman who is about to give birth to a child. Suddenly judgment will come upon the whole world. Many of us will be caught unexpectedly. We will have made insufficient preparation. We will not be ready to meet our Lord. Whether we are living when the Lord comes or not, when death comes to us, for all practical purposes, that is judgment. That is the end of the world, for our destiny is fixed and sealed then and there.

Events to Precede the Meeting

Even though I don't know the exact day when judgment will occur, I can tell you some events that are going to precede it. First, our Lord will come again... I would to God that I had the fluency of speech to impress upon your minds the fact that Christ is coming again. This is not a fairy tale, fabrication, or falsehood. This is fact.

Christ is coming again, and the Bible vividly describes His second coming... I am trying to get you to think, for you can lose your soul! Christ is coming again. He is going to take vengeance upon those who have not obeyed the gospel. Have you obeyed Him? Are you a Christian? Are you faithful and loyal? Do you put the Kingdom first in your life? What about it?... The dead will be raised; the living will be changed, and then this meeting will occur.

All Will Attend

People have all sorts of excuses for not attending church services. They *really* use the weather. When it's hot, it's too hot. When it's cold, it's too cold. When it's wet, it's too wet. When it's dry, it's too dry. Then, there is the problem of little Tommy having the sniffles on Sunday. If an eight-year-old has a slight cold, he can keep a family of nine from going to church. Everybody is so concerned about his needs they must all stay at home to wait on him hand and foot. If he has the sniffles Monday morning, that's rough because mother and daddy will both go to work. All of his brothers and sisters will go to school, and he will be left at home to manage by himself. Then, there is the headache that hits on Sunday morning. It arrives about 8:30 and it's unbearable for a few hours. Around 12:00 it vanishes. But about 5:30 in the afternoon it comes back again, and it's so severe you can hardly see. Then, about 7:30 it's gone...

You are going to be judged! You will give an account individually to God. We are not going to be judged congregationally. We are not going to be judged as families. We are not going to be judged as nations, but we are going to be judged as individuals. When you stand in the presence of God, you will not have regretted being an obedient Christian.

The Preacher and the Sermon

When you have a meeting, you must have a preacher. The greatest preacher who ever lived will speak at the meeting all will attend. Of course, I refer to Jesus. In 2 Timothy 4:1–2, Paul said... In Acts 17:31 the Bible says... Jesus is going to be the judge. Jesus is going to deliver the sermon on that occasion. And I know what he is going to discuss.

As a matter of fact, the sermon can be summed up in one word that has only five letters: W-O-R-K-S. Read Revelation 20:12. Or, listen when James said, "Faith without works is dead" (2:20). He also said, "Ye see then how that by works a man is justified, and not by faith only" (2:24). In Philippians, Paul wrote that we are to work out our own salvation with fear and trembling. Jesus, in writing to the seven churches in Asia, said at least seven times, "I know thy works." In Revelation 14:13... Over and over we read of works. We are going to be judged upon the basis of our works. Read what Jesus says in Matthew 25:41–43... What are those? Works! But still some contend that works are not important. Are clothes important on a cold winter day? I would far rather stand without any clothing on my body in the severest blizzard you can imagine than to stand before God without works! We are going to be judged upon the basis of our works. That will be the Lord's sermon.

Reaction to the Sermon

There will be various reactions to the sermon that I am preaching. When you leave, some of you will say, "I enjoyed it. I thought it was a good sermon." Some will say, "I didn't like it. I didn't appreciate his emphasis at a given point. I didn't like his closing remarks." That's your business. Go right ahead and criticize. Preachers criticize others. We ought to be able to take some ourselves...

After our Lord has spoken in the meeting of all meetings, there will be reactions to his sermon. Some are going to like it. Consider the five- and two-talent servants, whom you can read about in Matthew 25. Do you remember the story?...

The uncharitable will not be happy with Christ's sermon. In the Day of Judgment, Jesus will discuss feeding the hungry, giving water to the thirsty, clothing the naked, caring for strangers, and visiting the sick and imprisoned... If we don't take care of the needy, we will miss heaven.

After hearing the Lord's discourse, some will say, "Let us in anyway." Do you remember the parable of the wise and foolish maidens?... That is a picture of judgment. Many of us, after hearing what Jesus says, recognizing that we are going to be lost eternally, will say, "Lord, you must open up and let me in. You just have to let me in."

Then, there are those who will be unhappy because they have followed humanly devised schemes. They have not obeyed the will of the Lord. According to Matthew 7:21–23, Jesus will say, even to some religious people, "I never knew you."...

Confessions and Dismissals

The Bible says that it is appointed unto us once to die and, after this, the judgment. We have two divine appointments, death and judgment, and there is no second chance in between. On Judgment Day, no invitation song will be used to get people to accept Christ as Savior. The invitation, of course, is extended in this life. Jesus said, "Come unto me, all ye that labor and are heavy laden, and I will give you rest. Take my yoke upon you; and learn of me; for I am meek and lowly in heart: and ye shall find rest unto your souls. For my yoke is easy, and my burden is light" Mt. 11:28–30). The time for accepting the invitation is now, not then...

If you will allow me to press the figure a little, when our Lord has delivered the lesson, when the people have given their reactions to his sermon, there will be a dismissal prayer. In a few minutes, we will call on someone to dismiss us. We will all bow our heads and that person will say, "Dismiss us with Thy care and keeping and bring us back together tomorrow night at the appointed time," or words to that effect. Well, our Lord will lead the dismissal prayer. He will say, "Depart from me, ye cursed, into everlasting fire, prepared for the devil and his angels" (Mt. 25:41). He will also say, "Come,...blessed of my Father, inherit the kingdom prepared for you from the foundation of the world" (Mt. 25:34). Then, that assembly will be dismissed. We will go home. Some will go to a home of everlasting hell, from which there is no escape. Some will go to everlasting life to be with God, Christ, the angels, and all the worthies of all ages. In that home, there will be no sorrows, tears, unhappiness, or crying, for the former things will have passed away.

My friends, what you do with Jesus here will determine what he does with you there. We are a marvelously blessed people. This evening I ask you, "What are you going to do with Jesus?" You can sit here in the comfort of this air-conditioned auditorium and decide what to do with Jesus. But in the Day of Judgment the question will be, "What will Jesus do with you?" You will want him to receive you then; therefore, you must accept him now. Christians are hoping and praying that you will obey the Lord. Please come to Christ as we stand and sing.

Andrew Hairston

Andrew J. Hairston graduated in 1955 from Southwestern Christian College with an AA and BA He earned his BS and second BA from Paul Quinn College in Texas, and his BD and MTh degrees from Brite Divinity School at Texas Christian University. He holds a JD from John Marshall Law School, Master of Law from Woodrow Wilson College of Law , DMin from Emory University, and Masters of Judicial Studies from the University of Nevada at Reno. He holds honorary doctorates from Southwestern Christian College, John Marshall Law School, and Abilene Christian University.

Hairston has traveled extensively, including to Liberia, where he co-founded the Wells-Hairston Elementary/High School System. He has served as assistant Solicitor General of the State Court of Fulton County and Chief Solicitor of the Municipal Court of Atlanta, is a retired US Army Reserve Chaplain (Col.), retired Chief Judge of the City Court of Atlanta, and has served as Chairman of the Board of Directors of Southwestern Christian College.

Hairston is minister for the Simpson Street Church of Christ in Atlanta, Georgia (1961–), where he preached this sermon. As an African American minister, Hairston is a one-man mirror of the slow, painful journey of Churches of Christ from their once undeniably segregationist stance to the dawning awareness that the gospel is for all. This topical sermon, "A Divine Requirement: A Faith That Will Stand," begins as is common in African American preaching: with a direct statement of the thesis. He uses the KJV.

"A Divine Requirement: A Faith That Will Stand"

In his conversation and life with the Christian believers at Corinth, Paul knew that a weak, indefinite, or shallow faith of instability and shaky relationship with God would not be sufficient to hold or sustain believers in Christ. No, circumstances at Corinth demanded a strong faith, securely anchored on a well-built foundation that would enable the believer to stand against the storms and challenges Christians were destined to encounter.

In the Ephesian letter, Paul gives his readers insights into the faith needed and advised and urged them to "put on the whole armor of God" (6:11). He warned that they were not contending against the weaker challenges of flesh and blood, but against principalities, powers unseen, and against spiritual wickedness in high places. He urged the Ephesian believers to do "all" to stand and to therefore stand as expected by God. In this message, I seek to encourage believers to embrace the fundamental aspect of their involvement in the redemption of God through Jesus Christ and to become empowered to lead and to strengthen others in Christ.

It is in our sin-darkened world and age that we seek to challenge godly followers to bring the sinner, the errant, the ungodly, the haters, and the lovers of transgressions home to God. Advancing immorality, the challenge to develop our lives for God, the corruption of the believer, and lovers of all that God hates–these all suggest that our final moments are approaching. Immorality runs rampant; it has dared to set a new design for marriage and the family. The world urges Christians to throw their models away and adopt models that do not favor God in their place. It exploits the developing lives and threatens to deprive us of the security that has described our nation since its beginning.

We are in hard, challenging, and difficult times, when religion is being attacked, punished, ridiculed, and rejected. Clearly we need to join Paul in insisting on a faith that will stand, not simply in the wisdom of humans, but in the power of God. And to be sure, the faith we seek and are determined to possess lies beyond acknowledging God, the Son, and the Holy Spirit. The faith we seek is bound up in the wholeness of God's power and being. The faith we seek connects us to God in His[1] wholeness and gives Him preferential place with us and occupancy over the wholeness of ourselves, even to the extent of fatal surrender to God's will. Yes, in order for us to have a "faith that will stand in the power of God," our faith must be synonymous with God's to the extent that God accounts our faith as righteousness and gives us the power, like Abraham, to believe in God to the extent that "we stagger not" at the promise of God.

In these days in which Christ and religion are being abandoned and rejected, and God is being replaced by "freedom of choice," we must demand of ourselves, and present to the world, a faith that will stand in the power of God. One has said that the church is like a great ship on whose deck festivities are being conducted and enjoyed, while deep below the water line a leak has been sprung and the ship is gradually sinking day by day, even though the pumps pumping the excess water out are being worked day and night. That we, the church, are in trouble and threatened by our "slide rule faith" has become increasingly evident. And the threat is not only against our longevity; it is against our lives. For the sakes of our souls and lives, we must embrace a faith that will stand, not only in human wisdom, but definitely in the favor of God.

The Apostle Paul reminds us in 2 Corinthians 5:7 that we walk by faith and not by sight. But what is "that" faith by which we walk? Speaking for God from deep within the soul, the trials of experience, and the inspiration of the Holy Spirit, the author of Hebrews 11:1 says: "Now faith is the substance of things hoped for, the evidence of things not seen." THAT'S WHAT THAT FAITH IS!

And if that were not enough, "Through faith we understand that the worlds were framed by the word of God, so that things which are seen were not made of things which do appear" (Heb. 11:3). Yes, the creation of *all* these "things" in which we believe, experience, know, and accept lies beyond our explanation. And almost beyond our comprehension, we firmly believe them. Without knowing their origins and beginnings, we accept them as real. Further, the writer observes that without faith it is impossible to please God, and that those who come to God *must* believe that He is and He (God) is the rewarder of them that diligently seek Him.

In John 14:11–13, it appears that the disciples are experiencing difficulty with Jesus' understanding of His (Jesus') identity with the Father. According to Jesus, He was in the Father and the Father was in Him. The complexity of the Father/Son relationship was a matter of concern for the disciples. The challenge of building a faith that will stand is that the belief must be deeper than the disbelief and our *faith* must be stronger than the absence of evidence to support the truth of "what" we are called upon to accept.

The Complexity Considered

In the midst of the complexity of faith, Jesus suggested to His disciples to step over their inability to explain their thinking of the complex. They were encouraged to allow God's work to evidence itself in us and to constitute the proof of His sayings.

Jesus moved to a still higher level regarding their future productivity. "Greater works shall you do, because I go to the Father" (Jn. 14:12, preacher's paraphrase). Yes, while struggling with comprehending/accepting Jesus' explanation of God's active presence in Him and He in the Father, Jesus raises another seeming improbability of their understanding: the Father's doing greater works in them than He had done and was doing in Jesus. The disciples' differential or shortfall of faith or not understanding the relationship of Jesus with the Father or their lack of understanding of Jesus' statement that they would do greater works than He had done because He was going to the Father evidences that there was a need of their possessing a deeper faith and understanding of the true nature of the "greater works" that God would accomplish through them.

And there is still yet another startling case of the disciples needing to advance in their faith and understanding of "how" to become involved in the transmission of God's powers in their ministries. According to Mark 9:17–29, the disciples had failed in their effort to heal a son that had been brought to them for healing. In this instance, Jesus described his disciples as a "faithless generation" and asked that the son be brought to Him. The father begged of Jesus to have compassion on the child, to which Jesus responded, "If thou canst believe, all things are possible to him that believeth." The father responded, "Lord I believe; help thou mine unbelief," and Jesus proceeded to cure the child. After entering the house, the disciples inquired of Jesus why they were not able to cast out the demon, to which Jesus responded, "This kind can come forth by nothing but by prayer and fasting."

In the cases of Jesus' statement to the disciples regarding His being in the Father and the Father in Him, the disciples' doing greater works than He, and the disciples' failure to heal the child possessed by a spirit, we witness an absence of an enhanced and needed relationship with God and the failure of ministry. In these instances we see the ability of the disciples blocked, their insights restricted, and an absence of the required maturity. In these instances, the disciples needed a faith greater than the one they possessed. They needed a faith that would stand in the power of God. In these instances, we witness both the inability and need of the disciples to step over the bars to their faith into the ability to rest more fully on God in spite of their lack of faith and the restricting hindrances, and to experience the truly faith-structured life and live for God—such a faith that will sustain us in times of trials and doubts.

These instances illustrate that, in our relationship with God, *the depth of our faith and the extent of our reach are of critical importance.* We are always challenged to strengthen them and learn how to utilize these avenues of travel to pursue God's mission with us. And any "gap" in our relationship with God reflects our inability to be available to the movements of God. So we are in prayer asking God's help in deepening our faith and extending our reach.

And let us not forget the admonition of the author of the Epistle to Hebrews, "But without *faith* it is impossible to please [God]" [italics added to indicate emphasis]. And, above all, we will succeed. Our faith is inextricably bound up in "who" and "what" we are, what we hope to become, and our power to lean on and trust God.

It is through a faith that will stand that we discover God in our midst and in our lives. And it is through a lasting faith that we are, like father Abraham, justified or counted by God as righteous, that our hope is alive, that we believe beyond love and are made perfect through grace, that we know a truly lasting relationship with God and stagger *not* at God's promises. And it is through faith that we enter the Land of Promise as owners and not merely wanderers.

Again, in Romans 4:3, Paul argues that by "faith" Abraham was accounted by God as righteous—and not by his (Abraham's) works. Paul said in his recognition of Abraham's being justified by faith and not by works: "For if Abraham were justified by works, he hath whereof to glory; but not before God" (Rom. 4:2). Thus, of the two, faith and works, justification is by faith and not works. Thus, the believer's hope of salvation is faith and not works.

Paul and James wrote and discussed the role and importance of faith and works in the life of Christians. Paul said, "The just shall live by faith" (Rom. 1:17), while, "By the works of the law shall no one be justified in His sight" (Rom. 3:20, preacher's paraphrase). On the other hand, James assigns importance to works as a viable, necessary, and acceptable performance of one's Christian service. His aim is to stress the importance of the believer's moving his faith beyond the theatrical and philosophical, disciplined position to an active, practical, radical, and productive faith.

Paul's aim is to note that the believer's salvation rests upon an all-saving "faith" in Jesus Christ and His suffering, which is not through works of the law. Paul does not contend that works are not needed or that they have no relevance, but that faith though the crucified Christ is the source of the believer's salvation and, though important, work of the law is not the source of our redemption. On the other hand, James stresses the importance of the believer's living out his/her faith by "doing" what God calls upon him/her to do/be. Thus, Paul discusses the question of if the source of our salvation is faith in Jesus Christ or works under the law; and James speaks to the issue of an active, working, productive faith. Both faith and works are issues of critical importance considered by the apostolic angles from different viewpoints... Thus, for both writers, faith and works are important when properly understood by the believer. Accordingly, for Paul and James, true faith is inclusive of living out God's purposes according to His will. For "by the works of the law shall no flesh be justified in His sight" (Rom. 3:20, preacher's paraphrase).

According to Romans 1:13–17, it is essential that we deepen our understanding and grasp of biblical faith and its operations in the life of the believer. Faith is indicative of the total redemptive process forged by God for humanity. Far beyond being a common term and concept, faith is the fundamental, basic, and yet all-inclusive hope of the believer. It bears the holder safely across the invisible divide, and is the basic and long range connecting thread that ties the followers of God and their hope together from beginning to end. Without it (faith), the Hebrews writer says, one cannot please God (11:6). Without faith, salvation cannot be reached.

To all who would seek and search for a definition of faith, the Hebrews writer says it is the essence of the matter of which things consist. Without it, the thing does not exist. It is faith and not knowledge about faith on which we stand or fall.

The believer's gaining and possessing a strong and enduring faith is basic to the Christian's holding on in times of difficulty. The believer must acquire, possess, and live beneath a strong faith that will, without question, allow the believer to stand and deepen his faith beneath the power of God.

Because faith and what it provides may not have been pursued by the believer as the "true" and "only" foundation of our hope, we need to be clear in our message regarding the law and role of faith in our relationship with God. For some, faith is not simply a road sign but a true turning point and evidence of our deeper and lasting relationship with God. For clarity, I am saying that the Scriptures are clear in teaching that we are saved by faith in Jesus Christ by the will of God. And such faith is an all-inclusive word of God and not...anything less. Just as the Apostle Paul said in his letter to the Roman Christians: "For I am not ashamed of the gospel of Christ: for it is the power of God unto salvation to everyone that believeth; to the Jew first, and also to the Greek. For therein is the righteousness of God revealed from faith to faith: as it is written, The just shall live by faith" (Rom. 1:16–17). "Behold, his soul that is lifted up is not upright in him: but the just shall live by...faith" (Hab. 2:4).

And now, following my best effort to deliver God's word regarding our growing relationship with God, may His salvation be yours for the remainder of your pilgrimage with God's word.

Jim McGuiggan

Jim McGuiggan is a native of Belfast, Northern Ireland. McGuiggan and his family moved to Lubbock, Texas, where he attended Sunset School of Preaching in Lubbock (1965–1967). Upon the completion of his work, he returned to Northern Ireland and taught at the North Ireland Bible School for six years. He joined the faculty of Sunset School of Preaching in 1973, teaching in both the graduate and undergraduate programs.

This sermon was preached at the annual Abilene Christian University Lectures in 1988 and demonstrates Sunset's commitment to evangelism and grace. While McGuiggan's sermon is organized topically, he exemplifies a beautiful gift both in his rhetorical skill and his understanding of narrative logic. The sermon does not feel like an argument but a compelling drama that calls the listener to participate.

McGuiggan notes in the opening line of the body of the sermon that he resists the traditional way of supporting points in an outline through "proof texting." Rather, McGuiggan supports his topical outline with both theological depth and rhetorical skill. He paraphrases scripture throughout, except as noted.

"God's Self-imposed Mission"

Alexander was driven by the gods to Grecianize the world in their name. Before that mission was completed, millions had died in the wars. The Mongol leader Genghis Khan was impelled by a sense of divine mission which led him to slaughter about 40 million people[1]. A handful of leaders planned to liberate the world's oppressed workers, and recently we were told that between fifteen and 30 million people died in the Communist Gulag labor system between 1918 and 1956.[2] Hitler's "inner voice" of Providence urged him to set a world on fire, and more than 60 million perished.[3] Death bringers, all of them!

First-century Rome was a flea market of borrowed gods and conquered peoples— world of eyes sunk in fat, double chins; illiterate emperors; sodomy; wedding dresses priced at $200,000 and $834,000; an elite which fed on nightingale tongues and peacock brains while their pet fish fed on the flesh of learned slaves. A world of death, gladiator shows, and sixty million slaves. A morose, sexual deviant called Tiberius ruled this putrefying mass, while over in Palestine a young rabbi was heard to say: "I am the bread of life!"

Palestine was in an extended uproar. The priesthood was a sham. Hasmoneans warred against each other while foreigners got a stranglehold on the country. Religion was going up and spirituality was going down; bandits roamed the hills; and more than one would-be messiah died in the heat of the desert with a band of deluded followers. The nation groaned and withered—its face sunken and its ribs showing. A man in a restless crowd said: "I didn't hear that; what did he say?" and was told: "He says his father sent him into the world to bring us abundant life!" The world was discovering, one more time, that we can't live by bread alone, or anything else alone! They "lived" in a frenzy of activity (religious, political, cultural, and otherwise) to hide their deadness. The earth, a giant globular coffin, swung its silent way around the sun, and a young man prayed in a garden: "This is eternal life, that they may know you, the only true God." He said he came to do his Father's will! He said no one knew his Father except him and those to whom he revealed him. He brought out the meaning of God and insisted that God sent him to give life to dead people, abundant life, eternal life! If we can believe Jesus, God's self-imposed mission is to bring life!

The Scope of God's Mission: To Whom Does God Offer Life?

The scope of God's mission isn't discovered in just a number of independent proof texts like Mark 16:15, Matthew 28:19 and Luke 24:47. These bring into focus the message God has saturated the Bible with. The purpose of God is universal; it embraces all people irrespective of their ethnic, religious, or moral background. It's seen in the Bible's doctrine of monotheism. There is only one God, said Paul, and he argues justification by grace through faith for *all* on that basis. See Romans 3:29–30. "If there is only one God," Paul argues, "then all can be saved by grace!"

God's mission is seen in the Bible's doctrine of creation. God didn't create Abraham, the father of Israel and the father of all that believe (Rom. 4:11). He created Adam and Eve, the parents of all, everywhere. Psalm 33:5–8 calls all people to revere God, whose unfailing love fills the earth. Psalm 8 reminds us that God created humankind, and Psalm 136:5–9 says he created out of love! Despite the fall, we remain in the image of God (Jas. 3:9; Gen. 5:1–2, 9:6). God didn't create mere creatures; he created children (Lk. 3:38). The universal Fatherhood of God is taught in Scripture!

It's seen in the Bible's doctrine of covenants. After the flood, a covenant was made with all living beings (Gen. 15). The rainbow is a permanent witness to God's universal love of humanity. The covenant with Abraham, Isaac, and Jacob is never mentioned without universal blessing being talked of (Gen. 12:3; 18:18; 22:18; 26:4; 28:14).

The Mosaic covenant (Ex. 19:5–6; 24:6–8) created Israel as the world's servant. See Isaiah 41:8 through the end of the book. Israel (whether speaking of it as a full national entity, a righteous remnant, or the Messiah as representing what Israel was meant to be to the world) is reminded that she was to serve the nations of the world on God's behalf–bringing salvation and life to them.

The new covenant of Jeremiah 31:31–34 creates a new Israeli commonwealth of faith. This new Israel (with 12 new founders, new covenant, new mediator, new priesthood, new sacrificial system and new high priest) is the Church. Initially, it was made up of believing, physical Jews who were sent to the whole wide world, offering salvation and life under the terms of that new covenant into which all nations "were invited" (Heb. 8:6–13; Eph. 2:11–12).

God's mission is seen in the Bible's doctrine concerning the nations. In Acts 14:15–17, Paul insists that the Lord, who created all, allowed the world's nations to go their own wicked way. Still, God didn't wash his hands of them. He continued to speak to them by loving provision, filling their hearts with gladness. In Acts 17, Paul insists that God blessed all nations with life and possessions as an expression of his search for them. Even when we're told that God gave the Gentiles up (Rom. 1:24, 26, 28), we're not to think he utterly jettisoned them. We're assured (Rom. 1:32) that God bound all of us under sin that he might have mercy on all!

God's mission is seen in the biblical doctrine that Christ is the representative of all people. Christ wasn't made sin only for the Church (2 Cor. 5:21). His blood wasn't shed only for Christians (1 John 2:2). The ransom he became was for all (1 Tim. 2:6). We're expressly told that God's Son became human so he could submit to dying for the human race as the unique expression of God's love for them.

Personally without sin, Christ so identified with humankind that he publicly responds to John's call to repentance and joins the penitents being immersed by him. In solidarity with us, Jesus confesses humankind's sin and need of repentance. On the cross, becoming our sin-bearer and curse-bearer, he who knew no sin says: "I am one with them by loving choice. We confess that you are right about our sin. In me, as representative of us all, we humbly bear your just condemnation of our sin!"

Racism, in practice, makes God the God of only one race and not humanity! Radical nationalism, in practice, despises the truth that all people are created in God's image. Cultural or political elitism undermines the universal Fatherhood of God who longs to reconcile his created children with himself. Religious sectarianism and elitism create the unhealthy "we" and "they," as if the two groups before God were the innocent and the guilty rather than the forgiven guilty and the unforgiven guilty! First-century Israeli self-centeredness was a major obstacle to God's purpose to reach out for the world, and the Church's preoccupation with itself is too.

The Cost of God's Mission: Is God Earnest about It?

You can tell how earnest people are about a purpose by how much they are willing to endure to see it accomplished. God's earnestness is seen in his patience. His purpose to gift the human race with life is eternal in duration (Rom. 8:29). If God hasn't quit by now, he won't! After the flood, almost as if he were musing, we're told he said he'd destroy the world no more (Gen. 8:21). The reason he won't is peculiar. God's slowness, at times, to bring judgment is because he longs for everyone to be saved (2 Pet. 3:9) and he endures with "great patience" the objects of his wrath (Rom. 9:22).

God's earnestness is seen in his sternness. It is *life* God wants to give, not just pardon! His judgments are his love in action. Chastisement is an inevitable expression of God's love, not the absence of it (Rev. 3:19). Love by being is compelled to clean up the objects of its love. (The Bible calls this aspect of love *holiness*.)

God's earnestness is seen in the Son's earnestness. The Word called a halt to the unbroken worship of the heavenly hosts and became incarnate! Something was more urgent than his continuing to be worshiped. We can read in Philippians 2:5–8. A woman's womb and a cattle shed showed Christ was in earnest. He spent 30 years in living preparation for the final conflict. He wanted to save the world–this big, round, crowded world. He. Alone.

"Are you prepared to pay the price?" asked God with admiration in his eyes for the young carpenter. "To leave all you have, home and friends and quiet joy?"

And Jesus said: "I am."

Some months went by. "And are you still ready to meet the cost of it," enquired God, "to watch the crowds drift away, your followers desert you, the criticism and gossip become more vicious, the enthusiasm dying, and the sniggering growing louder?"

"Yes, yes I am!" Jesus quietly said.

A couple of years later, and the ugly shadow of a cross fell across his path. "And now?" challenged God.

"Nothing's changed!" said the sober young man.

By and by, they nailed him down and left him there to die. And God questioned, "Dare you pay the full price for it?"

And this earnest young man, dying, said: "I do, Father." That is what it means to be earnest!

God's earnestness is seen in his own willingness to absorb pain. This historical act at Golgotha was the price God was willing to pay for offering life and friendship to humankind (2 Cor. 5:19; Acts 20:28: the "church of God which he purchased") (NASB). God's Son, bearing in his body humanity's sin, revealed what God had all along been bearing on his heart.

Whichever theory of the atonement you favor, this much is clear: Sin causes God incredible pain! Our view of how Golgotha fits into God's dealing with sin may or may not be important. It's crucially important that we believe it does and that atonement involves at least this: Soul-wrecking pain for God! *We* can't sit by free from pain while our loved ones destroy themselves—can God? In the cross, God uniquely commends his own love to us (Rom. 5:8), but the cross didn't create the love of God. It was an expression of it. The pain felt there didn't begin or end there! And the love expressed there is beyond our comprehension.

And Hosea married Gomer. The first child he "sowed" was called by the name: "whom God sowed" (Jezreel). He was suspicious about the second child; didn't feel the same about it and called its name, "who knew no pity" (Lo-Ruhumah). He knew the third wasn't his, so he called it, "No kin of mine" (Lo-Amnii). (from Hosea 1:4-9). By and by, the woman ended up on the auction block. It's easy to imagine a friend of Hosea's knocking on his door to say: "Hosea, I know Gomer has been faithless to you for years, breaking your heart and shaming you. I just wanted to tell you I saw her among the slaves in Dothan yesterday. They're auctioning them tomorrow. She's finally getting her due!"

Good news to Hosea? Hardly! He got out his money and headed off to Dothan to buy her back. Easy? Yes and No. Painless? Never! Over in one act? No, sir! But it was God who sent Hosea to buy her back. It was in his own pain that Hosea learned the gospel.

Our Response to God's Mission: What Does All This Mean to Us?

It means the God who lovingly drew us into the Church, offers us life! Not just forgiveness, but a loving and redeeming relationship with him. We should gladly acknowledge that. It means the God who so loves us, so loves all humanity, without exception—national or individual, cultural or religious, racial or socio-economical. We must fervently embrace that. It means the God who graciously elected the Abrahamic community, the Israelite nation, and the Church eternally intended the elect to be his channel of blessing to humanity, which he also elected to create for loving fellowship with himself. We must soberly receive that. It means the God who unashamedly loves the human race will bear any pain in pursuit of humanity's redemption. He has borne it all along and will choose to bear more through the new Servant Nation (the Church) whose calling is to bear witness in proclamation and experience of the suffering and death of Christ, that it might bear witness to his resurrection.

It means it isn't enough to worship God. We must imitate him (see Eph. 5:1)... I'm fully aware there is no life without praising and adoring (worshiping) God! I'm simply (but poorly) saying that his worthiness doesn't lie in his commanding worship, but in the loving and selfless character that lies behind the command. And I'm saying we must be extremely careful not to substitute verbal adoration or creedal correctness for vital involvement in what he regards to be of paramount importance–the bringing of the Gospel to humanity in word and in way.

Conclusion

Those of us who by grace have said "Yes" to God as Lord have said "Yes" to what he cherishes and is in solemn earnest about. Our lives are to be spent, then, in pursuit of nothing less than that! We aren't called simply to be good or kind–we are called to confront people with God's offer to eternal life! We aren't called to merely make them happy or comfortable; our destiny is to work with God to bring people into a redemptive relationship with God! That, and nothing less than that, is the Christian's call.

Landon B. Saunders

Landon B. Saunders (1937–) is a graduate of Freed-Hardeman College (AA, 1958) and Harding Graduate School of Religion (BA, 1959). Since 1970 he has served as the president of Heartbeat, Inc. He is also a Presidential Scholar at Lipscomb University and a Fellow at the Caris Life Sciences Foundation. His work focuses on the communication of issues found in faith and culture. He is currently a member of the Brookline Church of Christ in Boston, Massachusetts, and resides in Norwich, Vermont. Saunders is European American.

In 1969, after ten years in local ministry, he took a world tour—visiting over 80 countries seeking answers to the eternal questions of faith and doubt. Upon his return, he founded Heartbeat, a media ministry that reached out to millions. Heartbeat ministries led to the *Feeling Good About Yourself* workshop, and other events focused on helping in the aftermath of disasters such as Hurricane Andrew and massive job lay-offs.

"…Now I See" is a sermon that represents Saunders' life work and the focal theme of his messages. In coming to know Jesus, who gave up divinity in order to incarnate humanity, one can know God. As Jesus sees others with the eyes of God, so too can we find God by seeing others as Jesus did.

This sermon was first delivered at the Minter Lane Church of Christ in Abilene, Texas, in 1974, and was refined in subsequent presentations. Saunders uses the RSV.

"…Now I See"

One of the most profound questions ever asked was this: "Do you see this woman?" (Lk. 7:44). A Pharisee had invited Jesus to his home. A woman in the city who was known locally as a "sinful" woman heard Jesus was there and came in uninvited. She began to bathe Jesus' feet with her tears and to anoint them with an ointment she had brought. The Pharisee thought this was terribly wrong and said to himself, "If this man were a prophet, he would have known who and what sort of woman this is who is touching him—for she is a sinner." (Lk. 7:39). So, he reasoned, sinners should not touch Jesus, and Jesus should not allow himself to be touched by a sinner.

So how are human beings to be viewed? Let's ask the question in light of current issues. When a child says to the parents, "I am gay," how are the parents to view the child? If you learn that an immigrant does not have documentation, how are you to view that human being? If the next-door neighbor worships at a mosque, how is that neighbor to be viewed?

These are the kinds of questions that have plagued many religious people throughout history. How do the religious often see human beings? Do they see others through the lens of Bible verses or through the lens of love? Given the example of Jesus, how is it that so many who claim to follow him get it so wrong?

Jesus changed the way human beings are to view other human beings. Paul, recognizing this, wrote, "From now on, therefore, we regard no one from a human point of view" (2 Cor. 5:16a). In our age of increasing pluralism, I can think of few questions of greater significance. "How are humans to be viewed?" is the single question that I can say, without reservation, has shaped my own life and work more than any other. It changed forever the way I see each human being I…meet each day. And it changed forever the way I see God.

One of the most dramatic places we see this at work is found in the story of the blind man recorded by John in chapter nine of his Gospel. This man had been blind since birth. He sat on the street and begged. People passed by, perhaps occasionally tossed him a coin, but no one ever *saw* him the way Jesus did. As the story unfolds, it reveals five ways the blind man was viewed.

First, there was *the disciples' view*. They saw in him a question, a question for religious discussion. "Rabbi, who sinned, this man or his parents, that he was born blind?" (Jn. 9:2). They didn't really see the *man*. They saw a religious question.

Second, there was *the neighbors' view*. They saw him as a label—"a beggar." Labels tend to diminish human beings. They reduce persons, because, with the label, comes an array of associations, of judgments and biases, prejudices and conclusions about that person. "He's an alcoholic." "She's a prostitute." Someone has said, perhaps rightly so, "All labels are libels."

Third, there was *the Pharisees' view*. They saw him—even after his blind eyes were opened—as a problem, a problem that challenged their religious views. For example, they questioned whether it was right to heal a person on the Sabbath. They said of Jesus, "This man is not from God, for he does not observe the Sabbath" (9:16).

Fourth, there was *the parents' view*. Their view was reduced to biological facts. "We know that this is our son, and that he was born blind; but how he now sees we do not know…, nor do we know who opened his eyes. Ask him; he is of age" (9:20–21). Even the parents, because of their fear of the power of the religious leaders, spoke only of physical realities, carefully avoiding any mention of the spiritual intervention of Jesus.

And then there was the fifth view, *the view of Jesus*. According to Jesus , he was born blind "that God's works might be made manifest in him" (9:3). This is true of every human being—whether blind or not. Every human being enters the world as a biological being, but there is a vast work that must be done if that human being is to grow into maturity–into love, mercy, kindness, and purpose. Jesus names this view–this process–"God's works."

Jesus teaches us not to see a human being as a religious question, or a label, or a problem, or simply as a biological result. We are to see each person as one in whom "God's works" are revealed.

But what does this mean? What are "God's works"? In its most succinct form, "God's works" are found in the expression, "You shall love your neighbor as yourself" (Mt. 22:34–40). That is how Jesus saw all persons.

This highlights a difficult, difficult problem. Do we see others as neighbors we love as we love ourselves, or do we see human beings through the lens of Bible verses? Let's look at three occasions when this question emerged.

First, look again at the story of the blind beggar. The disciples and the Pharisees saw him through the lens of Scripture verses. This led to confusion and controversy. Jesus saw him through the lens of the Great Commandment of love. This led to a wonderful change in the person's life. Who got it right?

Second, when the woman who had been caught in the act of adultery was brought to Jesus, a group of people (with verses of Scripture in their mouths) justified stoning her. Jesus, seeing her through the lens of the Great Commandment of love, said to her, "Neither do I condemn you; go and do not sin again" (Jn. 8:11). These are the words of love. Who got it right?

Third, when the disciples picked corn on the Sabbath day to alleviate their hunger, Pharisees saw them with verses of Scripture on their tongues and condemned them. Jesus saw them through the lens of love and blessed them. Who got it right?

The attitude of one who sees others through the lens of Bible verses seems to be, "If everyone knew Scripture as well as I do, they would see this person as I see them…treat them as I treat them." Contrast that attitude with the response of Jesus in each of these examples.

Wikipedia tells us there are 969 chapters in the Bible and 31,102 verses. If we go over the lives of our neighbors with the fine-tooth comb of 31,102 verses, the results will be ugly–we will be ugly, and our neighbor will have no chance of love from us. In contrast, Jesus said that the 23,145 verses in the Old Testament find their supreme focus in love of God–loving God totally and our neighbor as we love ourselves. This, he said, is the Great Commandment on which all Scripture hangs. If understood, this is very good news for us…and for our neighbors!

But if our view of our neighbor–whom we are to love as we love ourselves–is replaced by endless debate over this or that Scripture, then we will exist in a state of perpetual confusion. And, more than likely, we will end up on the side of those objectors in the stories of Jesus. This is bad news for our neighbor.

So if we look at each human being—whether gay, or immigrant, or the member of a different religion or a different race or different nationality—as Jesus saw them, our first and central response will be to love. We are to see another human being with hearts and minds that have been shaped in the image of Christ, with eyes that see persons as Jesus saw them, understand Scripture in the way Jesus understood, and are therefore able to love a human being, regardless of who it is or what they've done, in the way Jesus loved them.

The story of Jesus' meeting the Samaritan woman at the well beautifully illustrates this view (John 4). She had had five husbands, was a member of a different religion, yet was spoken to by Jesus in a way that thrilled her and caused her to run to all of her friends and say, "You have to come see this person." Jesus knew Scripture, knew her failings, and yet spoke to her out of a love that brought her nearer rather than judging and driving her away. He put the woman before the restrictions of the law. He perfectly followed the law's deeper intent.

People today are turning away from organized religion in record numbers. Young people who were reared in churches are leaving in droves. Are they turning away from the love we are describing? Or are they turning away from a kind of religion we've seen in those who objected to seeing others as Jesus saw them? We must examine ourselves; we must examine how we see others, how we love our neighbors.

So many times we are fearful to love, fearful that we will be perceived as accepting wrongdoing if we love and welcome. But the love Jesus teaches conquers all wrong. In the presence of that love…one has a chance!

Our world desperately needs people who know how to see others, others who are different. Our world does not need Christians and churches that are filled with angry speech, filled with condemnation and judgment— even contempt—for others. Our place is not to judge others. Paul says clearly, "God judges those outside" (1 Cor. 5:13). This relieves us of a terrible burden and frees us to meet each human being in love.

"God so loved the world…" (Jn. 3:16). In Jesus we see in human terms what that looks like. What a difference it makes to see human beings as Jesus saw them! No difficulty is insurmountable; no sin obscures the human being; no question blurs the demand to love. To love as Jesus loved is to know what to do, how to behave, with any human being one meets. No stammering. No hesitation. No delay. No problems or labels, fears or questions.

When we love as Jesus loved, any problems of life can be overcome. And the people we meet and know, because they have been loved with this love, will be able with one voice to cry out, "One thing I…know, that though I was blind, now I see" (Jn. 9:25).

Let us go forth and work the "works of God" while it is day.

Lynn Anderson

Lynn Anderson graduated with an AA from Freed-Hardeman University in 1957, a BA degree from Harding University in 1959, and a MA from Harding Graduate School of Religion in 1965. Anderson was the first to graduate with a DMin degree from Abilene Christian University, in 1990. He is the founder of Hope Network Ministries, serving for 21 yrs. During this time, he consulted with hundreds of churches, coaching leaders through transition and equipping them with skills necessary for community. Lynn also taught as a graduate professor at Abilene Christian University and Pepperdine University. His 60 years of ministry include 11 years of church planting in his native British Columbia, Canada, plus many years as Senior Minister in churches in the U.S. (19 yrs. at Highland Church, Abilene, Texas, and 5 at Preston Road, Dallas). He has authored 11 books, his most popular title being *They Smell Like Sheep: Spiritual Leadership for the 21st Century*.[1] He is European American.

"Places in the Heart" was first delivered at the Highland Church of Christ, Abilene, Texas, around 1978. It was one sermon in a series, "Jesus and People," drawn from the Gospel of John, chapters 1–10. The sermon is a dramatic retelling of the story of Jesus and the Samaritan woman at the well. At the climax, Anderson's central image is an empty water jar, carrying the primary message that the miracle for the woman is still available. He uses the NIV.

"Places in the Heart"

John 4:19–21, 23–26

My friend Clois often said, "There is always something going on behind what's going on." He meant that surface words or actions are merely symptoms of what is going on beneath the surface of life. But these surface symptoms often appear to be totally unrelated to the real and larger issues in the depth of a heart. Thus, conversation focused on surface issues often leaves the real issues untouched.

But in this conversation, Jesus gently moves from surface issues to the heart of the matter. Jesus and the woman both sensed that "something was going on behind what was going on" that day at the well. Jesus knew that the woman's search for water—and even for marital security—was only a surface clue to the profoundly deeper longings of her heart. So he initiates the conversation, "Could you give me a cup of water?"

The woman, on the other hand, feared that behind Jesus' friendly words lay either a come-on or some other sort of trap. So naturally, still suspicious, she probed a bit more: "How is it that you—a man and a Jew—ask me—a woman and a Samaritan—for a drink of water?" One wonders what tone colored her voice when she reminded Jesus that Jews have no dealings with Samaritans: *curiosity? hostility?* Did she spit the word "*Jew*" as if it were a four-letter expletive?

However, Jesus explained, "There is a well of special water—the kind that can permanently quench all thirst."

See the wistful look in her eye as she pictures a life with no painful encounters at the well? "Sir, give me this water so that I won't get thirsty, and…have to keep coming here to draw water" (Jn. 4:15). Listen to her heart! This man not only accepted her, but also seemed to respect her as she was. What is more, He offered her a way out of her past, a route that did not lead only to new burdens and another man's bed! *Can this man set me free? Dare I believe He could, somehow, actually give me a new start?*

But if this is what she imagined, the daydream of escaping her "ball and chain" of matrimonial failures seemed quickly shattered when Jesus said, "Go, call your husband" (Jn. 4:16). Why? What was Jesus doing? Was He trying to embarrass her into repentance? Hardly.

Jesus ached with the emptiness that had stalked the days and nights of this woman's life. And when she said, "I don't have a husband," she wasn't pretending things were different than they were. She was saying, "I don't even have a husband… I…I don't have *anything* at all."

At some special day in the past, she had celebrated her first wedding. Dreams radiant with joy. But before long, came that *other day,* when her husband took her to the door and announced three times to the whole neighborhood "I divorce you" (as was the divorce custom of the day). And she found herself suddenly on the street—alone, a dream shattered, destitute, facing prostitution or something worse.

Later, another romance came along and another marriage proposal. She went home with him, no doubt thinking maybe she had found a good man and a solid marriage this time. But a second husband also took her to the "divorcing door." How utterly devastating! But it got even worse: she had also a third failure, and then a fourth, and a fifth. Till, finally, on number six, a wedding ceremony seemed pointless.

When Jesus looked her in the eye and said, "I understand. You don't even have a husband," I do not believe it was a rebuke. Rather, I believe Jesus was empathizing, "You are the victim of at least five evil men! You've endured five heartbreaking experiences that have devastated you. And now you don't even have a husband. No security. No relationship. No love and joy. No home that you can count on! And you see no way this cycle will ever be broken."

So when the woman asked about the temple, she was not dodging Jesus' point; she was plunging right into the middle of it. She was saying,

"That's right. My life is so very empty. I desperately need God. Could you tell me where to find Him?"

Jesus had cut straight to the source of her pain. Authentic healing only comes when the real wound is treated. Jesus teaches us here the importance of cutting deeper than the superficial and lancing the real source. He is empathizing with the hopelessness that plagued the days of this woman's life. He is extending His hand to her, offering to enter the dark chamber of her world. *Jesus, do I see your thumb brush the corner of your eye?* "It must hurt, even after the pain of five desertions, that the man you now live with won't even give you his name."

This Samaritan woman and this Galilean carpenter are not standing toe to toe in some type of word game. No, they now stand soul to soul, Jesus the master surgeon and she the grateful patient. What Jesus sees here is not one wicked whore (as some are prone to assume, but Scripture does not say.) Rather, He saw a broken-hearted woman, stripped of nearly every vestige of dignity, but who is *still* hungry for God.

And He was looking at a person who mattered deeply to Him, and to His Father. And, possibly, her first glimmer of hope was awakened in her heart, because she stood face to face with the first man she ever met who didn't hurt her

Before you tag a person "divorcee," you might pause and consider the sting that word carries. When someone loses a mate to death, he or she grieves and we pull alongside him or her and grieve too. His or her heart is broken and something is gone that can never be replaced. But as excruciating as the pain will be, there is usually some dignity in that kind of grief.

But when one loses a mate through divorce, the same unutterable pain occurs. An unfillable void is created. However, there is no dignity in the loss and no real closure. So few comforters flow to the side of a divorced person to help them grieve. Few stand with them in the loss and loneliness. In fact, the opposite often occurs. Someone who already feels like a failure in relationships gets leveled to the ground by intolerance and lack of forgiveness. This grief has no dignity. Not only that, but the "corpse" is still walking around!

Let's multiply that cycle by five and see if we can fathom the gaping wound in the center of this woman's soul. She may not have been a bad woman at all. To me, she looks more like the victim of six *bad men.* Perhaps she was plain. Maybe she came from a poor neighborhood. Maybe she couldn't carry on a conversation. Maybe she was missing her two front teeth. We don't know why she was so rejected. Whatever the reasons, layer by layer the viciousness of these men had stripped her down until there was little left that was fine in her nature. Yet these men had not stripped away her hunger for God, her hope for a coming Messiah!

Ironically, those who have suffered the most often become the most spiritually insightful. Maybe it's because they have more reason for serious introspection—or because their desperation sharpens the focus of their search for a way out of their distress. Again, whatever the reasons, this woman's next comment reveals a long, tenacious pilgrimage in search of God!

"Our ancestors worshiped on this mountain, but you Jews claim that the place where we must worship is in Jerusalem" (Jn. 4:20). In other words, "I really do want to know God. But I don't know where to find Him! You people say He is in the temple. My people say He is on the mountain. I have investigated both places and I didn't find much 'God' going on in either one. You seem to have inside information: so, whom do I believe?"

What have you felt as you heard these words? You may have resonated with this woman. Possibly you, too, have long searched for God. Perhaps you, too, have found no answers for those questions that steal your sleep. Maybe, like her, you have heard the endless, pointless wrangling about religion among the "religious experts" and have walked away from a few visits to church feeling emptier than when you came. If so, I think you will like Jesus' response!

At this point, I picture Jesus becoming animated. He still gets excited today when He finds pure hunger for God in a broken human heart! I see Him forget His weariness, forget His hunger and the heat. I see Him gently lift the jar from the woman's shoulder, and motion for her to find a seat. And then He began revealing truths to her that up to this point He had revealed to no one else! That's right! The first person to whom Jesus revealed Himself as the Messiah is a racially outcast, five-times divorced, live-in girlfriend!

Let's paraphrase his response. "There is a day coming when the *place* of worship won't make any difference. You Samaritans worship what you do not know. You've been taught that going to the right mountain and performing the right ritual is how you find God. It isn't so. Relationship with God doesn't work that way."

One can imagine Jesus' finger punching the air as He continues. "True, salvation is from the Jews. But the day is coming…" He pauses and looks intently in the woman's eyes and says, "that day *has now come* when the 'where' and 'when' of worship will not matter. What really matters to God is genuineness in a worshiper. He cares about what is happening in your heart." Oh yes, Jesus saw her dark days. Felt her soul-hunger. "You are on the right track. You're on the right track! Your heart is hungry for God and you have never given up on your search."

Now if you think eavesdropping on this dialogue has been fun up until this point, listen to the woman's next few words: "I know that Messiah" (called Christ) "is coming. When he comes, he will explain everything to us" (Jn. 4:25).

Listen to that! Her question gives us a clue to the poor woman's heart. Remember, this is a Samaritan woman talking about the Messiah! Apparently this hope has kept her warm on all those cold nights. "In the back of my heart, for all these years, I've been dreaming of the day when God himself would come, hoping against hope that I could know Him."

Can you imagine what comes next? Don't miss the drama. It takes my breath away. Don't miss the pure joy and the mist in Jesus' eye as He moves yet a bit closer and says softly, "The one you've been waiting for? He is here. It's me."

I believe that is why she trashed her water jar. That is why she nearly ran over the band of disciples coming up the trail. That is why she stopped the first person she saw in the village and said, "Come and see a man who knows every dream I've ever dreamt and every tear I've ever wept. He saw my first wedding–white gown–flushed cheeks–romantic visions of a neat house on a quiet street–a baby babbling in the crib–He felt my delirious happiness.'

"And He felt the deep, searing, relentless pain that I felt when I was taken to the door that first time and my husband called the neighbors around and said three times 'I divorce you.' This man by the well heard me crying on my lonely bed night after night for all those years. Rejection after rejection. He knew why I finally settled for a 'live-in: a guy who didn't even give me his name.' He also knew those long nights when my heart cried out for God. That I have hoped for Him and longed for Him. *Could this man really be the Messiah?* It seems too good to be true, but I think I just gave a cup of water to God! Now this man has come and the chords that were broken will vibrate once more. For the first time in years, I feel hope!" Then the whole village, thirsty for living water, came running out to meet Jesus.

Be honest now, if the town tramp ran up to you and said, "Guess what? I just met a guy at the well who told me every bad secret I was hiding; come on out, and meet Him so He can do the same for you," do you think you and the whole town would rush out to the well? Not likely, right? But John says the whole town went out to see Him. They wanted to be valued as well. And understood. And forgiven!!

The living water does not flow to a *holy house* in Jerusalem or a *holy hill* in Samaria; and for this woman, not even to a *happy home*, or she could never have drunk it. But the living water flows to a *hungry heart*. The heart is the temple where God comes to live. It is also the vessel in which we carry home the living water. Jesus was looking for what was in this woman's heart. Love always sees the best; it always looks for the best. And Jesus saw the best in this Samaritan lady: a tender heart nearly buried forever under the rubble of the woman's broken life.

What happened then? The key that unlocks this story is found beside the well: The abandoned water jar. She had no more need to water the last dry sticks of a dead-end relationship. The abandoned water jar speaks eloquently. It says, "Jesus stirred a slumbering hope to its feet." It declares that this wounded woman found a joy so deep that she forgot to do what she came to do and took off to tell everyone the news, "The Messiah is here!" Instead of lugging heavy jars of tepid water to the house of a demanding human sponge, she piped in living water to all the hearts of a grateful, thirsty village.

Jesus' disciples came back from a grocery-shopping trip and found Him standing by the well (no doubt, with a big grin on His face) staring at the disappearing figure of a woman who was hotfooting it toward town. The disciples didn't know what happened. Jesus volunteered no explanation, and they lacked the courage to ask. One of them handed him a sandwich, and He turned it down. He seems too excited to eat. Who could eat at a moment like this? "Open your eyes," he told them. They looked up in time to see the excited woman disappear around the curve of the trail. "Look at the fields! They are ripe for harvest" (Jn. 4:35).

Before long, a crowd of Samaritans appeared around the same curve, with the same woman leading the pack. Smiling. Last time she came down that trail she was alone, carrying a heavy water pot and a heavier history of pain. This time, however, she comes with friends. This time she comes unburdened and jubilant. "There He is!" she cries. They have come to invite this newly found Messiah and His friends to their town.

Talk about creative! Imagine the captivating scene. A handful of young Jews walking into town with a group of curious Samaritans. On any other day, if these two factions were found together a fight would surely be brewing. But this time they are drawn together by a common hunch, a common hope, that this unassuming carpenter might...just might...be the one they've been looking for.

So the crowd headed back to town, following an odd couple: a Jewish man and a Samaritan woman; a rabbi and riff-raff; incarnate God and a single mother; a long-sought Messiah and a long-rejected misfit!

As we follow this Man-God on His brief earthly journey, we grow accustomed to His entourage; we frequently find Him flanked by assorted castoffs. Tax collectors, harlots, crooks, and thieves—they seemed to flow to Him. Somehow, they perceived that although He knew their darkest secrets, He was willing to forgive them. He felt their sharpest pain, too, and their deepest hunger—their longing for God! Somehow, they detected that He could bring cleansing to their lives, so stained with forbidden fruit, and freshness into their stale worlds.

Much ado is made over the way Jesus healed physical illnesses. We also cover our mouths in awe at the way He mastered the storm or sent a dozen shrieking demons into the deep. Appropriate response. But once we watch Him treat the gaping wounds of this nameless woman...once we see the balm that He could so carefully place upon the lacerated souls...that's when we are left most amazed. Here is where He performed His most majestic miracles and stilled His greatest storms: when He is stitching together the ragged lives of unwanted people.

Want proof? Look back at the well. The water jar is still abandoned. Want more proof? A whole town came out to meet the one who cared enough to notice. He calls us to open our eyes to look beneath the surface chaos into the hunger lingering at the depths of human hearts.

Paul Watson

Paul Watson (1939–) received his BA degree from Abilene Christian College in 1961, and his BD and PhD at Yale in 1965 and 1970, respectively. He taught at Erskine College in Due West, South Carolina (as faculty 1968–1974, and as dean of students 1974–1979), at Institute for Christian Studies in Austin, Texas (1979–1983), and at Pepperdine University (1970–1971). After moving to Durham, North Carolina, he spent 24 years preaching for the Cole Mill Road Church of Christ. In retirement, Watson teaches Bible (primarily Old Testament) and ministry (primarily homiletics) online for Amridge University in Montgomery, Alabama. Paul has also served as a board member for *LEAVEN* since 1989 and is a frequent presenter at national lectureships and preaching seminars. He is European American.

Paul Watson's sermon from Isaiah 56:1–8 represents his typical expository style. The sermon also uses Luke 14. He uses his own paraphrasing of Scripture, except where noted. This sermon was preached on October 31, 2004, at the Cole Mill Road congregation in Durham, North Carolina. The listener is caught up in the scene and, with just a few words, the poetry sings.

The original manuscript was scripted as dialogue, but due to space limitations the scripting is minimized here. The last third of the sermon is a dramatic retelling of a popular movie. The story carries the weight of concretizing the sermon without further reflection.

"The God Who Gathers the Rejected"

Isaiah 56:1–8; Luke 14:15–24

Few things in life hurt, sting more than rejection.

A child approaches another child at school and says, "I want to be your friend. Will you be my friend?"

And the answer comes, "No. Why would I want to be your friend?"

You go for a job interview, one you have prepared for, dressed for very carefully.

You give it your best shot; but, at the end of the interview you hear, "Thanks for coming in today; however, I don't think we can use you."

Rejection.

On the other hand, few things in life feel better than being accepted, and accepting. When my stepson Stan was in the sixth grade, his class got to play softball at recess, with two students serving as captains on a rotating basis. Everyone in the class enjoyed the game–none more so than Sally, who was perhaps the most uncoordinated child for her age the school had ever seen. Sally could not catch the ball; could not throw the ball; could not hit the ball. Otherwise, Sally was great. As you can imagine, no captain ever chose Sally if they could help it. Sally always came last—except this week, when Stanley burst into the house and said, "Mama! Guess what! It was my turn to be captain, and I chose Sally first of all."

Our sermon this morning is about rejection…and acceptance. Let us pray.

For the past two weeks we have been with Israel in Babylonian exile: looking forward to that time when the great promises of God would come true and Israel would be able to go home. Today we move into the last 11 chapters of Isaiah, which contain oracles addressed to a people who had done just that—who had returned home. After the Jews had endured more than a half-century of captivity, Cyrus the Persian conquered Babylon; And, within a year, Cyrus issued a great emancipation proclamation allowing all Jews who chose to do so to go home. It was an amazing event.

Those who did decide to return had problems once they got back "home." "What sort of community shall we be?" they asked themselves. "It's wonderful to start a new community, but what kind of community is that going to be? What shall be our priorities?"

We know from the prophets Haggai and Zechariah that they put the rebuilding of their own homes above that of rebuilding God's temple. It's a matter of priorities, don't you see?

Another question troubled them: "Who shall be included in our new community? Just those of us who have returned home from Babylon? What of our fellow Jews here in the land, whose grandparents never went into exile? Shall we include them? And there are a lot of 'furriners' (foreigners) here who have overrun our land. What about them? Are we going to run them off?" The question is, "Who belongs?"

The answers of this returned group tended to be exclusivist and fundamentalist: "Only pure-bred Jews," they tended to say. "Only those who keep God's Torah in minute detail." So what a surprise—and what a blow—it must have been for them to get these new messages from God in these last 11 chapters of Isaiah, beginning here in Isaiah 56:1-2, which sets the tone for what follows. "This is what the LORD says: Maintain justice, and do what is right; for my salvation is close at hand, and my righteousness will soon be revealed. Blessed is the man who does this, the one who holds it fast, who keeps the Sabbath without desecrating it, and keeps his hand from doing any evil."

Maintain justice. Do righteousness. Keep the Sabbath. How many times do the prophets ring out those words? We heard it back in Isaiah 5:7, at the end of the Song of the Vineyard, when Isaiah said, "My people are like God's vineyard, except they are not productive." In spite of all the care that God had given his vineyard, the vineyard had only produced wild grapes.

God said, through Isaiah: "I looked for righteousness, but found only bloodshed; I looked for justice, but heard only a cry – a cry of pain that arose from violence."

Righteousness and justice were two of Amos' favorite words as well: "Take away from me the sound of your harps, I don't care about your worship services" (Amos 5:23). "But let justice roll down like waters, and righteousness like an ever-flowing stream" (Amos 5:24, NRSV).

Favorite words of our Lord as well: "It's well and good for you to tithe those little garden herbs of yours—mint, dill, cumin. But more important still are the weightier matters of the Law—justice and mercy and faith" (Mt. 23:23).

God's will, as expressed in God's Torah, was much more than a list of "do's" and "don'ts." It was meant to cover *all* of life: To establish community. To establish relationships that were supportive, not competitive—relationships built on mutual respect, mutual concern, and mutual love.

And what about the Sabbath? This was not a "let's go to church and get it over with so we can have the rest of the day to ourselves" kind of commitment. Sabbath was part of those fundamental "expectations" God had for people that we call the Ten Commandments. Sabbath was to be a day of remembrance of God's powerful deliverance. And when Israel kept the Sabbath in this way—with all of its rich, full meaning in front of them—it would be a sign to their children, to their neighbors, to the world of who they were and to whom they belonged. "Blessed is the one who keeps the Sabbath and maintains justice and does what is right" (Isaiah 56:2).

But then who is that "one"? Who is to be admitted to the assembly of the people? Who belongs to that God-oriented community? Only those people whose bloodlines are pure, whose lineage can be traced back to one of the 12 sons of Jacob? Only the "good people," the "beautiful people," the "right people"? Not at all.

"Do not let the foreigner joined to the LORD say, 'The LORD will surely separate me from his people'; and do not let the eunuch say, 'I am just a dry tree'" (Isa. 56:3). Those words would have been mind-blowing to those people who were trying to rebuild their homes, their lives, their temple. "These folks, and folks like them—foreigners, outsiders, physically handicapped, nobodies—they belong as well—*providing* they observe the Torah of God."

What is so mind-blowing about this is that these are the very people who are excluded in Deuteronomy 23:

> No one whose testicles are crushed or whose penis is cut off shall be admitted to the assembly of the LORD. Those born of an illicit union shall not be admitted to the assembly of the LORD. Even to the tenth generation, none of their descendants shall be admitted to the

assembly of the LORD. No Ammonite or Moabite shall be admitted to the assembly of the LORD. Even to the tenth generation...

You shall not abhor any of the Edomites, for they are your kin. You shall not abhor any of the Egyptians, for you were an alien... in their land... The children of the third generation that are born to them may be admitted to the assembly of the LORD. (23:1–3a, 7–8, NRSV)

Some may come in sooner; some may come in later; some may never come in. But now God says: "They may all be included in my assembly. Eunuchs may have a memorial, even better than children of their own. Foreigners may bring their offerings, their sacrifices to my altar. My house shall be a house of prayer for all people."

God is a God who has great and wonderful expectations for his people: A way of life that is harmonious and fair. A way of life that is uplifting and deeply satisfying for all who choose to accept it–and that includes outcasts and rejects, the maimed and the strays.

And God's inclusion of folks such as these was not limited to this generation that returned home from exile; his inclusivity was meant to go on; and it still goes on, even today.

You remember Jesus' parable of the great banquet in Luke 14:15–24: "Someone gave a great dinner and invited many" (v. 16). It would be like receiving an invitation to dinner at the governor's mansion or the White House: "The President and First Lady invite you to join us for dinner..." But the original recipients turned down the invitation: The noble, the well-bred, the "beautiful people" offered their excuses. And the host said to his servants, "Find some street people – the poor, the homeless, the blind, the lame – and invite them to come to my banquet. And if that doesn't fill my house, go out into the country; search the lanes and the byways; and compel those whom you find to come in."

You heard the words of Peter from Acts 10 this morning as we came to the Table: Peter said, "I get it. I get it. They're OK, folks like Cornelius and his clan. They can enter the kingdom of heaven."

Paul said, at greater length, in Ephesians 2:11–22, "These folks, these Gentiles, are no longer aliens and strangers, but fellow citizens of God's kingdom and members of God's family."

"Thus says the Lord GOD, who gathers the outcasts of Israel, 'I will gather others to them, besides those already gathered.'" (Isa. 56:8, NRSV).

A wonderful contemporary depiction of this is the movie made a number of years ago called *Places in the Heart.* It is set in the 1930s in the small town of Waxahachie, Texas. The movie stars Sally Field as a widow trying to protect her house and land from foreclosure by the town banker.

The five of them—a widow, her two young children, a handyman who sleeps in the barn, and a blind roomer in the house—are now living together...as a community. The widow empowers the itinerant handyman by expressing her confidence in his ability to harvest the cotton so that they can be first to the cotton gin, win the first-place prize money, and save her home and land.

The widow herself is not solely interested in harvesting the cotton; she cares about the cotton pickers too. After they have worked all night picking cotton, she insists that they have breakfast before going back into the fields one last time to finish their work—even if it means losing the race for the prize.

Do you see what is happening in all of that? Community is being shaped. *Justice* and *righteousness* are being practiced.

The final scene takes place in the community church on a Sunday morning. The preacher has taken his text from 1 Corinthians 13, preaching about love. Down on the front row are the widow's sister and her husband. They have been in a strained relationship because the husband has been unfaithful. But in the course of the reading of the Scripture she reaches across the distance that separates them on the pew to take his hand, in a gesture of reconciliation. And then it is time to serve communion. Miraculously speaking, everyone is there: The widow's sister and her husband take communion together. Down at the end of the row is this "crazy lady" who lived out of her car but who disappeared in the tornado—somehow she's there. The banker and his wife are there. The four pickers from a travelling string band who came through town occasionally to play for barn dances—they're there. Of course, the widow is there, with her two children. Somehow the itinerant handyman has come back to town,

And he is sitting on the pew next to the blind man; and they share the tray as it is passed along to them. They pass it along in turn to the sheriff and the young black man who had shot him. Apparently they have been resurrected, and they are there. They are *all* there, together...

Gathered by the God who gathers the outcasts of Israel—even today. Amen.

Rubel Shelly

Rubel Shelly earned a PhD at Vanderbilt University. He preached 27 years with the family of God at Woodmont Hills in Nashville, where he also taught at Lipscomb University, Vanderbilt University School of Medicine, and Tennessee State University. In 2005 Shelly became Professor of Philosophy and Religion at Rochester College. In 2008, he was named President of Rochester College. In 2015, he returned to Nashville as Distinguished Professor of Philosophy and Religion at Lipscomb University. Shelly has published several books, most recently *The Lamb and His Enemies.*[1]

Shelley first preached "Loving Someone Who Isn't 'One of Us'" in 1980, fearful about how it would be received. Shelly told his spouse, "This may be our last Sunday at Ashwood! I must be satisfied with telling what Jesus did and making some obvious applications that don't fit my experience."

There were mixed reactions to the sermon. Shelly's own public pilgrimage of faith as a white male preacher reflects something of a microcosm of many other members of Churches of Christ. "Loving Someone Who Isn't 'One of Us'" starts with trouble in the world that is seen in the life of the church. Next, Shelly turns to a biblical story, simply letting the words of Jesus speak. Moving toward resolution, he brings listeners to a new non-sectarian faith. He primarily uses the NIV.

"Loving Someone Who Isn't 'One of Us'"

The best way for Churches of Christ to get clear about our mission in the world is to study the life of Jesus. Our goal is to be, in our corporate life, the continuation of who Jesus was in his personal life. So we must take our cues from him.

We see Jesus breaking down barriers by taking time for children, affirming the dignity of women, and receiving the people others avoid. He touches lepers and blind people. He receives Gentiles and makes a Samaritan the hero of one of his best-known parables. He rescues a woman about to be stoned for adultery. He eats with tax collectors and sinners. As you read those stories from the Gospels, however, you notice that the religious establishment is outraged by his behavior. They don't imitate him. They criticize him—and, eventually, *murder* him!

It distresses me greatly that churches generally have the same bad name with the general public today that I have just given the "religious establishment" of Jesus' time. That is, churches are typically viewed more as exclusive clubs than welcoming havens. More people say they find nonjudgmental acceptance in Alcoholics Anonymous than in churches. And if you are inclined to reply in a defensive mode that groups like A.A. are willing to tolerate every point of view and let people get by with doing anything they like, you are exposing the fact that you know nothing about how Alcoholics Anonymous functions.

Christ's church is supposed to be the place where the disenfranchised and rejected find acceptance. It was created to be the place where Jew or Gentile, slave or free, and male or female would all stand on equal footing. It is supposed to be a unified group in our fragmented world that models oneness among black and white, have and have-not, educated and illiterate, Democrat and Republican, American capitalist and Chinese communist. Is that how the world sees the church? Does the church bridge those great divides in human experience? Why, we can't even model unity among those of us who confess Christ as the Son of God and try to follow him!

Jesus not only challenged his disciples to love those who were ethnically or socially different from themselves but those who held different religious beliefs. Do you realize that the parable of the Good Samaritan points to both race and religion as distinctions between the wounded man and his rescuer? Ironically, Jesus made the Samaritan the hero of the story—a story he told to a Jewish audience.

Let's look at a love-your-neighbor passage. The circumstances that produced it are clear from the brief context in which it is set. The narrowness of his own disciples' views forced Jesus to confront them for their suspicion, hatred, and exclusion of someone whose experience of him was different from their own.

> "Teacher," said John, "we saw a man driving out demons in your name and we told him to stop, because he was not one of us."

> "Do not stop him," Jesus said. "No one who does a miracle in my name can in the next moment say anything bad about me, for whoever is not against us is for us. I tell you the truth, anyone who gives you a cup of water in my name because you belong to Christ will certainly not lose his reward." (Mk. 9:38–41)

John was guilty that day of what many of us have done over the centuries of church history. He equated being "one of us" with belonging to Christ. He was mistaken. Jesus rebuked his narrowness and told him to stop passing judgment on other people who were following him. Paul would later rebuke the church at Rome for the same sort of narrow-mindedness: "Who are you to judge someone else's servant? To their own master, servants stand or fall. And they will stand, for the Lord is able to make them stand" (Rom. 14:4).

I have a dear friend who pastors a Pentecostal Church. A while back he made this confession to me: "Rubel, time was that I would not have considered you my brother in Christ because of the way you were baptized. My church tradition took Acts 2:38 to be a 'pattern' that required us to say 'in the name of Jesus Christ' as a verbal formula when we immersed somebody. And because you were baptized 'in the name of the Father, and of the Son, and of the Holy Spirit,' I could not honor your baptism."

Can you imagine it? We both believed that Scripture was the word of God to humankind. We both confessed Jesus Christ to be Immanuel, God come in the flesh. We had both repented of our sins. We both believed it was necessary to be immersed in water for the remission of sins. But he thought my baptism didn't count because the "formula" somebody said when I was put under the water invoked the Trinity instead of the name of Jesus only! Can you imagine the arrogance of that?

Here's what I told him: "Dear Brother, I felt exactly the same way about you. Because of how I was taught to interpret Acts 2:38, I would not have considered you my brother in Christ. I could not honor your baptism. I can certainly forgive you your arrogance in judging me, if you will forgive my arrogance in judging you."

There are some Bible stories in the Old Testament that we used to tell with particular slants to make people think that God is a stickler for detail and eager to make an example of anyone who broke a rule. They were used in sermons to say that anybody who misinterpreted Scripture or failed to follow the biblical pattern down to its minute details had no hope of seeing God. So we told about "poor old Uzzah," who made an honest mistake with good intentions in touching the Ark of the Covenant, and was struck dead for his trouble.

We warned about "strange" and "unauthorized" worship practices in light of the Nadab and Abihu story in Leviticus 10, in which the two sons of Aaron were killed on the spot for some offenses they committed in their haste or inattention to the rules of the sanctuary.

God's instruction to us in terms of rules and commandments is to be taken seriously. A disciple listens and learns. A servant hears and obeys. As Jesus would later teach us, however, some disciples learn more and others less. And there are varying degrees of responsibility for servants, depending on their opportunities and potential. The sense of fairness we humans have comes from the fact that we are made in God's image, after all.

But if the servant thinks, "My master won't be back for a while," and begins oppressing the other servants, partying, and getting drunk—well, the master will return unannounced. He will tear the servant apart and banish him with the unfaithful. The servant will be severely punished, for though he knew his duty, he refused to do it. But people who are not aware that they are doing wrong will be punished only lightly. Much is required from those to whom much is given, and much more is required from those to whom much more is given (Lk. 12:45–48).

So we need not worry that lack of information and opportunity will be treated as rebellion. We need not worry that someone who does the best she can, under limited conditions, will be treated like the "irreverent" and "defiant" person. It is only deliberate, willful sin that one commits against God in defiance of his holiness for which there is no sacrifice left to atone (Heb. 10:26; cf. Num. 15:30).

The God who has revealed himself in Jesus deals with us as a loving father does a prodigal-but-dearly-loved child. We are not numbers on his judge's docket; we are the objects of his love as daughters and sons within the dysfunctional human family. Yet we need to understand that God didn't become kind, loving, and gracious after Calvary. Calvary happened because he has always been that way! And the horrible misrepresentation of those Old Testament stories already named–of Uzzah, Nadab, and Abihu–is perhaps easier to justify than the avoidance of certain stories that would have taught us not to understand them as they were being represented to us. Take just one example. It is a story a brother pointed me to when I was in Uganda several years ago.

Hezekiah became King of Judah at age 25 in the year 715 B.C. He was convinced that the horrible state of affairs in his kingdom was due to the sins of his ancestors. They had been punished by Yahweh for their faithlessness and rebellion in the face of all the prophetic warnings he had sent them. So Hezekiah set about to initiate a restoration of the spiritual life of the people. He called the priests and Levites together, commissioned them to refurbish the long-neglected temple at Jerusalem, and to reinitiate sacrifices to the Lord (2 Chr. 29).

Moved by a sincere determination to restore the ordinances of devotion, Hezekiah sent runners not only through all of Judah but into Israel as well to announce that Passover would be celebrated at Jerusalem. His intention was to call the people together "in large numbers" to keep the Feast of Passover "according to what was written" (2 Chr. 30:5). His plea to the Northern Kingdom is particularly poignant, for Israel has been devastated by the Assyrians and many of the kinfolk of those he called to Jerusalem for the festival were still mourning their fate. Listen to the language of contrast between rebellion and seeking, punishment and mercy:

> Do not be like your ancestors and relatives who abandoned the LORD, the God of their ancestors, and became an object of derision, as you yourselves can see. Do not be stubborn, as they were, but submit yourselves to the LORD. Come to his Temple, which he has set apart as holy forever. Worship the LORD your God so that his fierce anger will turn away from you. For if you return to the LORD, your relatives and your children will be treated mercifully

by their captors, and they will be able to return to this land. For the LORD your God is gracious and merciful. If you return to him, he will not continue to turn his face from you. (2 Chr. 30:7–9 NLT)

Now notice the outcome. People began streaming into the city from throughout the divided, scattered, and alienated people of the land. The priests began the Passover process with sacrifices for their own sins and then began to officiate for the people. Then, among some who arrived from distant areas too late to purify themselves for the Passover, a dilemma arose. In the midst of King Hezekiah's call for devotion to the Lord and careful obedience to his commandments, this happened: "Although most of the many people who came from Ephraim, Manasseh, Issachar and Zebulun had not purified themselves, yet they ate the Passover, contrary to what was written" (2 Chr. 30:18a).

Will the renewal program be compromised? Will it be necessary to punish and banish those who ate "contrary to what was written"? Will the king, priests, and consecrated people have to separate themselves from the ones who have broken the rules? Here is the prayer King Hezekiah prayed for them (Could it be appropriate to our time, place, and alienation in the larger Christian context?):

Hezekiah prayed for them, saying, "May the LORD, who is good, pardon everyone who sets his heart on seeking God—the LORD, the God of his fathers—even if he is not clean according to the rules of the sanctuary." And the LORD heard Hezekiah and healed the people (2 Chr. 30:18b–20).

God could heal our divisions yet, if we would learn to pray that way for one another. Race, economics, gender, religion, politics—we have turned all of them into points of distinction and division. And we have used religion with particular vengeance to pass judgment on one another. How utterly shameful.

No, it is not right that Christ-confessors who are not part of "our group" should be judged, opposed, and put out of business. Jesus said nobody who gives a cup of cold water in his name will fail to be rewarded by him (Mk. 9:38–41).

No, it is not correct to think we are right and everybody else is wrong. To the contrary, without thinking for a moment that we are perfect, we press toward the heavenly goal that sees perfection in Christ alone (Phil. 3:12–14).

Yes, we have every right—even the spiritual obligation—to live, teach, and share our convictions about Christ as our best effort to honor him, but never as judgment of others (Rom. 14:9–13).

Yes, we may and should pray the generous Hezekiah Prayer for those whom we think are defective in some part of their spiritual life—and ask them to pray the same prayer for us in our deficiencies (2 Chr. 30:18b–19).

Let's be known for loving one another, not squabbling. Let's meet our neighbors in service to them, not in confrontation. Let's love across the dividing lines of race and gender, economic status and religious affiliations, neither compromising our own beliefs nor judging another's faith. It is Christ who is the judge of all.

Samuel Twumasi-Ankrah

Samuel Twumasi-Ankrah (1958–) is the President of Heritage Christian College (HCC), founded by Churches of Christ, and accredited with government university status by Ghana in 2015. Twumasi graduated from Abilene Christian University with a MAR in 2000. He holds an EdD in Administration & Leadership from Biola University (2014). He is on the Board of Directors of the Rural Water Development Project, Ghana; and is Chair of the Board of Governors of Hope College (Fetteh, Ghana). He spent 20 years as pulpit minister of the Nsawam Road Church of Christ, the largest Church of Christ outside the U.S., combining preaching with teaching at HCC. He has led student mission trips to other African countries. He has spoken at conferences in Canada, United States, Brazil, Britain, and various African countries.

Twumasi's preaching reflects two influences. His didactic style and topical flow represent the missionaries' preaching style. Additionally, Twumasi's training at ACU focused on biblical texts. His exposition of John reflects the notion that if a preacher explains the text correctly, then the preacher has communicated the gospel appropriately.

"For God So Loved the World" was the Keynote Address during the 88th Abilene Christian University Bible Lectureship & Centennial Anniversary in 2006. This sermon is especially convicting coming to an American audience from an African voice. John 3:16 moves beyond being the denouement of a story or a proposition to an argument, but becomes a "mandate" for the church. He uses the NKJV.

"For God So Loved the World…"

John 3:1–21

In the third chapter of John's Gospel, the meeting between Nicodemus and Jesus is more than just an exchange between two individuals. It is a drama in which religion clashes with regeneration.

In Nicodemus, we see the futility of a religious faith based on human knowledge and perception; in Nicodemus we see the uselessness of holding on to human categories of what's possible and what's not; in Nicodemus we see a religious faith that says "by an external system of deeds, you will gain entrance into God's Kingdom."

From Jesus, we grasp an understanding that is entirely different from what we observe in Nicodemus. From Jesus, we understand that it is by means of the divine gift of grace that we receive new life (salvation) that God offers through Jesus Christ, His one and only Son. From Jesus' response to Nicodemus, we gain insight that it is not by means of what we do, regardless of how perfect we think our knowledge may be (because, essentially, whatever we know and do is like filthy rags before God), but rather it is by relying on Christ's death on the cross that we gain God's favor and are offered a place in the eternal Kingdom of God.

Being a prominent member of the religious ruling council of his day that had jurisdiction over every Jew in the world, and belonging to the camp of the Pharisees, Nicodemus was the spokesperson for a group known for splitting religious hairs.[1] Therefore, he comes to Jesus as an official voice representing an entire community of his religious affiliates.

I believe Nicodemus came to Jesus in all sincerity to learn more about God's amazing dealings with sinful humanity. However, as Jesus amplifies His response, we observe that salvation (or regeneration) is something that God prompts, not humans. And religion, on the other hand, is something that humans prompt, not God. And that explains why Nicodemus couldn't get his arms around Jesus' concept of spiritual rebirth or regeneration. In essence, Jesus is saying, "Nicodemus, there must be an inward cleansing that God will make possible through His Spirit when you believe in Jesus."

Nicodemus, resisting Jesus' offer, asks the question: "How can this be?" You see, his mind attempts to grasp the idea of being "born from above"; however he stumbles at the very entrance to understanding. And you can tell Nicodemus is going in the wrong direction when he asks the question, "How?" "How can this be?"

The "whats" and the "hows" have their place, but we must be careful not to settle for the religion of Nicodemus, as that approach to God amounts to putting God in a box.[2]

You see, Nicodemus attempts to resist Jesus' free offer of regeneration (spiritual newness) on his own terms. His imagination is not prepared for the kind of new life Jesus offers, and so he clings tenaciously to his own categories of what's possible and what's not—which is similar to what goes on among us in the Church today. In the Church, different groups have their own accepted categories of what is possible and what is not; we have our own categories of what's scriptural and binding and what's not; we have our own categories of what constitutes salvation and who is in the Kingdom as against who is not.

The sad thing is that, in the Church, some—in the name of defending "the truth"—will pay any price to vilify others who might hold categories that are seemingly different from theirs. And they do so without realizing that Jesus the Savior received Nicodemus in love and patiently dialogued with him although Nicodemus was resistant initially.

In John 19:39–42, the epilogue to the Nicodemus story demonstrates that the power of Jesus' offer of spiritual newness, made available through His death on the cross, will not be silenced by resistance, doubt, and fear.

We observe that at Jesus' death Nicodemus is empowered by faith and he assists in the burial of Jesus' body. Yes, Jesus' death on the cross has now opened new possibilities of new life to Nicodemus. Yes, grace and newness of life are made available even to those who try to say no.

You may ask, Just what is the driving force behind this amazingly free gift of salvation? The answer to that question is love: the indescribable love of God as recorded in John 3:16. Brothers and sisters, the bottom line of all our Christian religious enterprise is not our human knowledge or our accomplishment, neither is it the mere holding on to our most cherished traditions. Rather, the bottom line is God's love for sinful humanity and how we respond to it. Hence, the inspired writer states: "For God so loved the world that He gave His only begotten Son that [whosoever believe] in Him [will] not perish but have everlasting life" (John 3:16).

In the year 1970, a medical missionary and his family from the United States moved to the country of Liberia, West Africa.[3] After they settled in the village of Flehla, in the Lower Bong County, he was set to begin work. He preached his first sermon on Sunday and chose John 3:16 for his text. The translator was confused and said that there was a new word in the sentence he had never heard before. The word was *love*. In the Kpelle language, there is no word for love. The missionary was crushed–How do you preach the gospel and leave out the word *love*? His answer came from the Lord. Not long after this, a cholera epidemic hit the village. The tribal chief and elders were skeptical of the missionary and his medicine. They told the people not to receive medicine from the missionary and so people continued to die. One day, the chief gave permission for the people to try the missionary's medicine and the cholera stopped. Before long, the cholera spread to a nearby village, Gbeyata, where the tribal chief lived. He wouldn't let the missionary come with his medicine until someone in his own family died. One day there was a knock on the missionary's door. A messenger had come from Chief Sinatwa. He said the missionary could bring the medicine but he was to leave the "Book" behind. The missionary agreed and went and vaccinated the village against cholera.

While there, he saw many health needs in the village–infant mortality rate was high from malnutrition and disease and this missionary offered to help. Sinatwa, the tribal chief, reluctantly allowed the missionary to come and bring medicine, but wanted no part of the "Book." For the next two years, the medical missionary went to the village of Gbeyata and took medicine and cared for the people in their need. There were those here in the United States who felt that, because there was no "preaching" going on, that the missionary should stop. But the medical missionary felt that preaching was going on in that particular instance.

One night, after two and a half years, a messenger came from the tribal chief and asked the missionary to bring the "Book." The missionary went on a Friday night and preached his first sermon there based on John 3:16 and 17. Five people put on Christ in baptism, including Chief Sinatwa himself.

The Church stands today—as it always has—in a world that is spiritually and materially in a dying need. And in the midst of these miseries, the Church's constant mission is to interpret the event of Jesus Christ and to intercede in His name. As Christ was sent, so *we* are commissioned by God to go forth under the sign of the Cross into the marketplaces of our contemporary society to retell the story encapsulated in John 3:16.

Quite honestly, the sights and the sounds and the smells of the world that surrounds us are not always pleasant. In fact, the raw realities are intimidating, and the TV screens cannot accurately capture them. And many congregations and individual Christians are at a loss to know just how to respond.

- Did you know that, according to UNICEF, malaria[1] disease kills a child somewhere in the world every 30 seconds? Malaria infects at least 500 million people each year, killing 1 million, and 90 percent of those who die are in Africa.

- Did you know that of the 40.3 million people worldwide who are living with HIV/AIDS, women alone account for 46 percent of them? Of the 6.5 million people in developing countries who need life-saving AIDS medicine, only 1 million can get help.

- Did you also know that one third of the world's population (i.e., 2 billion people) have latent TB? Each year, nearly 2 million people in India develop TB, costing $3 billion; the World Health Organization (WHO)[5] says unless urgent action is taken, more than 4 million people in India will die of TB in the next decade.

- Did you also know that in my own country, Ghana, the doctor-patient ratio in the northern region is 1:66,000 (WHO)?[6]

- And how will you feel if I told you the water that people here in the United States use to flush their toilet is cleaner than the water some people somewhere drink? And even that they have to walk for miles to fetch…in gallon containers.

I am sharing this information with you purposely—to point out the fact that each life saved represents a little child, a mother or a father whom God loves and sent Christ to die for. Yet many of us are so preoccupied with skirmishes within our homes, churches, or college communities that we do not have the energy to confront the larger issues of our society.

My brothers and sisters in Christ, could it be that the seeming regression of growth in Churches of Christ in the West is due to spiritual inwardness and a loss of sight of the larger world that God so much loves?

As an African Christian and someone coming from a Third-world background, I've always wondered whether most of the controversial 20th-century doctrines originated from Europe and North America; theologies and doctrines that originated far away from the crowded cities of Lagos (Nigeria), Johannesburg (RSA), Cairo (Egypt), Seoul, Mumbai, Sao Paulo, Mexico City. I've always wondered whether the controversial doctrines emanating from Occidental Christian experience really speak to the realities confronting the non-Western societies that constitute the vast majority of the world's population. May I further ask, Is our present understanding of God's love...culturally bound, emotionally as well as intellectually? How can the love of God ever wrap itself around the entire globe?[7]

The biblical truth is that God loves the world and all its humanity the same—be they Arabs, Africans, Asians, Hispanics, whites, blacks, other people of color, Muslims, Hindus, New-Agers, atheists, denominational Christians, non-denominationals, et al. God loves them all so much that He did not withhold Jesus from them for any reason, but rather gave Jesus up to die for the salvation of whosoever believes in Jesus. The more difficult question is whether we love them.

Is it true, brothers and sisters, that the Church in the West and its people are using most of their energies and resources to protect themselves from the real world? ...That is exactly how it is perceived by people from outside America. What can we do to raise our level of commitment to God's mission for a dying world?

When all is said and done, the paramount question facing us individually as followers of Jesus, and collectively as the body of Christ, is whether we are willing to be "born from above"—to be regenerated in our minds and hearts like Nicodemus. ...Are we willing to sacrifice our comfort whenever that price is demanded?

In conclusion, brothers and sisters, I submit to you that God's love for the world through Jesus Christ has not changed. Therefore, we must rediscover a gratitude for God's love displayed so completely on the cross. And when we become genuine practitioners of forgiveness, when we understand our indebtedness to God whom we can never repay, we will recognize that God's love for sinful humanity demands our highest priority and sacrificial loyalty.

The Church is the vehicle by which to carry out the mandate of John 3:16. Let us therefore move ahead in confidence, knowing that the cross of Christ has gone before us and that the strength of God's Spirit upholds us—always asking ourselves the fundamental question: Are we willing to love the world the way God did in Jesus Christ?

Mark Frost

Mark Frost (1950–) has been in ministry since 1972, serving 34 years within a single congregation: the Trenton Church of Christ in suburban Detroit. Frost led the Trenton church through a period of long-term, sustained growth, facilitating the transition from a ministry staff of one to a staff of four ministers, and helping transform the leadership structure to make best use of the gifts of the multiple staff. He also began a small-group ministry and a Celebrate Recovery ministry at the Trenton church.

Frost has a BA in Bible and Psychology from Harding University (1973) and a MA in Biblical Studies from Cincinnati Christian Seminary (1980). He has served as an adjunct instructor at Rochester College and as president of the board of Michigan Christian Youth Camp. He has published several articles and sermons in the Rochester College Preaching Series. Mark retired from full-time preaching in May, 2012, but continues interim ministries. He is European American.

"You Can't Handle the Ruth" was preached April 20, 2008, at the Trenton Church of Christ in Michigan. It begins by stating the theme, "God has a master plan. His design is to bring about reconciliation in the place of alienation." Frost directly connects God's master plan to the theology of providence. He employs "identification" as a way for the audience to imaginatively put themselves into the story. He uses the NIV.

"You Can't Handle the Ruth!"

God has a master plan. His design is to bring about reconciliation in the place of alienation. He is always at work on that master plan, working through people who are open to his call. In the book of Ruth, God's work is woven through the normal events in people's lives: the experience of economic hardship, trying to make ends meet, searching for a job, buying and selling property, raising children, marriage, birth, and even death. We have a name for God's work in the ordinary events of life: *Providence*. When God works this way, we may not know what he's up to; indeed, we may not perceive his presence at all. But his providential work is no less important than his signs and wonders.

So let's watch God at work in the book of Ruth, which begins this way (at least in the MLPV: Mark's Loosely Paraphrased Version): "In the days when the judges ruled, there was an economic downturn in the land. Companies were downsizing and outsourcing jobs, gas shot up to four dollars a gallon, food prices were skyrocketing, home values were plummeting, good-paying jobs were disappearing by the thousands, and multitudes were losing their homes to foreclosure. And Elimelek, a man from Bethlehem in Judah, together with his wife Naomi and their two sons, went to live for a while in the country of Moab."

For Elimelek and Naomi, moving to a foreign country involved more than a mere cultural adjustment. In their minds, they were leaving God's country. As Israelites, they knew that they were God's chosen people and that Israel was the land God had promised them. And they were sure that if God were going to do anything, he would do it in and through Israel. I'm not sure we can imagine the sense of foreboding they must have felt as they left their beloved homeland.

What's more, they were going to Moab. Israelites had a lot of negative attitudes toward Moab. Why? Consider the following scenes from its history. Moab got its name from its ancestor, who was conceived in a drunken, incestuous encounter between Abraham's nephew Lot and his own daughter (Gen. 19:36–37). Later, when Israel came from Egypt to their Promised Land, the Moabites refused to let them pass through their territory (Judg. 11:17). Instead, Balak, the Moabite king, tried to hire a soothsayer named Balaam to put a curse on Israel (Num. 22). On another occasion, Moabite women seduced Israelite men into adulterous and idolatrous practices (Num. 25:1–3). Moreover, the Moabites' favorite god was Chemosh, who was worshiped by child sacrifice. No doubt Elimelek and Naomi were more than a little nervous about living in Moab, and especially about raising their sons there.

In Moab, their worst fears come to pass. Elimelek dies, leaving Naomi a widow. Her sons marry Moabite women, Orpah and Ruth, and then the sons too die. Shattered, Naomi sees no alternative but to return home. She urges her daughters-in-law to go back to their homes as well. Orpah takes her sensible advice, but Ruth pleads to go on with Naomi. Her pledge of loyalty is one of our favorite Bible passages: "Where you go I will go, and where you stay I will stay. Your people will be my people and your God my God. Where you die I will die, and there I will be buried" (Ruth 1:16b–17).

The most startling part of this is that Ruth claims the God of Israel as her God. That's surprising. After all, Naomi herself is not too thrilled with her God. She blames him for her misfortunes: "The Almighty has made my life very bitter. I went away full, but the LORD has brought me back empty… The LORD has afflicted me; the Almighty has brought misfortune upon me" (Ruth 1:20b–21). Who would blame Ruth for saying, "So much for *your* God; I'll stick with mine!" And yet, Ruth inexplicably chooses Naomi's God as her own. I can only suggest that Ruth is drawn to Naomi because of the quality of her character, and she recognizes that Naomi's relationship with her God is central to who she is.

So Ruth goes to Israel with Naomi. Her journey with God takes her into a most unwelcoming environment. She is a woman in a society that sees women as the property of men, totally dependent on them. She is a widow with no man to provide for her. She is childless. She is poor. Most significantly, she is a Moabite, and her adopted God had given the command that "no Moabite...shall enter the assembly of God" (Deut. 23:3). There could be no better formula for complete social ostracism than this!

But amazingly there is one Israelite who doesn't greet her with suspicion, disdain, and rejection, but with respect and honor. His name is Boaz. God had mercifully instructed farmers to leave part of their fields unharvested, so that poor people could pick the grain there—a practice called "gleaning." Ruth goes into the fields to glean and winds up in the field of Boaz. He singles her out for special treatment and protection. Ironically, he is her exact opposite. He is a person of privilege. For every disadvantage she has, he has a corresponding advantage. He is male; he is a landowner; he's wealthy; he's an Israelite, and a respected citizen at that. Why does he show such open acceptance and kindness toward her, in spite of such formidable societal deterrents? Is it sexual attraction? Is it romantic love? Neither. Rather, Boaz sees God at work in her. He says::

> I've been told all about what you have done for your mother-in-law since the death of your husband—how you left your father and mother and your homeland and came to live with a people you did not know before. May the LORD repay you for what you have done. May you be richly rewarded by the LORD, the God of Israel, under whose wings you have come to take refuge. (Ruth 2:11–12)

Seeing God's working in another person trumps all else. It overcomes prejudice, fear, hostility, and distrust—it even trumps a law that says, "no Moabites allowed!" Boaz sees God at work in Ruth, so he reaches out to her with a kindness that goes well beyond duty or hospitality. What he doesn't know is that God is going to use *him* to complete the work he's begun in Ruth's life—and that Boaz himself is going to receive a huge blessing by means of this powerless, disenfranchised foreigner.

Ruth goes at night to Boaz's threshing floor and does an outrageous thing: she proposes marriage to him! Her request—"spread your cloak over your servant," that is, over me (Ruth 3:9) – repeats the words Boaz used to describe God's care for her. Then Boaz, the child of privilege, the one holding all the power and influence, humbly submits himself to Ruth's request: "[D]on't be afraid. I will do for you all that you ask" (Ruth 3:11). No doubt, Boaz thought God's purpose was for him to bless Ruth by being her earthly protector, and surely that's part of the picture. But little did he know that God had brought Ruth into his life to bless *him*.

You see, up to this point, this has been a nice little story. It's a romance, a "chick flick" with a happy ending. But it's so much more. It's a story about God's working out his big plan. And we don't see that until the very end.

Boaz sees God at work in Ruth and agrees to become God's partner in protecting her. Because of his actions, the people of the town also accept her as one of their own, not as a rejected and ostracized foreigner (Ruth 4:13–15). But the real surprise is saved for last. "Boaz took Ruth and she became his wife. When he made love to her, the Lord enabled her to conceive, and she gave birth to a son... And they named him Obed. He was the father of Jesse, the father of David" (Ruth 4:13, 17). By showing kindness to the Moabite Ruth, Boaz eventually became grandfather to Israel's greatest king!

All through the book of Ruth, we've seen God's brush on the canvas, but we don't see the big picture until the very end. That's the way God's Providence works. And we don't really see the whole picture even at the end of Ruth. For that, we have to go to the New Testament, where God's angel announces "the rest of the story" to another young woman of humble origins: "Do not be afraid, Mary; you have found favor with God. You will conceive and give birth to a son, and you are to call him Jesus. He will be great and will be called the Son of the Most High. The Lord God will give him the throne of his father David" (Lk. 1:30–32). God had reached into foreign, despised, idolatrous Moab, put his hand on Ruth, and brought her into Israel, all as part of his plan to bring his own son Jesus into the world!

Now let's make some personal applications. First, we need to understand that our greatest service to God may not be performed among his chosen ones—other Christians—or in his "territory"—the church and its programs. Rather, our greatest influence for God may be among the irreligious people around us, people among whom we live and work who seem to care little for God. Consider Naomi. As a foreigner in pagan Moab, she lived the kind of life that made God attractive to Ruth. The result was that Ruth became a vital link in the chain that brought God's Son to Earth. The Apostle Peter underscores the importance of imitating Naomi's example: "Live such good lives among the pagans that...they may see your good deeds and glorify God" (1 Pet. 2:12). Consider the words of John Burke: "Generally, emerging generations do not ask, 'What is true?' They are primarily asking, 'Do I want to be like you?' In other words, they see truth as relational. 'If I want to be like you, then I want to consider what you believe. If I don't see anything real or attractive in you or your friends as Christ-followers, I don't care how "true" you think it is, I'm not interested.'"[1] How we live, especially among unbelievers, matters more than we know.

Second, we need to look for God's hand at work, even among the "Moabites" around us. Boaz had every reason—social, cultural, and religious—to shun and ignore poor Ruth. But instead, he saw God at work in her life and that made all the difference. What difference might we make if we actively looked for God at work, even in unexpected places? Consider the story of Liz Pence Garcia. Raised in a loveless home, she grew up to become an embittered atheist. A hard-nosed bank manager, Liz had an employee who was a believer and who constantly looked for God's presence. Liz was rude and hostile to this subordinate, making a special point to use profanity in her presence. One day this coworker invited Liz to lunch. She demolished Liz's defenses when she said, "I don't understand how you can be an atheist, because I see God in you!" Intrigued, Liz had to know more. Thus began a process that led Liz to surrender to Jesus Christ. And what a surrender it was! She has served as a missionary to the poorest of the poor in Oaxaca, Mexico, where she lived for two years in a rat-infested shed with a dirt floor. Currently she works with women suffering from trauma, depression, addiction, and from other effects of troubled lives and broken hearts—all because a humble believer saw in Liz what no one else did: the work of God's hand.

Do you frequently find yourself in "Moab"—surrounded by irreligious and profane people in your neighborhood or workplace? Do you find yourself longing to extract yourself from their midst so you can once again enjoy the fellowship of a close family of believers? *Of course*—that's a natural reaction. But understand that Moab may be the very place God needs you the most. He hasn't given up on the Moabites, and he may use you as a key component of his plan to reconcile all humankind to himself.

Mike Cope

Mike Cope earned a BA from Harding University (1978) and a MTh from Harding School of Theology (1982). He preached at Pine Valley Church of Christ in Wilmington, North Carolina; College Church of Christ in Searcy, Arkansas; and then Highland Church of Christ, Abilene, Texas (1991–2009). He then joined Heartbeat Ministries as Executive Vice-President to engage in ministry online. In 2012, Cope became the ministry outreach director at Pepperdine University. He also taught at Abilene Christian University for over 15 years. Cope recently began a co-preaching role at the Golf Course Road Church of Christ in Midland, Texas. He has published several books, most recently *Megan's Secrets: What My Mentally Disabled Daughter Taught Me about Life*.[1] He is European American.

Employing Paul's narrative strategies in this sermon, Mike represents a perspective of the New Homiletic. While Paul is often neglected by the New Homiletic generally, Churches of Christ have majored in the epistles. Many early works of the New Homiletic so emphasized narrative genres that imitating discursive texts in the pulpit did not attract many practitioners. Preachers and scholars in the Churches of Christ have helped connect the New Homiletic and Paul's writings.

"Great Is Thy Faithfulness" was preached on April 4, 2016, at the Golf Course Road Church of Christ in Midland, Texas, as part of an ongoing series on the book of Romans. Cope uses the TNIV.

"Great Is Thy Faithfulness"

Imagine taking a vase this morning and filling it with marbles. You drop one more on top, and it looks full. But now drop in BBs until, once again, it looks full—only, this time, it seems packed. But now pour in sand until not another grain can be added. And then slowly pour water in. Now your vase is full.

That's what our text is like this morning. Three chapters that are dense—full of the larger story of Scripture—and challenging. In my theological library I've got a lot of books that might help us (along with several that would probably just confuse us!).

But I want to pull out one of my wife's children's books. *Zoom*—a delightful book that is just pictures—begins with a red, teeth-shaped object. But page-by page, the "camera" is pulled back so that you get a larger picture of what you previously saw. You realize that the teeth-shaped object is a rooster's comb…which is on a fence with children watching…and is part of a village…that turns out to be a toy village that a little girl is playing with…which is really just the cover of a magazine that a boy is holding… and so on. Click, click, click. Your perspective zooms outward until you barely see the Earth from a distance.

In Romans, we've seen Paul zoom in close, like in Romans 3:21–31. But this morning, we zoom out–way out–to hear Paul tell the story of Israel in light of what he now knows about Jesus. And as I said, it's thick wading. He has at least 45 partial or whole quotations (or at least echoes of passages) from all over the Old Testament: from Exodus, Leviticus, Deuteronomy, Psalms, Isaiah, Hosea, Joel, and so on.

And he presses for an answer to a question that many of us don't spend a lot of time thinking about: Has God been faithful to his promises to Israel? Frankly, it's a bit more than we want to think through at times. Give us a few morsels of advice to help us make it through the week; perhaps a "Precious Moments" experience that will warm us; a devotional thought or bit of moral wisdom that we can take like a daily multi-vitamin.

But Paul–the apostle to the Gentiles–thinks it's essential that we ask this question. So often in his letters as he moves around the Mediterranean world, he's rethinking the great themes of the Old Testament in light of the Risen Lord whom he had met. He rethinks Israel, law, circumcision, temple, and the land promise–because, now, knowing the crucified and risen one, he has to read backwards. So he zooms out in Romans 9, beginning with the patriarchs: Abraham, then Isaac and Rebekah, then Jacob and Esau. He carries the story forward with Moses and the Exodus and then the prophets.

If you aren't careful, you wind up thinking that he is talking about some kind of election where God has determined who will be saved and who will be lost. But that isn't what "election" is about. For Paul, election is a calling, a trust, a responsibility. God is working like a potter to shape his people for a purpose: to undo the sin of Adam. Out of love for people–and with wrath because his world is broken–God calls a people to carry his blessing to all nations.

And as Paul tells this story, we realize that there is a goal to it all: Israel's Messiah. We saw back in chapter 4 of Romans that God is making good on his promise to Abraham. But as it turns out, it's not through all those who share DNA with father Abraham; it's through the descendant who was the Messiah of Israel and Lord of the whole world!

Now the people of God whom God is electing to reach the whole world are those who put their trust in this Messiah–both from the Jews *and* the Gentiles. There is a remnant of physical Israel that has followed Jesus; and there are many Gentiles who've been grafted into the family tree. Before their very eyes, "Israel" is being transformed from an ethnic family into a worldwide family who are committed to Jesus.

Paul opens our long section, Romans 9:6–8, saying that there are two Israels: physical Israel and faith-filled "Israel."

It is not as though God's word had failed. For not all who are descended from Israel are Israel. Nor because they are his descendants are they all Abraham's children. On the contrary, "It is through Isaac that your offspring will be reckoned." In other words, it is not the children by physical descent who are God's children, but it is the children of the promise who are regarded as Abraham's offspring.

Paul sadly admits that many of his fellow Jews haven't placed their faith in the Messiah yet, but the door remains open. He eagerly hopes that many of them will, through trust in the faithfulness of Jesus, be grafted back into that tree of blessing (11:24).

We've seen from the very first of this series that Paul is trying to unite the believers in Rome. Some are pagan converts who grew up on the stories of Roman or Greek gods, goddesses, and heroes; others are Jews who grew up hearing the words of the Torah.

But by zooming out and giving the larger perspective of God's mercy to rescue the world (11:32), Paul reminds them that this faithful God—the one who has, indeed, been faithful to his promises to Abraham—is setting all followers of his Messiah into one family.

Many of you know that my family of uncles, aunts, cousins, nieces, and nephews isn't, perhaps, your typical West Texas family. We are white, Latino, and African-American. We are (by birth) American, Uruguayan, Jamaican, Iranian, Jewish, and Vietnamese. I have first cousins named Ilya Hooshie Broomand and Anahita Marica Broomand; my uncle is Iraj Broomand. And then there's Aunt Carol (who didn't get such a cool name as the others!). We are family through birth, adoption, and marriage. Being family doesn't mean we agree on everything. Like other families, there's always a chance at Christmas that someone will pull the pin out of the grenade known as "presidential politics"! But we are nevertheless one family.

Before the Messiah, many in Israel made the mistake of trusting certain badges: circumcision, law, Sabbath-keeping. It was almost as if just having Abrahamic DNA made you a part of the family. But Paul shows that this is God's story: a story of pouring out his mercy for the sake of all, a story of redeeming people through the Messiah, a story of people of all tribes and languages coming by faith.

Here's part of what we need to hear as a church: so many things that *could* divide us *shouldn't* divide us. Our unity doesn't come from having the same backgrounds or the same perspectives on everything. It doesn't even come from lining up perfectly with our doctrinal beliefs. We've been made one by God through the one Messiah, Jesus.

And we also need to hear that we have a set mission: this faithful God is using us to reach his whole world.

In the middle of this long passage from Romans 10:9–17, Paul talks about the beautiful feet of those who will bring this healing message of Christ to the world:

> If you declare with your mouth, "Jesus is Lord," and believe in your heart that God raised him from the dead, you will be saved. For it is with your heart that you believe and are justified, and it is with your mouth that you profess your faith and are saved. As Scripture says, "Anyone who believes in him will never be put to shame." For there is no difference between Jew and Gentile—the same Lord is Lord of all and richly blesses all who call on him, for, "Everyone who calls on the name of the Lord will be saved." How then, can they call on the one they have not believed in? And how can they believe in the one of whom they have not heard? And how can they hear without someone preaching to them? And how can they preach unless they are sent? As it is written, "How beautiful are the feet of those who bring good news." But not all the Israelites accepted the good news. For Isaiah says, "Lord, who has believed our message?" Consequently, faith comes from hearing the message, and the message is heard through the word about Christ.

You have beautiful feet; Paul says! Not because they're shapely or because you've had a pedicure, but because those feet carry the person who embodies and announces the story of Jesus as he or she enters into God's beloved world.

Well, this is quite a perspective. When we let Paul zoom all the way back to see the sweeping story of God's love, it can leave you speechless. What can you say to all that? It's almost as if the only possible words are doxology:

> Oh, the depth of the riches of the wisdom and knowledge of God!
> How unsearchable his judgments,
> and his paths beyond tracing out!
> "Who has known the mind of the Lord?
> Or who has been his counselor?"
> "Who has ever given to God,
> that God should repay him?"
> For from him and through him and to him are all things.
> To him be the glory forever. Amen. (Romans 11:33–36)

Dean Barham

Dean Barham is a teacher and attorney in Nashville, Tennessee, and recently finished his DMin degree at Lipscomb University in missional and spiritual formation. He is European American. Previously, Dean served as the preaching minister for the Woodmont Hills Church in Nashville, and an adjunct professor in ministry and Bible at Lipscomb. He has been married for 25 years to his wife Melanie; they have three wonderful children: Christine, David, and Luke. Before moving to Tennessee, Barham served as campus minister for the Broadway Church of Christ in Lubbock, Texas, serving Texas Tech and Lubbock Christian University. He was also an instructor in Bible and ministry at Lubbock Christian University. Before this, Dean earned a law degree from the University of Virginia School of Law and practiced civil litigation and constitutional law. His greatest passion is to live and tell the story of a Man who wouldn't stay dead.

"Beyond the Wilderness" was first preached in July 2013 at a Conference on Preaching at Lipscomb University on the theme of the Exodus as a paradigmatic narrative. Barham uses the NRSV. The sermon was written considering the preacher's home church, Woodmont Hills Church in Nashville, a congregation with a rich heritage in the Stone-Campbell Movement. The church values family and mission, choosing its present location because it is strategically located at the intersection of diverse communities.

"Beyond the Wilderness"

Exodus 3:1–6

Life used to be easier when I understood God. "God is great, God is good," we used to say in one of our earliest forms of liturgy. "God is great, God is good." Clear. Simple. Conceivable. We defined our God at the beginning and we've sought to define him ever since. In everything from books, creeds, to "now," trendy church websites, we've been clearly articulating our understanding of God for ages.

The only problem with all this is that, from time to time, God actually shows up. And the God who shows up and meets us in our world is often quite different from the God we've captured in our words.

In the classic text we read today, God shows up...to a person named Moses, who's had 80 years to define his notion of God. And what is most intriguing to me in the story—and I suspect you noticed it too—is the fascinating detail of *where* God chooses to show up. The text says, God meets Moses "*beyond* the wilderness." He meets him at *Horeb,* the mountain of God; but at this point Moses has no idea that this mountain is anything other than what its name literally means: "a desolate wasteland." So God shows up in a bush, in a desolate place, *beyond* the wilderness.

Why here? Why here, I wonder?

If God wanted to reveal his power and highlight Moses as his true servant, wouldn't it be better to start outside an Egyptian temple? God could surround the place with a host of angels and shut down the entire business. Can you see the reaction of the crowd, if Moses stood there, flanked by angels with swords of fire? I can see the Egyptian mother leading her little flock to the altar of Ra, and she stops and cries out: We must "turn aside and look at this great sight!" (Ex. 3:3).

Wouldn't that be a more fitting introduction? Kind of like the episode with Dagon in 1 Samuel, when the Ark of the Lord gets introduced to the Philistine temple and Dagon keeps falling down—literally. Now *that's* an appearance.

But God shows up in a bush, in a desolate place, *beyond* the wilderness.

Why not on the streets where slaves are forced to fashion bricks of injustice for the monuments of a consumer-driven empire? Imagine the walls of these national icons falling down. As every stone hits the ground, it drives home the new reality of God's freedom, much like with Jesus on the streets of Jerusalem with a woman caught in adultery. Now that's an appearance.

But in a bush, in a desolate place, *beyond* the wilderness?

Eyes are the Window to the Heart

And I wonder what Moses is expecting to *see* out there on this day. We can't know, of course; but we have some hint, because you *can* tell a lot about a person's heart from where they direct their eyes.

I recall my freshman year at Virginia Tech. I had a class in a movie theater downtown. I only remember two things about that: the smell of the doughnuts on the walk to class, and where the professor directed his eyes. He taught the class for an hour and a half at a time, lecturing nonstop, and not once did he look us in the eye: he looked over our heads the entire time—a feat made even more remarkable by the fact that the rows of seats sloped down in the room. He looked over us, past us, almost as if he wished he were somewhere else. I don't even remember his name.

On the other hand, I recall one of the few times when I got to drive with my family to church on Sunday morning. Just a few weeks ago, we pull up to the light and I realize my wife is not paying any attention to my spellbinding summary of the day's sermon. In the 30 seconds we are there, she is looking past me, into the eyes of the homeless man selling a newspaper. As she does each week, she speaks to him, buys a paper, and reaffirms his worth. His name is John.

You can tell a lot about a person from where they direct their eyes. Follow the eyes. Moses is looking for something in that desolate, wilderness place, and we don't know what it is, but we *can* see his eyes. Follow them with me; follow his eyes—because they move in the story—and that makes all the difference.

In the beginning of the story, Moses looks *at God.* The text says: "... the LORD appeared to him in a flame..." (Ex. 3:2a), and Moses says to himself, "I must turn aside and *look* at this *great sight*" (3:3a). Perhaps what Moses is expecting is the kind of God-appearances we all seem to long for: a dazzling display of divine force—a God he can see, a God he can know, a God he can name.

Moses *begins* by looking. Language of vision and sight dominate this story—he goes to see, to gaze, to "behold" the vision of God. But just as he begins to get comfortable, to perhaps define what he sees, God's voice *arrests* Moses: "No further! Remove your shoes" (a common practice when you entered a temple in those days). "This ground," God thunders, "is sacred" (preacher's paraphrase).

And right there, beyond the wilderness, a common thorn bush becomes an altar and a desolate wasteland becomes a sanctuary. And in this holy moment, Moses' eyes move. The text tells us: "Moses *hid his face*, for he was afraid to *look at* God" (3:6a). At the end of the encounter, Moses turns his eyes *away* from God. And maybe that's precisely what has to happen first—before he can really *see* God. Before he hears the name, he turns his face; before he receives the call to march forward on the mission, he falls on the ground; before he beholds God's glory in the tent or on the mountain, he *lets go* of the encounter with the Divine. There, beyond the wilderness, in the desolate place, Moses chooses *not* to see God.

Moments like this are why, for ages, people have seen Moses as a model of what some call "the way of *un*knowing." A way of seeking to know God by detachment, distance—coming to know who God *is* first by learning what God *is not.*

So perhaps we could learn something before we get too much further on our "Doctorate of Ministry" journeys; perhaps we begin the way Moses does here: by *not* looking—by turning away from our profound ideas about who God is and what he does in the world. Maybe we begin again by allowing God to surprise us—allowing God to reveal to us, not who he *is,* but *who he is not.* We would do well to follow Moses' eyes.

Sometimes Turning Away Is the Right Way to Turn

We must, because sometimes turning *away* is the *right* way to turn.

I had just prayed the final prayer over the fresh grave of a 19-year-old boy, the only son of one of my dear friends. The funeral and the graveside service were over, except for one final element. One of the pallbearers thought it would provide a personal touch for him to put the first shovelful of dirt onto the grave, and then let the professionals finish the job. He did, but then something happened. A college student grabbed the shovel and took a turn...then another...and another. Before long, nearly everyone was coming, some forgoing the shovel and thrusting their hands into the trailer of dirt, to cast their final offering into the tomb.

But this part of the scene I will never forget: the boy's father got up from his seat under the tent, walked to the trailer, and began shoveling piles of dirt, one after another. Finally, in an act that spoke beyond words for everyone present, he *threw the shovel down* onto the trailer and walked away.

I wish I could tell you that since then, he's come to *see* the grand redemptive purpose for it all; that all questions are answered, and all doubts dispelled; but I can't. It's still hard. His journey is still in the desolate place, beyond the wilderness. But as much as my soul aches for him, my heart also burns with anticipation—because, in that moment, I saw a shovel become a sacrament and a pile of dirt become an altar. God *was* there. Beyond words. Beyond definition. Beyond knowing.

I can still see him walking away—but that walk is not a walk of despair. It is a walk *deeper into the wilderness with God.* And for all of his struggle, he is not afraid to begin a new discovery by *unknowing,* and he's not afraid to start over by *letting go.*

And I can't wait to learn what Name he will hear and what mission he will embrace, now that he has turned in great humility in the face of the staggering otherness of God.

SECTION TWO

CHRISTIAN CHURCHES/
CHURCHES OF CHRIST

Orientation to Preaching in the Christian Churches/Churches of Christ, 1968-2018

by Joseph Grana II

The first *Living Pulpit of the Christian Church* published in 1868 included 28 male ministers. The original intent was that the *Living Pulpit* would be represented by "Living Preachers." However, between sermon submission and publication, David Staats Burnet passed away two days after his 59th birthday. "His discourse was already partially in type, and the engraving nearly ready. Under these circumstances, it was thought best to retain him in the book, although the original intention was to have no one appear in it but living preachers."[1] Burnet's introductory biography ended up being much longer than those of any of the other sermon writers.

The comments concerning each writer included Moore's commentary and evaluation. For instance, writing about Thomas Munnell, Moore states, "His preaching is chiefly practical, and always instructive and entertaining, though not remarkable for logical arrangement, rhetorical finish, or oratorical display. He is a much better writer than speaker."[2] In regard to J.W. McGarvey, he declares, "As a teacher, he has very few superiors... But Brother McGarvey is also an excellent preacher, and, as a pastor, has been eminently successful. He has a kind, generous nature, but is not very demonstrative. He attends to his own business."[3] Moore's comments are candid: sometimes complimentary and sometimes caustic.

In contrast to the above, the Christian Church stream has chosen 13 sermons as representative of the past 50 years of preaching. Among the 13 are two women known for their pulpit presence and communication gifts. Laura Buffington (Miamisburg, Ohio.) and Jodi Hickerson (Ventura, California.) use creativity and imagination in their sermons while using props and role-playing the characters in the story, and using contemporary images such as comparing Jesus' miracle of feeding the five thousand to a "kid's Happy Meal."

Two of the sermons are from deceased preachers. One might say they still provide a "living pulpit" through their writings and recordings of sermons. Russ Blowers (Indianapolis, Indiana) and Myron Taylor (Westwood, California) are well-known "pulpiteers" who have made a lasting impact on Christian Churches and Colleges.

Also included within these selected sermons are profound and practical sermons from preachers of large congregations and megachurches. Weekly numbers in their congregations range from eight hundred to twenty-thousand-plus in attendance. These leaders have had a tremendous impact throughout the country and the world: Cal Jernigan (Mesa, Arizona), Bob Mink (Moreno Valley, California), Bob Shannon (Atlanta Christian College), Glenn Elliott (Tucson, Arizona), Bob Russell (Louisville, Kentucky), Mark Scott (Ozark Christian College) and Gene Appel (Anaheim, California). Their sermons are insightful and challenging. They communicate in a way to fill the heart and the head.

Two of the "living pulpit" preachers have been college presidents: LeRoy Lawson (Hope International University) and Marshall Leggett (Milligan College). These educators have been pastors of local churches, leaders of institutions, and presidents of the North American Christian Convention. In their "golden years," they are looked to as leaders in our movement and sought out for wisdom and counsel. These 13 preachers are European American.

Evangelism has been and is a major preaching focus for the past 50 years. A concern for people to make a commitment to Jesus and be baptized has not gone away. What has changed is that during the early years of this period of time most churches encouraged baptisms every Sunday. Now there is more of a push for a "Baptism Sunday." These "special" Sundays are usually held once a quarter or twice a year. In the meantime, church attenders are encouraged to indicate making a decision for Christ by raising their hand in the worship service and, then, coming to a session for instruction.

The themes have changed regarding approach. For many years, an exegetical, book-by-book focus was the norm. A preacher would go through an Old Testament book, then do a topical theme, cover a New Testament book, and return to a theme. In more recent years, a more general, topical approach has taken over. Instead of one focal text, many texts are used to make the point of the message. Life issues are the themes. Four to six weeks constitutes a series, not three months or more, in a particular book.

The topic of the Restoration Movement or the Stone-Campbell Movement is seldom, if ever, addressed. Restoration principles are taught, but not as coming through the Movement, but simply as biblical teaching. There is little interest in the heritage's history. There is little identification of a "Christian Church" related to any other "Christian Church." Most of the congregations are truly independent. The pastors are aware and participate with others in the movement, but the "common" church member would have little, if any, idea of the non-denominational denomination!

Use of media is the norm in churches today. Where, in the past, there were more skits, today the use of video has taken over. Many churches are adept in the use of big screens. Some of these screens are 40 feet long and almost as high. Pictures, PowerPoint, YouTube, self-created videos are almost expected to hold the interest of today's congregation, which is media driven. Some preachers have the congregation use their phones to participate in the sermon. Churches have replaced the hymnal with words on a screen. However, there are often not just words, but pictures or moving graphics accentuating the message. In many churches, use of the screen is very professionally done. "Worship Center" or "Auditorium" has replaced the nomenclature of the "Sanctuary." Creativity of décor, lighting, and arrangement of chairs (instead of pews), are used to create different ambiances. Clear pulpits, round tables, and no pulpits often free the preachers of nonverbal communication that may create barriers for the congregation.

In the past 50 years, the number of megachurches has greatly increased. In fact, the definition of megachurch has changed from Lyle Schaller's range of "over 1000" attendees to today's description of "over 2000." For years, the signal megachurch for Independents was First Christian Church in Canton, Ohio. During the P.H. Welshimer days, the church had over 1000 attenders. In 2015 it still had 1442. Now, however, 58 Christian Churches have an attendance of more than 2000. Two of these churches, Christ's Church of the Valley in Peoria, Arizona, and Southeast Christian Church of Louisville, Kentucky, have more than 20,000 people in their weekend services.

The sermons presented in this volume are biblical, challenging, and inspiring. Their varied approaches to topics and texts are good representations of the "Living Pulpit" of the Independent Christian Church.

Russell F. Blowers

Russell F. Blowers was born June 26, 1924, in Zanesville, Ohio, and died November 10, 2007, in Indianapolis. He was a World War II veteran of the Eighth Air Force. After returning from the war, he married Marian Eagon, and completed an undergraduate degree at Ohio University in advertising and commerce. Subsequently, he was called into ministry and went to Christian Theological Seminary (then Butler University School of Religion), completing a MDiv in 1960; later, he received an honorary doctorate from Milligan College. He was for 46 years the minister of East 91st Street Christian Church in Indianapolis, during which time he mentored many younger ministers and was active in various other ministries, including the Billy Graham Evangelistic Association and the North American Christian Convention. He served as a trustee for Milligan College, Emmanuel Christian Seminary, and Christian Missionary Fellowship.

Pastor Blowers' sermon, on "The Anatomy of a Preacher's Heart," was prepared following heart bypass surgery in the summer of 1978 and preached at East 91st Street Church. He was already a close friend of his cardiologist, and became a good friend of his heart surgeon, who briefed him on the anatomy of the human heart. He preached this sermon on various occasions in churches and conventions. One of his personal favorites, it reflected on the anatomy of the preaching ministry itself, for which he had a deep passion, using metaphors from cardiology, about which he learned so much during his health crisis mid-career. He uses the RSV.

"The Anatomy of a Preacher's Heart"

1 Timothy 4:6–10

I'm not here this morning to serve up an autobiographical homily, nor am I here to dish out good advice. My all-time favorite cartoon printed years ago in the *New Yorker* pictures two clergymen conversing in a luxurious library. The older of the two says to the younger, "Drawing upon my considerable experience, Andrews, my advice to a young man ambitious of success in our profession is to steer clear of two subjects: politics and religion." I promise you I will not lay advice upon you but only offer some thoughts from my heart and mind to yours.

Two institutions are being sharply denounced in our time, and the funeral orations for both are being written: the City of New York and the Church of Jesus Christ.

Cole Porter flippantly wrote the song: "I Happen to Like New York."

I happen to *love* the church! I happen to love the ministry—that incomparable calling of an inadequate person to an impossible assignment for an indefinite period. I like to breathe the air of it; I like to drink deeply of the highs and lows of it. I even like the stink of it—the hurt and loneliness, and the disappointments of it, the joy and glory and ecstasy of it! Oh, who among us in this family of faith does not admit that, apart from Jesus Christ, we are nothing? And who among us has not had those moments of soul-wrenching self-inquisition? Breathes there a preacher with soul so dead, who never to oneself hath said, "One more crisis like that and I'll switch to insurance or real estate"? The apostle may have been able to be all things to all people, but most of us have a peck of trouble being a few things to some people. But still, we love it! Praise God that we are associates in the Christian mission.

The anatomy of a preacher's heart.

Take a peek into that remarkable muscle. A young Indianapolis cardiologist helped me describe its function:

> The most important function of the heart is to pump blood to its near neighbor, the lungs, and to its neighbors farther away—as far away as the head, hands, and feet. The heart itself is divided into four rooms or chambers. The upper right (the atrium) receives blood from the rest of the body. This muscular chamber pushes the blood into the lower right room, the right ventricle, which, in turn, pushes the blood into the lungs where oxygen enters the blood. The blood returns to the heart, but this time to the lower left room, the left atrium, which, in turn, pushes the blood into the upper left room, the left ventricle. From there, the blood goes to the rest of the body.

The heart serves two functions: it collects and distributes life-giving blood to the body. It receives and it transmits. It takes and gives. The cycle must be complete...no input, no output.

Now check the heart of a preacher—not the pulsating muscle, but the person.

The heart of the preacher must be filled.

Colossians 3:1 says: "If then you have been raised with Christ, seek the things that are above, where Christ is, seated at the right hand of God." It is essential that we ingest the life-giving word:

- That we take in power in prayer,

- That we fill these minds with the fruit of scholarship (not just flush them with the sermons of others),

- That we collect in our spirits the message of life in Jesus Christ until fire burns in our bones.

Our cardiologist continues, "A heart attack is an *infarction*–when one of the coronary arteries that feeds the heart becomes clogged,…part of the heart is deprived of nourishment, and part of it dies." If we are not constantly fed and nurtured, if we preachers are not daily taking into our minds the truth, we will cease to be a channel of that truth. We will dry up; we will be frustrated and unfulfilled; we will be open to moral failures; and, in our emptiness, we will wander like desert Bedouins from church to church, and thus the whole body fails.

A preacher's heart must receive power, sometimes through suffering.

Through these years God has chastised me in love, for I am a son, not an illegitimate offspring. In the personal agony of a daughter's death, I found that everything I'd been telling people at funerals was really true. In the fickleness of church members who abandoned ship when I needed them; in those times when my jealousy of others rebounded and broke my envious spirit; in my personal struggle with indolence; in my silly efforts at empire-building and self-serving; in those high moments of radical confrontation with the Lord, when I see myself as less than zero, an earthen vessel full of cracks and chips–in all these traumas God has filled my heart anew with the power of the Holy Spirit.

The heart of a preacher must beat with the rhythm of the great heart of Christ.

If it does, it will be big enough to include those who march to a different theological drummer. I have refused to be encased in the straitjacket of isolationism. I've tried to keep from having that open mind in which everything falls out, but I have been willing to associate with other evangelicals–not just to steal them from their tradition–but to love them and let them know what God has given to me about the faith once delivered to the saints. I hate sectarianism with a passion, even when it's our brand…*especially* when it's our brand. We are free people. We need more mavericks in the ministry–those who stand for principle even though it may mean not being invited to give the homecoming sermon at dear old alma mater–even though it may mean the politics of our non-denomination may keep you from being called to that church you've always wanted. But be prepared for the flak and for the mud to hit the fan if you stand free. My understanding of church has always freed me to associate with many families of God's disunited and disengaged people. When one's heart is flooded with love, the mind with sound doctrine, and the soul with the security of his presence, all is well.

The heart of a preacher must send its roots deep into the wells of the Spirit.

In that superb passage in 1 Corinthians 9, Paul writes of self-discipline, as Olympic runners who race for a gold medal, "but I beat my body and make it my slave, so that after I have preached to others, I myself will not be a castaway." (v. 27. preacher's paraphrase). A castaway is something that cannot bear a test—counterfeit, worthless, disqualified. I cannot be real, alone. There is no sufficiency in me. I cannot subsist for a day without dropping my bucket deep in the spring of the Spirit. Our people need to see us walk into that pulpit or into that hospital room or into that classroom with the smell of Christ upon us.

I have lately been reading again Andrew Murray's *Abide in Christ*. As that great classic reminds us, Jesus did say, "Come unto me" (Mt. 11:28, KJV), but in John 15:4 he says, "Abide in me." Abiding in the Vine is not an option for the preacher who would draw new life from the Lord Jesus, life that Jesus can translate into words and service and love that will nurture the body and feed the flock.

So, then, the heart of the preacher must be filled, and the heart of the preacher must give its contents away.

Just as this muscle squeezes oxygenated blood to the dependent body, so does the minister of Christ pour out the gospel and its related truth to the church. And this is a continuing process. Once is not enough. The blood comes back for more oxygen, more food, again and again. For this reason, those of us who are pastor-teachers have the world's most exciting, demanding, exhausting function!

But the preacher's own heart must not be given away to just any common cause.

One cannot be involved in every crusade that comes down the pike without being used up and tied up. I'm all for giving time to those projects and involvements in which we can be God's servant in a secular setting, but we've got to be careful we're not being used by the world. Billy Graham and Richard M. Nixon were friends for years, but Billy had no idea what was going on. Mr. Nixon deleted all the expletives when he was around the Reverend. But I'm speaking primarily of those good causes that can sidetrack us from our real calling.

In the 1950s, I humbly agreed to take on the entire world communist movement. I was an expert on Marxism-Leninism. I read things by Lenin that he didn't even write. I spoke at so many church dinners on anti-communism that my stomach still locks up when I see ham and green beans. I was so busy for a time explaining communism that I awakened one day to discover it was replacing the proclamation of the gospel. So I phased out. I'm still as anti-communist as ever, but one can be sucked into divergent activities that are subversive to the church's mission.

A preacher's heart must be invested in his preaching.

"Woe to me if I do not preach the gospel!" (1 Cor. 9:16). Everything about me must go into my preaching! It's foolish to assume you can preach without being heard and seen. The great Boston preacher of the 19th century, Phillips Brooks was on target when he thought of preaching as communicating truth through personality.[1] Piously you may pray that your hearers will not see you at all, but that is quite impossible. "We preach... not ourselves" (2 Cor. 4:5a), to be sure, but we preach *through* ourselves, and while the message is not dependent upon ostentation, loudness, flamboyancy, and charisma, the messenger is essential. The preacher is transparent to the discerning Christian. The preacher must have heart.

The Eu'tychus Syndrome (sleeping in church—Acts 20:9) is going to take place whether Paul or Russ is doing the preaching. Some minds are so deprived of a good blood supply or so mentally constipated by indifference or unbelief as to render them impervious to the Word. But there is no excuse for boring people to death either through a lot of heat and little light, or through humdrum delivery of a draggy, burdensome essay.

A church dignitary once asked British playwright and actor, David Garrick, why the theater was reaching the many, while the church reached the few. Why, considering their respective messages? Garrick replied: "The reason is that we make fiction appear to be true, while you speak truth as though it were fiction."

A preacher's heart must be consistent with the truth being preached.

A preacher who can't handle the elders and comes home and takes it out on his family is in trouble. Preachers who are Jekyll in the pulpit and Hyde at home risk the possibility of turning their own children into infidels. Those who compliment the youth group as the greatest and neglect to tell their own children is destroying them. Preachers who tell their congregations how much they love them, but don't tell their own spouses are counterfeit.

Finally, a preacher's heart must be sustained by the power of the resurrection!

Philippians 3:10: "...that I may know him and the power of his resurrection, and may share his sufferings, becoming like him in his death..."

Last spring, I stood on the wind-worn Oregon coast with Bill Richardson and Dennis Helsabeck, there where the Pacific waters have thundered against the rocks for countless centuries and hewn out crevices with the power of a million chisels...a coastline where the air currents are so swift and relentless that the trees are all bent eastward and twisted into freakish shapes. I stood there for a long time watching the waves of the ageless sea roll with rhythmic fury at the beaches...felt the east-bound winds, watched the sun go down but not out...saw the stars turn on... I watched the power of God's responsive creation perform before my very eyes! And then the thought possessed me: a power greater than all this natural action is resident in me–the power of the resurrection! To know Jesus Christ and the power of his resurrection is enough–for Paul...for you...for me.

Marshall Leggett

Marshall Leggett has been an honored statesman for the Restoration Movement for over 60 years. He is a graduate of Milligan College and Christian Theological Seminary. He has been awarded honorary doctor degrees from Milligan College, Kentucky Christian College, and Midwest Christian College. Marshall pastored local churches from 1948–1982. He preached at Broadway Christian Church, Lexington, Kentucky, for 16 years. For 15 years, he served as president of Milligan College, where he is presently the chancellor. Marshall was president of the North American Christian Convention in 1971.

Christian baptism, as a part of life in Christian Churches during the past 50 years, has been a source of disagreement, contention, even division. The purpose of this sermon is the hope that Christian baptism will not be so much argued and debated in the next 50 years but will be something to be received and celebrated–because of the precious, precious promises it carries in Scripture. He uses the NIV, except as otherwise noted.

"Blessing of Christian Baptism"

It was after Easter morning services at First Christian Church, Canton, Ohio, where I served as Youth Minister, and I was visiting with a family when a little ragamuffin-type boy came up and yanked at my coat to get attention. I turned and told him to wait a minute. A minute later there was another yank, which met with the same response, and a minute later another yank. The family and I decided our visit was over and I turned my attention to him.

He was so excited he couldn't stand still. "Guess what! Guess what! My big brother got bathtized this morning!" The little fellow didn't pronounce the word right, but he had good reason to be excited about his brother's bathtizing, because Christian baptism is a blessing for three reasons:

- It carries with it precious, precious promises.
- It is cause for celebration–Hallelujah!
- It is the seal of our salvation.

The first persons to receive the blessing of Christian baptism were from a large gathering in Jerusalem for Pentecost in Acts 2, a pivotal chapter in the Bible. The Holy Spirit came in power as Jesus had promised. Peter preached the first gospel sermon, and, using Hebrew history and prophecy, he convinced many that Jesus was the Messiah. He concluded saying:

> "Let all Israel be assured of this: God has made this Jesus, whom you crucified, both Lord and Christ."

When the people heard this, they were cut to the heart, and said
to Peter and the other apostles, "Brothers, what shall we do?"
Peter replied, "Repent and be baptized, every one of you, in the
name of Jesus Christ so that your sins may be forgiven. And you
will receive the gift of the Holy Spirit." (Acts 2:36–38)

Can you imagine the relief these people must have felt? *Forgiveness!*
Not just for this sin, but for *all* their sins–a new start! Then Peter added an
addendum, which is more than just "icing on the cake," but was a profound
promise: "And you will receive the gift of the Holy Spirit," that was to lead
them as they followed Jesus in his Way.

Two precious, precious promises that came with their baptism, but
there is a third. Later, Acts says, "Those who accepted his message were
baptized, and about three thousand were added to their number that day"
(2:41). They became charter members of Jesus' new body, the church; that
made them recipients of three precious promises.

Now let's turn our attention to the eighth chapter of Acts to find another
blessing. An angel came to Philip the Evangelist and told him to go down
to the road that led from Jerusalem to Gaza, where he found an Ethiopian
riding in his chariot, reading from Isaiah. The Holy Spirit told Philip to
hitch a ride in his chariot, and Acts says, "he preached unto him Jesus" (v.
35b, KJV). They came to a body of water and the Ethiopian said, "Look,
here is water. Why shouldn't I be baptized?" (v. 3).

This is an inference, but an obvious one. Somewhere in "preached
unto him Jesus," Philip must have told the Ethiopian about the blessing of
baptism, or he would not have known to ask for it. Christian baptism is a
part of the gospel message, for it is good news.

Romans 6 carries a precious, precious promise: "Or don't you know
that all of us who were baptized into Christ Jesus were baptized into his
death? We were therefore buried with him through baptism into death in
order that, just as Christ was raised from the dead through the glory of the
Father, we too may have a new life" (vv. 3–5). Does this not sound much
like being born again by the water and the Spirit, as in Jesus' conversation
with Nicodemus in John 3?

Saul of Tarsus received the blessing of this "new life." No one needed
forgiveness more than Saul, who was implicit in the stoning of Stephen and
had papers to persecute Christians in Damascus. You know the story–how
he was struck down on the road. Jesus said, "Why do you persecute me?"
Saul asked, "Who are you, Lord?" He knew to whom he was speaking.
Jesus answered, "I am Jesus..., whom you are persecuting" (Acts 22:7–8).
And he was told to go into the city and he would be told what to do. At this
point, Saul was not forgiven. We know that he repented with such intensity
that he did not eat a bite or drink a drop for three days, and he still was
not forgiven. Then Ananias came to him and told him what to do, "Why

tarriest thou? Arise, and be baptized, and wash away thy sins, calling on the name of the Lord" (Acts 22:16, KJV).

This is that precious, precious promise: "a new life"–the slate wiped clean by the blood of the cross. The persecutor became the apostle. God even changed his name from Saul to Paul, and from that point he is never again referred to as Saul. He was a new creation, a precious, precious blessing.

Much more can be said about the precious, precious promises, but we must move on because Christian baptism is cause for celebration. Hallelujah!

Celebrating Christian baptism is biblical: Acts 2, they received it gladly; the Ethiopian went on his way rejoicing; when the Jerusalem church learned about the baptism of Cornelius, it glorified God; the Philippian jailer was baptized and invited Paul and Silas into his house where his wife cooked them a meal. Knowing they were itinerant evangelists, I'm sure it was fried chicken, mashed potatoes, and a slice of lemon pie–which is the historic cuisine for itinerant evangelists. Then it says, the jailer set a meal "before them, and rejoiced, believing in God with all his house" (Acts 16:34b, KJV). It sounds like they had a party.

However, some people think the celebration can be carried too far. First Christian Church, Johnson City, Tennessee, has been a great church for many years. My parents and I worshiped there when they came to dump me on the Milligan College campus to become a student– and it was where, later, I spent 15 years of my vocational ministry. One Sunday morning after the invitation hymn, the minister asked the Johnson City congregation to be seated because the young people had a baptism. The high school students came and gathered around the baptistry. When their friend was baptized, they did not applaud or say, "Amen." Instead, they shouted, "Right on! Right on!" One of our professors got up and walked out with her son, saying, "I don't think I'll ever come back."

It was sometime later I was leading a midweek service at the Olivet Christian Church, Norfolk, Virginia. When I finished, the presiding elder asked the people to remain seated–"The young people have a baptism." Olivet is not a large church, but it had a big bunch of young people. When the youth minister baptized the teenager, it was not, "Right on!" but almost in unison the bunch shouted, "You da man! You da man!"

Now I'm not sure I'm ready for, "Right on!" and, "You da man!" but every time I witness a baptism, I feel like singing "Now I Belong to Jesus." I've never been asked to lead singing at a church service, but this is my opportunity and I'm going to take advantage of it. I know I'm speaking to a sophisticated and aristocratic audience, but let me ask you to lay aside your inhibitions and sing with gusto. Like Lawrence Welk, a-one, a-two, a-three: [Here the preacher led the congregation in singing "Now I Belong to Jesus."[1]]

Christian baptism is a precious, precious promise, because it is the seal of our salvation. In Bible interpretation, there are types and antitypes. A type is an event or person in the Old Testament that illustrates a truth or person in the New Testament. The apostle Peter uses Noah and his family being saved in the flood waters in Genesis of the Old Testament to illustrate a truth in the New Testament. He writes, speaking of the flood, "In it only a few people, eight in all, were saved through water, and this water symbolizes baptism that now saves you also–not the removal of dirt from the body but the pledge of a good conscience toward God. It saves you by the resurrection of Jesus Christ" (1 Pet. 3:20b–21).

The key word here is "pledge," that carries the connotation of a seal. Peter uses the Greek word *eperotema,* which is a business and legal term in the Greek language. For example, you have a document you want finalized. So you take it to a notary public who has you sign the document in the presence of two witnesses, then she signs her name and takes her seal and clamps down on it. The seal means that the document is finalized, finished, complete. Old-time monarchs used to do it with their ring and wax. They would put wax on the paper, then thrust their ring into it that carried the family crest.

This is the role Christian baptism plays in our acceptance of Jesus as our Savior and making him the Lord of our lives; it finalizes, finishes, completes,...*seals* our new relationship with him. It enables Peter to say *twice* "baptism saves."

This in no way diminishes the importance of faith. Ephesians 2:8 says, "For it is by grace you have been saved, through faith..." It is faith that opens the door. People cannot be baptized without faith; they can be immersed, but that is not Christian baptism without faith. I would also include repentance, because at some point people must recognize that they have sinned, are sinners, and the only way they can be saved is by the grace Jesus purchased with his sacrificial death upon the cross.

In the book of Acts, there is a sense of urgency between accepting Christ as Savior and Christian baptism–Acts 2: "the same day"; the Ethiopian: "what doth hinder me"; Saul [pre-Paul]: "immediately...he was baptized,"; and the Philippian jailer: "the same hour of the night" (all KJV). Christian baptism was not an appendage to accepting Christ; it was and is a part of accepting Christ. It has been shown even in our day–when people understand the connection between accepting Christ and baptism, they are anxious to receive it.

Jeff Vines was minister of Christ's Church of the Valley in California. The church had grown rapidly and new members had come from many denominations. He thought, "We have a lot of people here who follow Jesus as Lord and Savior, but they have never been taught about baptism...or at least don't understand what it's all about. So, I thought, I need to teach what the Scripture says about baptism and see what happens."

He decided to have a weekend of church services to emphasize baptism, which was daring because, if it failed, he would look bad. However, the church bought into it and preparation began: two portable baptistries were bought; they went to Big Lots and Target to buy towels and wiped them out; black T-shirts were purchased for modesty purposes; garbage bags were made available for driving home in wet clothes; et al.

Vines wanted to make his sermon simple and short. He said, "Your sin separates you from God. God's not expecting you to be perfect—just that you are sorry and turn and start living his way. Then, trust Jesus to forgive you of your sin. And finally, be baptized."

He went on to say, "I had three goals in mind. One, I wanted them to see that Jesus commanded it: repent and be baptized. Two, I wanted them to see that there are nine conversion experiences in the book of Acts, and all nine began with someone making an internal commitment that Jesus is my Savior and ended with the external act of baptism. All nine. The third thing I wanted them to see was that there's no gap. You become a believer, you repent, and then you're baptized. The examples I used were the Philippian jailer and the Ethiopian eunuch."

The invitation was given. 482 responded and were baptized, and the following weekend 119 more were baptized. An elderly gentleman came up to Vines and said, "I've been going to church all my life, and I've never experienced this before. All these people..." He said it with a tear running down his cheek.

What does this say to me? It says that when people accept Jesus as their Savior and make him the Lord of their lives, they will jump at the opportunity to be baptized.

There is one more Scripture I must mention, because we are going to sing a chorus. It is 1 John 5:7–8, "There are three that testify: the Spirit, the water and the blood; and the three are in agreement." To testify is to give witness. The Spirit is the gift of the Holy Spirit that enables people to see Christ living in Christians, and that is a witness. The blood is the Lord's Supper. Paul said, "For whenever you eat this bread and drink this cup, you proclaim the Lord's death until he comes" (1 Cor. 11:26), and that is a witness. The water is Christian baptism. We are buried with Christ, into his death, and as Christ arose from the dead, we rise with "a new life." It is a beautiful, dramatic witness to the good news of the gospel.

Let's stand and sing our chorus. I will be standing here with three of our leaders. Let me urge you, if you have never received Christian baptism, to lay aside your timidity and step forward. Nothing would give us more pleasure than to visit with you about the blessing of Christian baptism and how it can be a witness to your faith in Christ.

Robert Shannon

Robert C. Shannon was born in 1930 in Corinth, Kentucky, the son of a farmer. He graduated from Cincinnati Bible Seminary and did further study at Tusculum College, Georgetown College, and Lutheran Evangelical Seminary. His pulpit ministries were in Kentucky, Tennessee, Ohio, Florida, and California. For eight years, he worked behind the Iron Curtain lecturing in seminaries, colleges, and churches. He taught preaching at Atlanta Christian College before retiring to the Blue Ridge Mountains of North Carolina, where he served several churches in interim ministries.

Bob watched the style of preaching change over 50 years and tried to adapt to the changes. As a pastor, he saw many life situations that could and should be addressed, and with his training and background in biblical preaching, he searched for Scripture that addressed those situations. Because the church in Florida, his longest ministry, was filled with winter visitors each year, he felt that sermons should target widely felt needs rather than local situations, and timeless needs rather than timely needs–but, often indirectly rather than directly. This sermon was preached in Florida around 1981, using the KJV.

"The Fox and the Lamb"[1]

Luke 23:7–12

In literature, the fox has always stood for cunning and the lamb for innocence. In Aesop's fables, it is the fox who guards the grapes he cannot eat. It is the fox who deceives and eats the gingerbread man. The expressions have become proverbial: "Sly as a fox." "I outfoxed him." "The Prince," said Machiavelli, "must be a lion; but he must also know how to play the fox."[2] The fox stands for craftiness, cunning, and cruelty.

The lamb is always the symbol of gentleness and innocence. "Gentle as a lamb," we say. It was said of one that he was "a lion in the chase" but "a lamb at home." In the lodge ritual of a large fraternity, the lamb is the badge of innocence. In the writings of Blake, the lamb is also the badge of innocence.

The Bible describes Herod as a fox and Jesus as a lamb. The Pharisees had come to Jesus earlier with a warning. "Get thee out, and depart hence: for Herod will kill thee" (Lk 13:31).

Jesus said, "Go ye, and tell that fox, Behold, I cast out devils, and I do cures today and tomorrow, and the third day I shall be perfected" (Lk 13:32). In other words, "I am keeping my schedule."

No one was more deserving of that title, "fox." When his father, Herod the Great, died, he left most of his territory to another son and only little Galilee to Herod Antipas. Herod hurried to Rome to try to influence the emperor against his brother, but failed. Against another brother, he was more successful. He seduced Herodias, his brother's wife. Eventually, he shipped his first wife home and married Herodias. His sister-in-law became his wife, and she was already his niece. So the sin became a triple sin. It was that sin that John the Baptist fearlessly denounced. That was the reason Herodias demanded and got the prophet's head on a platter.

Nor was any person more deserving of the term "lamb" than Jesus. His introduction by John the Baptist contained just those words: "Behold the Lamb of God, [who] taketh away the sin of the world" (Jn. 1:29b). Never was a person gentler with children, with the sick, with the sinner. Never was anyone so innocent. "He did no sin; neither was guile found in his mouth" (1 Pet. 2:22, NIV). Pilate's verdict is the only verdict. "I find no fault in him" (Jn. 19:6d).

How perfectly He fulfilled Isaiah's prediction – "...led as a sheep to the slaughter, and like a lamb dumb before his shearer" (Acts 8:32). We must not suppose that His silence in our text was a deliberate fulfilling of the prophecy, but rather that the prophet saw before what would, in fact, be the case.

Small wonder that in Revelation Jesus is pictured as "the Lamb" again and again. Small wonder that our songs reflect that thought so often:

"Dear dying Lamb, thy precious blood shall never lose its power."

"Are you washed in the blood of the Lamb?"

"Near the cross, O Lamb of God!"

In this text, the fox and the lamb meet. Picture the scene. There sits Herod with all his soldiers arrayed behind him. How powerful he seems. How weak he is.

Jesus is standing alone. How weak He seems. How powerful He is. Herod has his bodyguards and all the palace crowd around him. Jesus is alone. Five thousand ate His loaves and fishes by the sea, but none of them is here now to defend Him. Twelve sturdy disciples had accompanied Him for more than three years, but none of them is here. He has friends: Nicodemus and Joseph of Arimathea. But they are not present to rise to His defense. If you were there and asked to join the winning side, you'd pick Herod at once. All the power of the Roman Empire is behind that puppet from Galilee. The carpenter seems a poor choice by comparison.

Yet the career of one ends in obscurity. The career of the other ends in grandeur. Indeed, if it had not been for Christ, most of us would never have heard of Herod. The fame of Christ has spread around the world and down the ages, and He is today the most powerful person of human history. Herod's life sputtered out in the obscurity of exile in France. How quickly glory fades and power evaporates!

Yet we keep supposing that the answers to world problems lie with the Herods of the world and not with Jesus. The world keeps betting on the fox and not on the Lamb. We ourselves often think that the odds favor the Herods of the world; that the odds lie with power, not with humility; that the odds lie with wealth, not with poverty; that the odds lie with cunning, not with innocence.

Once, on a boat, the disciples discovered that no one remembered to bring a picnic basket. There was only one loaf for all 13 of them. Jesus said, "Beware of…the leaven of Herod" (Mk. 8:15b). They pondered that cryptic remark. Was He upset because there was no bread? What did He mean? He spoke it not only for them but for us. Jesus knew that through all time people would turn to Him for guidance. To us today, He says, "Beware of the leaven of Herod."

Beware of the sins of Herod. Lust and cruelty are in the world still. Beware of the idle and flippant curiosity of Herod. Beware of the irreverence of Herod that makes us mock holy things.

Beware of the tendency to talk when silence would be better. If Herod had only known the true situation, he would have kept silent. If he had known that he was in the presence of the King of kings, would he have dared to demand a miracle? Would he have dared to play the little game of masquerade? Would he have dared to mock and ridicule?

King Henry VIII went to hear Latimer preach. The great man began by giving himself some public advice: "Latimer," he said, "be careful what you say. The king of England is here." He added, "Latimer, be careful what you do not say. The King of kings is here.³"

In this text, the fox and the Lamb meet. And it is the fox who is afraid.

Verse 8 hints at this, and Luke 9:7–9 makes it plain. Herod had never gotten over the execution of John the Baptist. No doubt, he secretly admired the man. He had spoken rashly at the birthday party, promising the seductive Salome anything she wished. When the request was for the head of John, Herod was, says the Bible, exceedingly sorry. Herod never forgot how weak he had been, how he had been manipulated, how cruel he had been.

When Jesus came along, so like John, curiosity arose in the heart of Herod—and turned to fear. What if John had indeed come back from the dead!? What if he were only biding his time for vengeance? How sin makes people afraid!

Jesus' silence seems fitting. He would not remove from Herod that fruit of sin he so fully deserved. Let him wonder. Let the anxiety smolder.

Jesus is remembering how desperately John had sent word from prison to find reassurance that his life had not, after all, been in vain. And the cruel and needless execution of that great preacher must have surely filled Jesus' heart with strong emotion. He may have kept silent because He dared not speak. So strong was that emotion, He may not have trusted himself to say anything. To speak would calm Herod's fears. Silence only makes them grow deeper.

Herod's fear is also mixed with a certain curiosity. Again, look at verse 8. Everybody likes to see a magician perform his tricks. Many like to believe there is something supernatural about it. It amazes us how willing, how anxious, people are to believe in magic.

The reports that have come to Herod about Jesus are exciting. He wants to see those miracles of healing. But how would that look? Imagine, the governor of Galilee going out to some hillside to watch a carpenter teaching and healing! Of course, his position would not let him do that. But now he has a chance at last to satisfy his coarse curiosity about Jesus, and Jesus properly will not honor it.

We may sometimes come to the Bible with such an unholy attitude. The Bible is far, far more than an old curiosity shop. If all you are interested in is viewing its curiosities, then stay away. We must come here as Moses did before the burning bush, without our shoes, recognizing that this is holy ground.

People do strange things when they are afraid and frustrated. Some whistle. Others laugh. Herod is in the second category. Verse 11 says that he "set him at naught." That is translated by some as "made light of him" or "treated him with contempt." They ridiculed Him, made fun of Him, and mocked Him. They put on Him a gorgeous robe. He could have struggled against the ugly charade, tried to shake off the robe, cried out, "Stop it!" But Jesus never lost His dignity. He bent to receive that robe with all the grace and bearing of a king. Never in His life had He worn anything half so fine as that. How odd it looked over His rough Galilean garments. Yet never a man deserved to wear it more than He.

In the story of the crucifixion, people kept unknowingly doing appropriate things. Judas betrayed with a kiss. Did not Jesus deserve the loving kisses of the world? The soldiers gave Him a reed for a scepter! Never did a man deserve more to hold the scepter of power! Pilate put up a title: *King.* He put it in three languages so that no one would miss the joke. What is more appropriate than that the Lord of all humankind should be identified trilingually?

So here, though the scenes make our blood run cold, there is a cruel appropriateness to it all. Herod and his soldiers play their little game of charades. Does he hope to provoke Jesus to speech? Is he bored with palace routine? Is it some devilish streak in his nature that prompts such action? We cannot know. We recoil from the scene. Herod and his men soon tire of it. In the gorgeous robe, Jesus is sent again to Pilate.

But let us not miss the importance of verses 9 and 10. The tendency when one is accused is to answer back—quickly, firmly, at length. Why does Jesus offer no defense? Perhaps it is because some charges ought not to be dignified with a defense. Years ago, when everybody was hunting communists, it was not hard to find pages of accusations hurled at high public officials. Often they were silent in the face of such slanders. I wondered why. I even sometimes naively thought that their silence proved their guilt. I am older now. I know what Jesus obviously knew all along. One does not dignify every charge with an answer. Some accusations are not worthy of an answer.

So as charge after charge is hurled against Jesus, He stands calm and unruffled in dignified silence. We admire Him far more for that than if He had shouted, "Lies! Lies! They're all lies! You made that up!" True enough, that would have been, but Jesus would have lost something of dignity and honor and maturity. And, looking at the scene today, we know He did exactly right. He ignored those clamoring voices as if they were no more than wind in the trees. Thus went the first meeting between the fox and the Lamb. It was not the last. Herod and Jesus met again. This time Herod was the prisoner in the dock. This time Jesus was the judge. This time it was Herod who was speechless.

Myron J. Taylor

Myron Jackson Mabry Taylor was born on March 26, 1924, in the coal mining town of Goodwill, West Virginia. Even though neither of his parents had gone to high school, he and all three of his siblings attended college. Myron enrolled at Johnson Bible College, Knoxville, Tennessee, in June of 1942 to prepare for a ministry of preaching.

Myron preached for several different congregations while at Johnson and graduated in 1946. He attended Butler University School of Religion. He received his BD degree from Butler in June, 1956. Pastor Taylor preached in Gosport, Indiana; Mays, Indiana; Toledo, Ohio; Portsmouth, Ohio; East Point, Georgia; and Westwood, California.

Johnson Bible College honored him in 1980 with the DMin degree. He served as adjunct professor of preaching at Emmanuel School of Religion (now Emmanuel Christian Seminary at Milligan), offering a preaching course during summer terms for 26 years. Taylor retired from the Westwood Hills church in 1999, after which he edited and published five books of his sermons, essays, and lectures on preaching: *Preacher of the Gospel,*[1] *Proclaiming the Risen Lord,*[2] *True Faith and Sound Learning,*[3] *Where God Meets Us,*[4] and *One God and Father of All.*[5] Myron Taylor passed away in 2015. This sermon, which was preached at Westwood Hills, uses the NRSV.

"The Sacrament of Continuance"[6]

1 Corinthians 11:23–32

The sermon today is the last in a short series during the season of Pentecost on the nature of the church in our time, and especially our Christian Churches. Our purpose has been to be as explicit as possible as to what a Christian Church is. We like to think of it as a movement within the great Church pleading for the unity of all Christians based on the Christian gospel for the sake of the mission of the church in the world. We spelled that out in three sermons. A part of that larger series, and as a kind of sub-series, we have developed three sermons on the sacraments. Today we deliver the last of those sermons on "The Sacrament of Continuance–The Lord's Supper." In Christian baptism, we have the sacrament of initiation. In the Lord's Supper, we have the sacrament of continuance.

When we talk about sacraments, we need to understand the relationship of God to the natural (material) world. God created the world of nature and called it "good." God loves the world he has made. God uses the natural world to contact us and speak to us about the reality of the spiritual world. "Symbols of the natural world become vehicles of the heavenly world."[7]

Jesus' parables of nature tell us that God is the God of nature, that the whole world is his and is fitted to speak to us of him: "Consider the lilies of the field, how they grow: they neither toil nor spin, yet I tell you, even Solomon in all his glory was not clothed like one of these" (Mt. 6:28–29). Jesus uses the "symbol" of the lily of the field to tell us that we need not worry because God cares for us. We use "symbols" all the time as we worship God—words, music, gestures, ritual action, standing, kneeling, clasping our hands, closing our eyes, bowing our head. Christian symbolism "uses seeing, feeling and tasting as often as hearing in describing the experience of the divine presence."[8] To understand the Christian faith, we need symbols that can be seen and touched and tasted; and, so, we have water and bread and wine and all the actions of the sacraments—the death, the burial, the resurrection of baptism; and the tearing of the bread,…the pouring out of the cup, the Elders standing in the place of Christ, the passing of the blessing in the Lord's Supper. "God loves matter; He invented it" (C.S. Lewis). God uses matter in which the natural elements become sacraments, by which God comes to us with his grace to bless us and give us his gifts. Sacraments operate through human faith. By God's gracious action on our behalf in Jesus Christ, we come to trust him and to open our lives to him. Out of our faith—our loyal fidelity to Jesus—we come to the Lord's table to experience again the mighty act of God in expressing his love for us in the death of Jesus on the cross. At the cross as no other place we see the love of God laid out before us. Jesus did not die to make God love us, but to show us his redeeming love, his holy love. A sacrament is something, usually quite ordinary and common, which has acquired a meaning and a significance and a value far beyond itself.

In the Celebration of the Lord's Supper, there is a sense of the Real Presence of God. In this human action, there is divine action. What do we mean by the Real Presence?

It is important to note that there are several degrees or modes of the divine presence. For instance, we believe in the omnipresence of God. There is a sense in which he is everywhere present. Yet we say that God is with those who trust him and obey him in a way in which he is not with others. We say God's presence is with us at some times more than at others. We speak of entering his presence in worship, and we ask him to come and be with us and grant us the privilege of his presence. We say that when two or three are gathered in his name, he is there in the midst of them. And now we speak of his Real Presence in the keeping of the Supper. What does that mean?

(1) God has a certain spiritual relation to his whole creation, even the material world, in the sense that its very existence and functioning from moment to moment depend upon his will. God can make the

material world the vehicle of his coming to us–the manifestation of his presence with us.

(2) There is a further degree of this presence in the relationship between God and us, because now there is the beginning of a personal relationship, in the sense that it is only through our being approached and addressed by God that we are a person at all–a responsible human being. There is a distinction between an individual and a person–an individual is one going it alone; a person is one in relation to God–a person is in fellowship. In that fellowship God's presence is known by the Holy Spirit.

(3) There is a still further stage when we humans respond to God's divine address by personal faith and obedience, so that God is especially present to the faith of the believer–or, better still, to the faith of a fellowship of believers in worship, where two or three are gathered in his name.

(4) All of this reaches its climax in the keeping of the Supper, where God who was incarnate in Jesus uses the symbolism of the Lord's Supper as a special means of awakening the faith of his people that they may receive him, since faith is the channel by which God's most intimate presence comes to us in this earthly life. The presence of God in the Supper is not in the elements but in the action–truly and really present to the faith of the believer. It was not so much the bread as the breaking, not so much the elements as the actions, that were symbolic. P. T. Forsyth wrote many years ago: "[T]he act was more than a symbol or parable. It was more than emblematic. It was donative (a gift). It was symbolic in the great sense, and really sacramental. It does more than mean, it conveys what it means."[9] The body and blood of Christ are "spiritually present to the faith of the receiver"[10]–that is the most Real Presence conceivable for a divine reality in this present world. The most objective and penetrating kind of presence that God gives us is *through faith*. Paul's prayer for his friends at Ephesus is "that Christ may dwell in your hearts through faith" (Eph. 3:17). That is how Christ dwells in our hearts in this present world. The sacrament of the Lord's Supper, by giving us not only words, but visible and tangible elements, should draw our thoughts away from ourselves to that great divine reality, which is ever nearer and more truly real than the things we can see with our eyes and touch with our hands. The Lord's Supper is truly the sacrament of the Real Presence.

There are three dimensions of the Supper which will help us experience the profound depth of our worship. **First, there is a memorial feast.** Here we are led into the holy of holies of our faith and stand before our Lord as he died for us on the cross. The Lord's Supper takes us to Calvary. Here we celebrate the Church's corporate memory of the episode of the cross: "For as often as you eat this bread and drink the cup, you proclaim the Lord's death until he comes" (1 Cor. 11:26). He may have meant that the action of the taking and breaking (tearing) the bread and pouring out the wine is a dramatic representation of the death of Christ. Paul wrote to the Galatians: "It was before your eyes that Jesus Christ was publicly exhibited as crucified" (Gal. 3:1). When did that happen? The Galatians were not in Jerusalem when Jesus was crucified. They did not see Jesus die on the cross. Yet Paul says Christ had been publicly exhibited, as crucified, before the eyes of the Galatians. When did that happen? When they celebrated the Supper, they saw Jesus Christ again in his death on their behalf. Some scholars think the Greek phrase "you do show" means you do announce or "proclaim" or even "recite." The statement may mean "whenever you celebrate the Lord's Supper, you recite the story of the passion." If so, it would indicate that in Paul's time it was the custom to recite that whole story at the Lord's table, and this might well account for the fact that the part of the Gospel story which narrates the final scenes is out of all proportion fuller and more detailed than all the rest of the story; all the details were faithfully preserved because, from the earliest days, they were being continually recited in the worship of the church. The Lord's Supper takes us into the past, as the death of Jesus becomes again very real to us.

Second, the Lord's Supper makes Christ very real to us in the present moment. "Do this in remembrance of me" (1 Cor. 11:24, 25). Some have translated these words: "Do this for my re-calling." The Hebrew (Eastern) sense of memory is quite different from our Western concept of memory. Our view is that we think of one who once was with us but is now gone from us. Our view presupposes a sense of absence. The Hebrew concept of memory is that, when we think of those gone from us, they are made present again. That view presupposes a sense of presence. In *Adam Bede,* George Eliot writes: "Our dead are never dead to us until we have forgotten them." There is a sense in which our Lord is present with us in the keeping of the Supper. His presence is not in the elements, but in the action—our faith meeting the breaking of his body (the bread) and the pouring out of his blood—his life (in the wine).

Third, the Lord's Supper presents to the church not only a present enjoyment and a memory of the past; it also has a looking forward into the future. At the institution of the Supper, Jesus said: "I tell you, I will never again drink of this fruit of the vine until that day when I drink it new with you in my Father's kingdom" (Mt. 26:29). Here, in ringing tones, is expressed the future hope of the Christian. Oscar Cullman maintains that the early Christian prayer (which was so early that it was handed down in its Aramaic form) *Maranatha,* "Come, Lord," had both a future sense and a present sense. It meant, at the same time, "Come and grant us now your presence in our worship" *and* "come to us in power and glory at the consummation," so that the note of Christ's Real Presence in the action of the Supper and the note of his future coming are blended into one.[11]

There is a remarkable and oft-quoted passage from the pen of C. H. Dodd, which dramatically sums up what we are attempting to say:

> In the Eucharist, therefore, the Church perpetually reconstitutes the crisis in which the Kingdom of God came in history. It never gets beyond this. At each Eucharist, we are *there*–we are in the night in which He was betrayed, at Golgotha, before the empty tomb on Easter Day, and in the upper room where He appeared; *and* we are now of His coming, with angels and archangels and all the company of heaven, in the twinkling of an eye at the last trump. Sacramental communion is not a purely mystical experience, to which history, as embodied in the form and matter of the Sacrament, would be in the last resort irrelevant; it is bound up with a corporate memory of real events.[12]

One reason we keep the Supper is because we are pilgrims and strangers in this world, and all our human journey is a pilgrimage toward something that lies beyond, some supernal reality, the kingdom of God in its consummation, where sacramental symbols will no longer be needed because God himself will be its temple–we will see him face to face.

One result of our recovery of a deep and strong sacramental theology will be this: we shall learn to approach the Lord's table, not looking inward into our own souls and striving to work up some effect in the realm of feeling and emotion, but looking beyond ourselves to the One who is waiting to be gracious to us, the One who answers before we call and hears while we are speaking, the One who in his grace and love is as near and as real as the bread which we see with our eyes and touch with our hands. The Lord's Supper is the sacrament of continuance–the means by which God keeps our hearts and minds on Jesus Christ and his death for us.

Cal Jernigan

Cal Jernigan serves as the Senior Pastor of Central Christian Church of the East Valley, Phoenix, Arizona, a church where he has been on staff for the past 30 years. Central Christian is a multi-site church in the Phoenix area that currently has five campuses and sees over ten thousand people gather together every weekend for worship and teaching. Cal's ministry was born out of a love for students, out of which he spent his early years developing his teaching and leadership gifts. Cal received his Bachelor's Degree from Pacific Christian College (now Hope International University) and his Master's Degree from Fuller Seminary. He and his wife Lisa have been married for 38 years and have two grown children who are both in the ministry, and six grandchildren. This sermon has been preached a number of times, most recently on February 14, 2016, at Central Christian Church in Mesa, Arizona, and broadcast to their multi-sites. Rev. Jernigan uses the NIV.

"There's More to Life than Me!"

It is one of the saddest statements in the Bible. What it says should never be said of anyone. What makes it even worse is that, once it's established, it's permanent. It will never change. I hope and pray it doesn't happen to me. I hope and pray it never happens to you.

Before I show you the statement, let me give you the setting. It's found in a verse that involved one of the Kings of Judah, a man by the name of Jehoram. To understand Jehoram, you must know a little about his family.

Jehoram's dad was also once the King of Judah, a man named Jehoshaphat. He was a good man who did many good things. Mostly, Jehoshaphat trusted and depended on God, and to this day we still tell stories about his courage and his laser-clear focus. He was a good man, to be sure. Jehoram's son, however, was not. His name was Ahaziah. He was the exact opposite of his grandfather Jehoshaphat. Also a king, Ahaziah was neither a good man nor a good king. He aligned himself with the wicked King of Israel—a man named Ahab. Ahab and his wife Jezebel were notoriously evil. Ahaziah wanted to be accepted by them. Ahaziah was a bad man wanting to be accepted by bad people. We can maybe feel a little for him, as he never had much of a role model in his father, Jehoram. But this isn't true of Jehoram.

So what was so bad about Jehoram, the man in the middle of these three generations? Just listen to the following verse and let its truth soak in. It is found in 2 Chronicles 21:20. "Jehoram was thirty-two years old when he became king, and he reigned in Jerusalem eight years. He passed away, to no one's regret, and was buried in the City of David, but not in the tombs of the kings."

He passed away to no one's regret? No one's? Not one person regretted his dying? No regrets anywhere? Not from anyone? Not to his wife's regret? Not to the regret of any of his kids? He didn't have any friends who were saddened by his passing? Did they bury this King of Judah in a place of disgrace because no one cared to show him any honor in his death? What does a person have to do to live such a life and end it so ingloriously? How bad do you have to be?

The legacy of Jehoram is simply dismal. Here's the reality: every life tells a story and every life both builds and leaves a legacy. Your legacy is what you pass on to the generations that come after you. Your legacy is what your life contributed to the good of others, or to the ill of others. Ahaziah was Jehoram's legacy.

Here's something you can count on—after you die, your name will come up in someone's conversation. You will be talked about. You will be remembered and your life will be recalled. The big question, though, is what will people think about when you come to mind? Your legacy is much more than just your reputation; it's your reality. Your legacy is the summation of the days of your life. Your legacy *becomes* what you really *were* while you yet lived.

When, then, should you give thought to your legacy? Wisdom would suggest that you think it through long before you die. Long before. Since knowing when our lives will end is not something that we can easily know, I suggest the best time to think about it is now. Right now, Immediately. No…even *sooner* than that.

Today we're going to talk about the choices facing us as we decide how to live our lives. Will we live our lives for ourselves, or for others? Jehoram clearly never gave much thought to others. He died to no one's regret because he lived to no one's benefit. This is not the life God wills for us. He has something much better in mind. For now, we'll just call it "the life that is truly life."

The Disease of Our Age

Historically there has always been no shortage of things that can ruin your life, or rob you of your life. Some of these have been on a grand scale, and others have been on a more personal scale. On a grand scale, for example, there have been major epidemics that have destroyed large numbers of people in a very short order. A few examples would be:

- Between 250 and 262 A.D., a pestilence raged all over the Roman Empire. It was known as the Cyprian Plague, and in some Italian cities, 80 percent of the population died out. In Rome alone, it is said that 5000 people a day died. Historians and scientists estimate that one half of the human race died in those 12 years.

- The Black Death ravaged Europe in 1347 and 1348. About 1.5 million people died, about one fourth of Europe's population.[1] Worldwide, as many as 75 to 200 million died.[2] (These may be conservative estimates of its toll!)

- In 1918–19, a flu epidemic killed between 50 and 100 million people around the world. The disease killed more people than WWII.[3]

Today we might worry about contracting AIDS, the bird flu, or cancer. Of course, the actual list is much longer. Some diseases attack people of a particular age group, nationality, race, or sex. Some show no discretion whatsoever.

But there is one disease that has been raging untreated on this planet ever since the beginning of time. It's very personal and it's ravaged many people. The evidence of its existence is everywhere. You see it in the world (as you might expect), but tragically it's also very common in the church. You see the path of its destruction; and few, if any, would deny its reality. It's "the disease of me." Its greatest symptom is self-centeredness.

Self-centeredness is when the only person that you worry about is yourself. It's when really all you care about is you. In a sense, we are all infected with this to some degree or another. It's something we all have to keep in check. Some, however, seem to be less than concerned about it. Today, more people than ever are living only for themselves, and more people than ever are feeling a deep sense of emptiness in their lives.

Perhaps you can recall this little ditty from the past. It's called "Three Guests," by Jessica Nelson North:

I had a little tea party
This afternoon, at three.
'Twas very small—
Three guests in all—
Just I, myself and me.
Myself ate all the sandwiches,
While I drank all the tea;
'Twas also I who ate the pie,
And passed the cake to me."

What a lonely and tragic way to live your life. What an all-too-common occurrence. Me, myself, and I. The three musketeers of madness. The most unholy of all trinities. If ever there were a root of most dysfunction and unhappiness in our lives, this would be it.

In the recent past we dubbed an entire generation the "me generation." While this is understandable, it also is a bit unfair. We've always been about "me." But if you listen to the lyrics of music these days, you can't help but hear it. Fewer and fewer lyrics are about "us" and "we"… More and more are about "I," "me," and "mine." Talking about ourselves has become our favorite subject. You can't miss it in our conversations.

All of this reminds me of a married man who received several sessions of intensive counseling to improve his marriage. As the sessions progressed, he reported to his wife, "Darling, I got a wonderful insight today. I learned that I'm constantly talking about myself, and that this has to change. So, from now on, I need you to talk more about me." This is why it's been said the one nice thing about egotists is they don't talk about other people.

The mantra of our age could simply be summed up: "Live for me and live for now." The question that is constantly asked, if not thought, is, "What's in it for me?" You hear this in our expressions: "Look out for number one!" or, "Take care of yourself!" or, "You should have it your way!" or, "Expensive, but you're worth it!"

Perhaps this is, in part, the result of living in a world in which we tell all children that they are "special." We make them repeat it often so we build up their self-esteem. We've done a really good job at this! They've heard it and they've come to believe it. I think nothing sums it up better than these words by the actress Shirley MacLaine:

> The most pleasurable journey you take is through yourself…[T]he only sustaining love involvement is with yourself… When you look back on your life and try to figure out where you've been and where you're going, when you look at your work, your love affairs, your marriages, your children, your pain, your happiness—when you examine all that closely, what you really find out is that the only person you really go to bed with is yourself… The only thing you have is working to the consummation of your own identity. And that's what I've been trying to do all my life.[1]

Is this all there is? Self? Just self? Just me? When you stop to think about it, the word itself is truly disgusting—*selfishness.* Is there anyone more pathetic whom you meet than a totally selfish person? Is there anyone you are less drawn to? Is there anyone whom you respect less? When is the last time you've heard someone brag about how selfish they were?

So let me ask you a simple question: Who is your favorite self-centered person? Think about it. Come up with one. Think of a self-centered person you enjoy being in the presence of. So if you're ready for a revelation…let me tell you who your favorite self-centered person is: You are! You're it! There is no other self-centered person you enjoy being around (or can even stand to be around!). The irony of all of this is that the last thing most of us would ever want to be called is selfish. If we were called this, we would surely deny it. We would verbally defend ourselves from its charge. We would be insulted! *They're* selfish–I'm not! But are we living selfish lives? What would an impartial jury decide?

An Alternate Possibility

Against this backdrop, I want to ask you to use your imagination to think about a different way to live. Try to think about what the world would be like if people intentionally sought to apply the following two verses to their lives. Trust me, it's going to take some imagination.

Philippians 2:3–4–" Do nothing out of selfish ambition or vain conceit, but in humility consider others better than yourselves. Each of you should look not only to your own interests, but also to the interests of the others."

First Corinthians 10:24–"No one should seek their own good, but the good of others."

When I read these verses, I can't imagine anything that sounds more appealing to me. Hard–yes, but, oh so appealing! I can't think of anything more attractive than living in a society where people actually look out for each other. I doubt there could ever be a more significant compliment paid to you than that you were incredibly focused, not upon yourself, but rather upon others. I would love to be known as a person who lived for others, not for myself. These thoughts are intriguing, and they are inspiring! If this is so, why would we not pursue this as our life's goal?

Let me continue to drill down on this. I don't think there is anyone we are drawn to more than the person who lives for others. I don't think there is anyone we hold more respect for. Think for a moment of the late Mother Teresa. Once, when Mother Teresa was passing through a crowd in Detroit, a woman remarked, "Her secret is that she is free to be nothing. Therefore, God can use her for anything." Does life ever get any better than when you are surrounded by people who are actively looking out for your best interests?

This reminds me of a story I once heard my friend Dave Stone tell. It's actually something Robert Roberts of Cambridge University writes about. It has to do with a fourth-grade class in which the teacher introduced a game called **"The Balloon Stomp."** A balloon was tied to every child's ankle, and the object of the game was to pop everybody else's balloon while protecting your own. The last person with an intact balloon would win the game. The concept was: if I win, then you lose. The nine-year-olds entered the spirit of things vigorously. When the battle was over in a matter of seconds, only one balloon was still inflated. And, of course, its owner was the most disliked kid in the room. A second class came later that day and was asked to play the same game–only this time the class was filled with developmentally disabled children. With this group, the Balloon Stomp proceeded quite differently. When the instructions were given, it seemed the only idea they grasped was that the balloons were supposed to be popped. But instead of fighting each other off, the children got the idea that they were supposed to help one another pop balloons. They formed a kind of balloon-stomp co-op. One little girl knelt and held her balloon carefully in place–like the holder for a field goal kicker–while a little boy stomped it flat and then knelt and held his balloon still for her to stomp. On and on it went, all the children helping one another in the great stomp. When the very last balloon was popped, everybody cheered–and everybody won. The question you have to ask is this: "Who got the game right, and who got the game wrong?"[5]

While this is extremely appealing, I have a hard time imaging anything harder to accomplish than for the church to live lives focused on others. I also can't think of any more powerful force. It would be a game-changer. What would this take? We would all have to "lay down" our self-interests, and trust those around us to watch out for us. We would have to become a lot like Jesus–which reminds me of something Dave Platt once said: "While the goal of the American dream is to make much of us, the goal of the gospel is to make much of God." When we make much of God, we tend to make much of others.

The Call to Discipleship

All of this now brings us to the heart of the matter, which is the heart of the gospel–what it means to be one who follows Jesus. Who is a true disciple? The church these days has lots and lots of people who show up and attend, many who give money, many of them do many things that look rather spiritual, and, yes, most of them claim to be Christian. While this is certainly true, we all know attending a church and doing a few activities doesn't make you a Christ follower.

I find it interesting that Jesus himself clearly spelled out what it means to be one of his disciples. He wasn't vague concerning this. He wasn't obtuse about it. What he said, he said in the absolute clearest of terms:

Then he said to them all: "Whoever wants to be my disciple must deny themselves and take up their cross daily and follow me. For whoever wants to save their life will lose it, but whoever loses their life for me will save it. What good is it for someone to gain the whole world, and yet lose or forfeit their very self?" (Lk. 9:23–25).

It has been argued that this is one of the least-taught teachings of Jesus. When was the last time you heard a sermon on this passage? I'm not sure why we are so reluctant to tell people what Jesus himself said were the conditions of following him. It actually forms a perfect three-part sermon: (1) Deny yourself, (2) Take up your cross daily, (3) Follow me. Wow! Simple outline! Powerful concept!

But here's something to wrestle with: When Jesus said, "If anyone would come after me," was he stating a commitment to aspire to, or was he stating the minimum required commitment? While I can certainly call myself a Christian if I don't agree to this, I doubt I really am one. If I think his demands are excessive or extreme, or too difficult, and I choose to release myself from them, I surely am revealing to others that I am not a follower. In other words, I cannot come to Christ on my own terms while refusing to accept the terms that he laid out. Surely there are consequences to deciding to call myself a Christian using my terms, even though my terms are quite different (more liberal) than his terms.

All of this has much to do with listening to Jesus—listening, and then *doing* what he says. In Matthew 7:24–27 Jesus said:

> "Therefore everyone who hears these words of mine and puts them into practice is like a wise man who built his house on the rock. The rain came down, the streams rose, and the winds blew and beat against that house; yet it did not fall, because it had its foundation on the rock. But everyone who hears these words of mine and does not put them into practice is like a foolish man who built his house on sand. The rain came down, the streams rose, and the winds blew and beat against that house, and it fell with a great crash."

When we hear what Jesus says, our values change. Our priorities are reprioritized. We do things differently. Against his wisdom, we are all subjected to no shortage of voices that motivate us to instead seek to gain all that the world has to offer. But it all comes at a price. There are things we must surrender to have what the world offers.

Not too long ago, Steve Jobs died. He was 56 years young; such a young man, really. One could argue he was just hitting his stride. At the time of his death, his company had more cash on hand than did the U.S. Government. If there was ever anyone who "gained the whole world," it would be him. But what good is "the world" to someone as they lie dying? It kind of seems like this idea of gaining all this world has to give, and then dying, is likened to winning the lottery of which the prize is priceless art, only to discover that the day you won, you went blind.

Again, let me remind you that Jesus wasn't vague. He laid out three "essentials" to prospering spiritually. Let's look at these each a little more closely.

The first is that we must deny ourselves. What exactly does this mean? I think it means what we all intuitively know it means. It means I must get over me! I have to quit feeding my self-centeredness. I must quit justifying my self-centeredness. I have to quit ignoring my self-centeredness. It means I have to take seriously the attacking of my innate tendency toward being a self-centered person. For me to accomplish this, I have to declare war on the fleshly, self-serving part of my personality. There is plenty there to work on!

The second thing he said is we need to take up our cross daily. The cross in Jesus' day had only one purpose; it was the instrument of death. The cross was a permanent statement…for once you died on it you were "fully" dead. There was a total and clear finality to it. But this is where "cross carrying" becomes a bit more complicated for us. What Jesus was calling us to do was not just to die once, but rather to die *over and over.* Every day: Today. Tomorrow. The day after that. This is what I believe is behind Paul's teaching in Romans 12:1–"Therefore, I urge you, brothers, in view of God's mercy, to offer your bodies as living sacrifices, holy and pleasing to God–which is your spiritual worship." A living sacrifice means that I can be on the altar today, but not tomorrow. I can crawl off and remove myself from future sacrifice. Because I'm not permanently dead, I am called to "die," yet every day I "live."

Thirdly, Christ said to follow him. This means we are to emulate the example he set. Just as he lived to give his life to others, we too are to live to give ours away. It means we are to go where he went, and we are to do what he did. We are not just to show up in these places, but rather we are to do so with the heart of Christ. We are to be where he would be, and be as he would be.

The Great Big Why?

Why would Jesus expect this of me, and why would I agree to do it? The answer to this is surprisingly simple: because there is more to life than me! I am not the center of the universe. This life isn't about "my story," but rather "his-story". The sooner I grasp this truth, agree with it, align my life to it, and live by it,…the sooner I will be living life as God wanted me to live it. This is what it means to "gain it all"!

Let's be perfectly clear about a few things:

To be a disciple of Christ is to be an apprentice of Christ. When I decide to follow him, I become a learner of his heart and his ways. This is more than listening to lectures from or about him. It is more than just reading books and gleaning insights. I must be a "student" in the fullest sense of the word and realize that unless I "do" what he instructed, I really haven't learned anything.

Jesus said it this way in Luke 6:40: "A student is not above his teacher, but everyone who is fully trained will be like his teacher." This raises the question: "How close is the resemblance?" Could anyone, by watching my actions, ever confuse me for him? For me to truly resemble Christ, I need to align my life to his. There is no way around this. Anything less is just compromise.

Sadly, as I think about this, I can't help but recall how just the other day I cut a lady off while getting on the freeway. Please understand, I had my reasons for doing so! There were two lanes merging into one and it was obvious how God designed this to work: one car from this lane; one car from that lane. Except, this lady in the next lane thought her lane got two cars for every one of ours. So she tried a power move and sought to force her way in. I, however, drive a big truck and I wasn't about to allow this injustice. Let's just say I ended up in front of her. Yay for my team! Except, then it all came into focus for me and I realized what a total jerk I had been as I forced my way ahead. I felt ashamed of myself and realized I really don't think that's how Christ would have handled it. I was ahead, but I was so far behind. It's hard to live like you aren't the most important person on the planet.

Here is where we begin to grasp what Jesus clearly grasped. Not everyone was going to choose to follow him. Let's take a moment and read together John 6:60–66.

> On hearing it, many of his disciples said, "This is a hard teaching. Who can accept it?" Aware that his disciples were grumbling about this, Jesus said to them, "Does this offend you? Then what if you see the Son of Man ascend to where he was before! The Spirit gives life; the flesh counts for nothing. The words I have spoken to you—they are full of the Spirit and life. Yet there are some of you who do not believe." For Jesus had known from the beginning which of them did not believe and who would betray him. He went on to say, "This is why I told you that no one can come to me unless the Father has enabled them." From this time, many of his disciples turned back and no longer followed him.

Notice, carefully, that Jesus didn't sweat it, or panic, or negotiate. He didn't recant his charge. He clearly knew there was a price to following him. If I'm honest, as a leader, I sometimes ask too much of someone. They stammer. They reconsider being involved. More than once I have had to modify my demands, lest I overwhelm them and lose them. Jesus didn't do this.

The way of Christ is the way of sacrifice. We can't have followed Jesus very far if we haven't been called to sacrifice our will for the will of God. I think this is clearly what Paul was referring to in Galatians 2:20 when he said, "I have been crucified with Christ and I no longer live, but Christ lives in me. The life I live in the body, I live by faith in the Son of God, who loved me and gave himself for me." And again, in Philippians 1:21, "For to me, to live is Christ and to die is gain." It's as if he were saying, "Come and die so you can truly live!" Perhaps this is what Dietrich Bonhoeffer meant when he said, "When Christ calls a man, he bids him come and die."[6]

In the spirit of full disclosure, I think we need to understand something else Jesus said. It's found in Luke 14:27-33.

> "And whoever does not carry their cross and follow me cannot be my disciple. Suppose one of you wants to build a tower. Won't you first sit down and estimate the cost to see if you have enough money to complete it? For if you lay the foundation and are not able to finish it, everyone who sees it will ridicule you, saying, 'This person began to build and wasn't able to finish.'

> "Or suppose a king is about to go to war against another king. Won't he first sit down and consider whether he is able with ten thousand men to oppose the one coming against him with twenty thousand? If he is not able, he will send a delegation while the other is still a long way off and will ask for terms of peace. In the same way, those of you who do not give up everything you have cannot be my disciples."

Let's be clear, before you choose to enter a battle, size up what you're up against. Before you build something, count the cost!

It seems to me that much of the problem in America is that Christianity has been marketed. It has been offered as a quick fix to all of our problems. It has been promised to be the answer to all of our dilemmas. The problem with marketing Christianity is simply that marketing is the process of convincing someone they need something they don't think they need. Marketing is about making a product sound better or more effective than it is just so you'll get people to cooperate and someone can make a profit from you.

Learning to follow Christ is a "lifetime" process! One of the greatest things about Christianity is that you simply can't master it! You never arrive! It's not like becoming an Eagle Scout, or earning a college degree, or achieving a black belt in Karate. Once you earn these things, you can call them yours for life. They can't be taken away from you. When you are 76 years old, you can still say you have a black belt in Karate. In fact, just saying it would keep people from messing with you...regardless of how old you were! It doesn't matter how committed to Christ I was yesterday; I need to recommit myself to him today.

Conclusion

Again, we must ask ourselves, "Why would I want to do this?" There's only one reason. Just one: It's simply because "there's more to life than me." There really is!

So Paul admonished Timothy to teach the concept of living for others to his followers. Be like Christ. Humble yourself. Take up your cross daily.

Follow. "In this way they will lay up treasure for themselves as a firm foundation for the coming age, so that they may take hold of the life that is truly life" (1 Tim. 6:19).

Let me remind you of the reason Jesus came. While we might offer many ideas as to what the reason(s) might be, we don't have to. Jesus said it himself, very clearly: "I have come that they may have life, and have it to the full" (Jn. 10:10b). Jesus came to teach us how to live, and this involved learning how to order our priorities. He set an example for us to follow. He spelled out clearly what it means to be one of his own. When we do this, we can be assured that the outcome will be lives lived intentionally. We will live lives of influence.

So we started with the story of King Jehoram. A life lived to no one's benefit and ended to no one's regret. A tragic life.

Contrast that with the life of Jesus. Think of how many people worship, adore, and seek to emulate his life today. It seems like the influence of Jesus grows with every passing year. There are more Christ followers today on the planet than at any other time in history. What was his secret? He lived for others and he died for others. His life was about blessing others, not seeking to be blessed—to serve others rather than seeking to have people serve him.

Let me quote the British journalist, writer, and Christian apologist Malcolm Muggeridge: "I can say that I never knew what joy was like until I gave up pursuing happiness, or cared to live until I chose to die. For these two discoveries, I am beholden to Jesus."[7]

So ask yourself: Do I live for anyone else's benefit? Are there people who would testify to this? Does my life feel empty? Do I sacrifice my needs for the needs of others?

I encourage you to follow Christ. Choose to be like him. Be very much like him! You'll be amazed at the impact your life will make. In doing so, you'll discover there is more to life than "me"!

Jodi Hickerson

After high school, Jodi Hickerson spent time living in Haiti with Northwest Haiti Christian Mission. Then she served at Southland Christian Church in Lexington, Kentucky. After marrying her husband Mike (with whom she now has three amazing daughters), Jodi joined the staff of Heartland Community Church in Rockford, Illinois, where she served as a Teaching Pastor and on the Programming Team. In 2011, the Hickersons moved to Ventura, California, to plant Mission Church. Mike serves as the Lead Pastor and Jodi is a Teaching Pastor and Programming Director at Mission. Jodi is quite clear: being a part of what God has done and continues to do at Mission has been the faith adventure she cannot imagine missing out on!

She preached this message several times, mostly to church congregations in the U.S. (in Chicago, Ventura, and Las Vegas). The first time was in October of 2011 at Mission Church in Ventura, with the emphasis being that there were a lot of unchurched people in the room or people far from God. The desire was for people to know the God that Jesus reveals to us, that God meets us where we are and isn't afraid of our mess, that grace is more powerful than shame, and that as the church we ought to meet people right where they are too, knowing that we all desperately need the grace of God! She uses the NIV except as otherwise noted.

"The Crossing: Life Verse"

Romans 8:1

Have you ever had one of those moments where you couldn't believe what just happened just happened?! I like to call those "that just happened" moments—you know, those moments where you stand back and say, "Wow!…that just happened," or, "Dang!…that just happened." I was thinking this week about some of these kinds of moments that have happened recently…and I'm going to need your help with this… When I say the event…you reply with your best: "That just happened!" Okay? Here we go:

That just happened list:

UK winning eighth National Basketball Championship

KeSha's "TiK ToK" sells more copies than any Beatles song

People are still watching *America's Got Talent*

Lebron gets a ring

Lakers fans are now rooting for Steve Nash

And there were all kinds of "that just happened" moments in the life of Jesus. I mean, think about what the disciples must have thought. There was this one time when Jesus took a kid's Happy Meal and fed 5,000 people… "That just happened!"

Or, when he got up from a nap in the bottom of a boat, and there was this huge storm blowing and everyone on board was terrified…and he stood up in the boat and told the wind and waves to stop and they did… You know the disciples on that boat had to be thinking… "That just happened!"… When he opened the eyes of the blind,…can you imagine being the blind man? One second you can't see and the next…"That just happened!"… When he reached out and healed a person with leprosy that no one else would even touch,…I bet the people on the street just gathered around like, "Dang! That just happened!" And it doesn't just show up on the pages of Scripture either.

I can tell you from experience that there were so many people in my life that saw this confused, people–pleasing, lying, manipulating, conning, insecure, impure, materialistic, cheating, hanging-with-the-wrong-crowd girl encounter Jesus and watch him change her life. It was as if jaws dropped and they were saying, "That just happened!" Did that just happen? Is that who I think it is? I can even remember getting a phone call from an old friend that I used to get in trouble with, and he said to me, "So, what, you've seen the light now or something?" And my answer was, "Yes." And it was, and still is, a miracle.

Well, today we are continuing in this series called "Life Verse," and our verse that I would love for all of us to have memorized, to have etched into our hearts this morning and really begin to believe, is Romans 8:1, "Therefore, there is now no condemnation for those who are in Christ Jesus."

Let's say that out loud together.

That is some good news. And I thought today that what we would do is dive into a story. To get to the heart of this verse,…gather around with a crowd of people at one of these "that just happened" moments where Jesus illustrates the truth of this verse as only He can through His encounter with a woman down in the dirt:

> Jesus returned to the Mount of Olives, but early the next morning he was back again at the Temple. A crowd soon gathered, and he sat down and taught them. As he was speaking, the teachers of religious law and the Pharisees brought a woman who had been caught in the act of adultery. They put her in front of the crowd.

"Teacher," they said to Jesus, "this woman was caught in the act of
adultery. The law of Moses says to stone her. What do you say?"
They were trying to trap him into saying something they could
use against him... (John 8:1-6a, NLT)

Okay, so just so we can get a little context of what's going on here,...
Jesus was gaining some popularity—that just happens when you're healing the
sick and opening blind eyes—and the Pharisees (who were some of the Jewish
religious leaders) didn't like it one bit. These were people whose spiritual
blindness never let them see Jesus for who He was... And so they knew
that with Jesus teaching in front of the temple there would be a big crowd
there...lots of witnesses... Because these leaders had been trying to get rid
of Jesus for a while now—this was all a political game to them—they wanted
more than anything to destroy his credibility with the people. And so they
try to trap him by using this woman—because, if Jesus were to say that the
woman should not be stoned, they could accuse him of violating Moses' law.
If he were to urge them to execute her, then they would report him to the
Romans, who did not permit the Jews to carry out their own executions...
However, Jesus is fully aware that this is nothing more than a trap.

Not to mention that it's more than a little suspicious. Jewish law required
that they bring both the man *and* the woman in a case like this...so where's
the guy? I mean, I've watched enough of *Law and Order* to know that this
was a setup... They "found" their girl... I don't know, maybe they arranged
for some guy to get with her...or maybe they just knew that she had that
kind of reputation,...so she would be easy prey... Maybe they had been
watching her for a while... However it all played out, this was some sort of
setup—How else do you "catch someone in the act"? They knew who she
was, where she would be, at what time. They used her.

They don't at all see the intrinsic worth of this woman; they just use
her as a pawn in their religious chess game. They have no concern for
her... She's only a means to their end. So they set her up,...grab her in the
act,...pull her out of the house,...drag her through the streets with nothing
on but a sheet she grabbed in desperation on her way out, and they throw
her down in the dirt in front of all these people...and Jesus. There is no
doubt that what these guys did was arrogant, self-righteous, judgmental,
scheming, and heartless.

But then there she was... She had to feel so embarrassed, ashamed,
guilty, exposed, dirty, used, trapped, condemned, and afraid. This was
the last group of people she wanted to be undressed in front of—religious
leaders, a group of people who had gotten up early to hear a sermon. Can
you imagine?

And then there was Jesus. A popular rabbi and teacher, What would
he think? What would he do? And Jesus, in this moment, doesn't start a

trial; he doesn't defend himself or begin to cite religious law; instead... verse 6b: "Jesus stooped down and wrote in the dust with his finger" (NLT).

We're never told in Scripture what he wrote down in the dirt... Some think he was writing down different sins for the crowd to see, so that they would be convicted of their own sins in this moment... Others believe that since God had written the Ten Commandments with *his* finger, and Jesus was writing those with his finger—*that's* what Jesus was writing... Had everyone there kept all of those?

I don't know, but I do know that the coolest part for me is simply that Jesus stooped down. Why? Because that's where *she* was: down in the dirt. While everyone else is towering judgmentally over her as she sat ashamed down in that dirt, just trying to cover her nakedness, Jesus "stooped down."

And I think that maybe as he knelt there in front of this downcast woman, who's avoiding eye contact with anybody—she's just staring down at the dirt—maybe, just maybe, what he was writing was for *her*... Maybe he stooped down to write so that she could see. Maybe he was writing down the Aramaic words for the emotions she was feeling: *ashamed...swept away... worthless...unloved...dirty...filthy...guilty...* God loves you... I think that if it had been a moment for the religious leaders, the Pharisees or the disciples standing around, John would have told us what Jesus wrote. I think this was a moment for her.

Obviously, the Pharisees weren't all that interested, because verses 7–8 say, "They kept demanding an answer, so he stood up again and said, 'All right, but let the one who has never sinned throw the first stone!' Then he stooped down again and wrote in the dust" (NLT).

Right back in that moment with her. Right back on her level. And the ironic thing is that Jesus, though he was tempted in every way we are, he never sinned. No one else in that crowd of people would have been qualified to throw out the first stone, except for the One doodling down in the dirt.

And, side note: I need to remember that more... I think we all have the tendency at times to stand over fallen people—rock in hand, you know—and throw out self-righteous judgment and disgust,...like, "Can you believe they did that?" We do it with people that we're close to—friends, family... We do it with people we don't even know—politicians, celebrities...

It is good for me to be reminded that I've got my own stuff. It may not end up on TMZ or ever make the cover of *Star* magazine, but Jesus had to get down and pull me up out of the dirt, too...and I have no right to throw stones at anyone.

Verse 9: "When the accusers heard this, they slipped away one by one, beginning with the oldest, until only Jesus was left in the middle of the crowd with the woman." Rocks all around in the dirt. Her accusers leave, and there they are—Jesus and this woman...both on their knees in the middle of the street... Can you imagine the emotions going through her mind at this time? Put yourself in her shoes for a moment... What are you feeling? *Confused. Ashamed. Dirty. Grateful.* I imagine that she can't stop the tears... They're just hitting the ground, making little dark circles in the dust right next to where Jesus has been writing.

Verses 10–11: "Then Jesus stood up again"–I'm guessing he helped her up, too–"and said to the woman, 'Where are your accusers? Didn't even one of them condemn you?' 'No, Lord,' she said. And Jesus said, 'Neither do I. Go and sin no more'" (NLT).

Even though the evidence is pretty overwhelming,...I'm the only one who is qualified to make this call, and I do not condemn you. You're not guilty; you are not condemned... You have been forgiven... Now go and live, grateful for this second chance... Don't go back your old way of life,... because it doesn't have to be like this... You don't have to go searching for "love" like that anymore... You are standing right in front of unfailing love... You are accepted... You are significant... You are priceless... You are so worth it that the God of the universe stooped down in the dirt to be with you... Go and sin no more.

And you know she had to be thinking,..."That just happened!"

Now I don't know what's going on in your life as you walk in here this morning. But I want to let you know a couple of things...

One is that there is a different crowd standing around this place today. Maybe you, too, have thought that the last place you would want to be exposed is in front of a bunch of church people–that if people here really knew what you had going on in your life, if people in your life group really knew your struggles, your reputation, they would judge you, they would reject you. You need to know–I know the leadership of this church, and that is so far from the heartbeat of this place. This is not a place full of "better than," superior, religious people just waiting to catch you, find you out, and throw stones.

This church is made up of all kinds of people, with all kinds of baggage, and history, and struggle...and the one thing everyone has in common is that Jesus had to stoop down in the dirt for every one of us. This is a safe place for you to walk into, no matter what you have going on in your life. Different crowd...

I also want you to know that there is an accuser after you, too... The Bible calls Satan the enemy of our souls, the father of lies, and our accuser–because Satan is the one who tries to keep us down in the dirt...tries to keep us from ever changing, ever living out that grateful second chance that God offers us;...because, just when we are about to believe that Jesus could change us...that our lives could be different,...Satan whispers to us,... "No, it can't... Come on,...you're not gonna change... You're not gonna ever leave this... You're not gonna ever stop."... And, again, whispers to us,... "You are a loser... You are a drunk... You are an addict... You are a pervert... You're a liar... You are so stupid... You are so worthless... You are so filthy... You are unlovable... You are so alone–always have been and always will be... Face it, that's just *who* you are."

Satan throws these accusations at us, so that, instead of believing that now there is no condemnation for those who are in Christ Jesus,...we feel condemned to carry around a load of shame for who we are.

And man, carrying around that shame, that can really take us out...

"The difference between guilt and shame is very clear in theory. We feel guilty for what we do. We feel shame for what we are. A person feels guilty because he *did* something wrong. A person feels shame because he *is* something wrong"–Lewis Smedes.[1]

And that is what our enemy, our accuser, wants us to believe: that we are something wrong... You see, Satan can't do anything about the fact that Jesus can forgive sin...can't do anything about the fact that God can redeem us, save us, restore us... But the accuser will settle if we just stay down in the dirt, feeling guilty, feeling condemned–unchanged, and paralyzed by our shame.

We have a different crowd surrounding us than this woman did, a different accuser trying to keep us down, but we have the same Jesus. And he still stoops down to meet us where we are. Maybe you don't know that about God. Maybe you've thought that if you approached God with your stuff he would be disgusted by you. Angry with you. That he would condemn you. Maybe you think that you need to get your life cleaned up first before you come to him.

You need to know today that God is not afraid to show up right in the middle of your mess. He's not. He's bold enough to deal with your dysfunction. Fearless enough to walk with you through an addiction. Heroic enough to lift you up out of the abuse you may have known. Humble enough to stoop down in the dirt and meet you wherever you are.

That is our Jesus. That's his track record; that's his reputation. And he will do that for any and all of us. No one is exempt. No one is too far gone. All you have to do is look at the life of Jesus...because there have been times in my life when:

I have wanted to be in.
To be in the "in" crowd,
In the loop, in the know, among the proud,
Not left out, but to be allowed
To be in.
I have wanted to be in.
Wear clothes that are "in" style

A trendsetter and versatile,
Just the right cut, and a perfect smile,
I have wanted to be in.
To be looked at as someone who has much,
All the "in" music on my iPod touch,
Own the latest and greatest stuff and such,
I have wanted to be in.
But, I have felt aggravated,
Frustrated,
Unappreciated.
Slated,
As someone who is underrated,
Unimportant, unknown, unseen,
Average, mediocre, routine,
Beneath, below, beyond a chance,
Inconsequential. Insignificant.
But, Jesus, he met people like me,
Took notice of a blind man and made him see,
Saw a locked-up kid, and set him free.
Told little Zacchaeus to get out of the tree,
Felt it when a desperate woman touched His cloak,
Kneeled beside a dead girl and up she woke,
Hung out with the down and out and broke,
Offered hope to the forgotten with just the words He spoke.
Touched a man with leprosy who others would mock,
Touched the mouths of the mute and at once they could talk,
Forgave a woman at a well, who was the laughingstock,
Came to be The Shepherd of a wandering flock.
In the company of sinners is where He would eat,
Defended an adulterer and made her accusers retreat,
Made followers out of those who were crooked cheats,
Let the tears of a prostitute anoint His feet,
And suddenly,
dramatically,
miraculously,
undeniably
They were in.
In His story, In His truth, In His grace,
In His purpose, In His eyes someone great,
And I have wanted to be in.
And since the day I met with Him,
He took all that I had been,

All my fear, my shame, my sin,
And changed my life by letting me in.
By the grace of God, I am in, and by the grace of God, you can
be in, too.[2]

I've heard it said that: "Justice is getting what we deserve. Mercy is not getting what we deserve. Grace is getting something we could never deserve."

Romans 6:23 (NLT), "For the wages of sin is death, but the free gift of God is eternal life through Christ Jesus our Lord." The wages of our sin is death... That's the penalty, that would be the condemnation—it's life or death for us, just like for that woman; but, through Jesus, God gives us mercy to not get what we deserve.

And he doesn't stop there... No, he lets us in—in on his grace, in on another chance, in on the opportunity to change, to live a full life on this earth and spend eternity with him... that is something we could never deserve... That is grace.

Romans 3:23 (NIV), "For all have sinned and fall short of the glory of God." All of us. We've all sinned. We've all messed up. We've all been down in the dirt... but check out the rest of that passage... Romans 3:24-25a (NLT), "Yet God, in his grace, freely makes us right in his sight. He did this through Christ Jesus when he freed us from the penalty for our sins. For God presented Jesus as the sacrifice for sin. People are made right with God when they believe that Jesus sacrificed his life, shedding his blood." I love that—that God, with undeserved kindness, declares us not guilty, but righteous. When we were trapped, caught, guilty, condemned, and ashamed...God made a way for us to be made right with him! And his name is Jesus.

Maybe you are here today and you don't know Jesus. Listen, he still stoops down for you. He is not afraid of your mess. He is not disgusted by you. He is not angry with you. You are not too dirty, too filthy for him. He is not towering over you with judgment. He wants to meet you right where you are today. There is mercy for you. There is grace to live a different life.

Or, maybe, for some of you, you've believed that at some point, or you're starting to, but you can't seem to get up out of the dirt because you've been listening to and believing your accuser. You've been buying in to the lies that you are worthless, that you couldn't get in with God. You think that, sure, maybe God can forgive me, but I'm still me. I'm still guilty. I'm still used. I still did what I did... It's not like I can change.

This verse, Romans 8:1, is such an important one to me, because for a long time I lived with thinking like that. I lived with some shame that I didn't think I could ever be done with, that I was just condemned to carry with me. But let me tell you what I've learned, what I'm still learning...

And that's that, while Shame can be a dangerous enemy to our souls...

Shame has an enemy, and it's called grace.

Shame towers over me and tells me I am defective. Grace stoops down and tells me I am valuable.

Shame says that because I am flawed I am worthless. Grace says that even though I am flawed I am priceless.

Shame believes that the opinion of the crowd is what matters. Grace believes that the opinion of God is what matters.

Shame leaves me alone and isolated. Grace gives me a relationship like no other.

Shame makes us hide. Grace sets us free.

Shame keeps us down. Grace picks us up.

Shame is the language of our accuser. Grace is the language of Jesus.

You see, Jesus did not stoop down for me, he didn't get in the middle of all my mess, so that he could forgive me and just leave me there, unchanged–still condemned, guilty, ashamed, and down in the dirt. No. Psalm 40:2–3 (NLT):

> He lifted me out of the pit of despair,
> out of the mud and the mire.
> He set my feet on solid ground
> and steadied me as I walked along.
> He has given me a new song to sing,
> a hymn of praise to our God.
> Many will see what he has done and be amazed. [Dang! that just happened!]
> They will put their trust in the Lord.

And today could be a "that just happened" moment for you, like it was for this woman. And if it is,...it won't be the last, because following Jesus, doing life with him, is about ongoing transformation... By his grace we're always changing and learning to live the life of the grateful second chance...

If you walked in here today feeling caught, trapped, guilty, filthy, unworthy, ashamed, condemned,...I want you to know my God...who wrote this down with his finger about you,... "I have swept away your sins like a cloud. / I have scattered your offenses like the morning mist. / Oh, return to me, / for I have paid the price to set you free" (Isa. 44:22, NLT). "As far as the east is from the west, so far has he removed our transgressions from us" (Psalm 103:12, NIV). "I, even I, am he who blots out / your transgressions, for my own sake, / and remembers your sins no more" (Isa. 43:25, NIV). "I'll forever wipe the slate clean of their sins." (Hebrews 10:17, Message).

"So now there is no condemnation for those who belong to Christ Jesus" (Rom. 8:1, NLT). Where are your accusers? Does anyone condemn you? Neither do I.

He wants to help you up today and let you know… You're not guilty anymore. You're not filthy anymore. You're not condemned anymore. You're not labeled anymore. I love you. You are mine.

Bob Russell

God has blessed Bob Russell with a life much different from any he could have ever imagined. As a young man growing up in northern Pennsylvania, Bob intended to become a high school basketball coach in his hometown. During his senior year of high school, however, Bob realized a desire in his heart to enter the ministry. Soon thereafter, he enrolled in Cincinnati Bible Seminary, where he graduated in 1965.

At just 22 years of age, Russell became the pastor of Southeast Christian Church in Louisville, Kentucky. That small congregation of 120 members grew into one of the largest churches in America, with 18,000 people attending the four worship services offered every weekend in 2006 when Bob retired. Now, through Bob Russell Ministries, Bob continues to preach throughout the United States, provide guidance for church leadership, mentor other ministers, and author Bible study videos for use in small groups. An accomplished author, Bob has written over one dozen books. His latest book is *After 50 Years of Ministry: 7 Things I Would Do Differently and 7 Things I Would Do the Same.*[1]

Bob and his wife Judy of 50 years have two married sons, Rusty and Phil and seven grandchildren with whom they enjoy spending their time.

This sermon was preached at Southeast Christian Church on August 30, 2009, using the NIV.

"Why I Love the Church"[2]

Oh, thank you. Thank you so much. The church of Jesus Christ is not very popular with some people today. There are politicians who don't like churches because we don't pay taxes. Some individuals despise the church because they were wounded by somebody in the church years ago, and they believe everybody in the church is phony. Others don't like churches because they see us as too judgmental, trying to impose our values on everyone else. A local Internet sports blog was discussing a current moral issue in athletics, and one contributor wrote: "I'm sure all the people at Six Flags Over Jesus will be taking a hard line on that issue." And what followed was a stream of comments, over a hundred of them: some attacking this church, some defending it.

You know, as wonderful as this place is, there are still some people who do not have a favorable view of it. I think there are people who don't know very much about churches at all who have a poor perception of the church, because they've been influenced by negative media stereotypes. Most of the time in movies, the churchgoer is portrayed as a fun-hating legalist, or a rank hypocrite, and it seems to me that newspapers sometimes sensationalize the failures of church leaders. You've read the headlines, "Minister Admits That He Lied About Teen's Death," "Pastor Indicted for Misappropriation of Government Aid," "Priests Arrested for Molesting Children," "Preacher Urges Congregation to Bring Guns to Church," "Governor Who Campaigns for Family Values Has an Affair," "The Daughter of a Vice-Presidential Candidate Who Attends a Charismatic Church Gets Pregnant Out of Wedlock." You get the impression that if the secularists can just prove enough people in the church phony, then they are vindicated in their own unbelief.

But it's not just the people outside the church who disparage the church. There are a lot of attacks in recent years from within. There have been several very influential Christian books recently that have portrayed the church as totally ineffective and irrelevant and indifferent. One author claims that he found more genuine fellowship in a commune than a church, and he apologizes to the world for the church's past transgressions. And let's be honest, some of the criticism is valid. The church is made up of very imperfect people–like you and me. But I have this genuine concern: over the last three years, I've met a lot of very sharp young preachers who are passionate about winning the lost, and they reason that since their generation views the church as totally phony, they need to completely distance themselves from yesterday's congregations and reinvent church. In their minds, it is: "Change it totally, or the church will die." And you visit their church services, and it sometimes seems like the more bizarre the better. They advertise it: "This is a church for people who don't like church. This is not your mother's church." Now some of the changes that are taking place across the country are necessary and very positive. Some are extreme and ludicrous. I saw a cartoon in a Christian magazine in which the preacher was out front of the church building changing the sign from "First Baptist Church," to "Faith Boutique."

Reasons to Love the Church

Reason #1: Because of Its Founder

Well, I've about had it with all the attacks against the church, and I'd like to talk today about what's *right* with the church, why I love the church. You know, you can focus on the 5 percent that's bad about your mate and make yourself miserable in your marriage. The Bible says we are to think about what is good and lovely and pure, so let's think this morning about what's right with the church, and I hope you'll leave today feeling better about the church; but, more importantly, you'll be better equipped to defend it when it's attacked. I love the church because I love its founder. Jesus asked His disciples, "Who do people say that I am?" And they said,

"Well, some say You're a prophet." "Who do you say that I am?" And Simon Peter said, "You're the Messiah; You're the Christ". And Jesus said, "That's right, Peter. On this rock, on this truth, that I am the Messiah, I will build my church" (see: Mt. 16:13b–18a).

[Pastor Russell displays a wallet.] I have an affection, somewhat, for this old wallet. It's worn and meaningless to most of you, but this is a wallet that belonged to my dad, who died almost 15 years ago. There are some things that I appreciate simply because they belonged to him. And if you love Jesus, you're going to love the church, because He loved it. Ephesians 5:25b says, "...Christ loved the church and gave himself up for her..." Now folks, it's very important that we understand that Jesus did intend to build a church. In some hip Christian circles today, it is the "in thing" to trash the church and dissociate yourself from the established church. You'll hear people say, "Well, I'm a Christian, but I'm against organized religion," or, "I have a relationship with Jesus, but I'm not involved in the institutional church." And they suggest that, in the Bible, the term "church" was just an invisible, universal body of believers. Everybody who belonged to Christ was a part of the church. And He wasn't referring to a local church where there are budgets and buildings and bureaucracy and boring sermons.

For example, in the book *The Gospel According to Starbucks* the author suggests that you may find more genuine fellowship in your church, maybe just a small group of people who meet at the coffee shop and talk about Jesus. You'll find more genuine fellowship there sometimes, he says, than you would in a church that goes through a ritualistic service. But the New Testament makes it clear; when Jesus said, "...I will build my church..." (Mt. 16:18), He intended it to be a visible body with structure and definition. There were elders in the church who were the overseers of the body. There were teachers who were to edify the body. The New Testament church was told, "Don't forsake the regular assembly together where you receive communion, and where you pray together and where there's an offering, and you are instructed" (preacher's interpretive summary of Acts 2:41-47). The church was visible enough that, when one member suffered, everybody else suffered too. When one strayed, the others were to hold that person accountable. It was defined enough that some in the world despised it and persecuted it. The church was not just a few people casually getting together at Starbucks; the church was at the very center of the purpose of God. The Bible knows nothing about an unchurched Christian. In Acts 2:41, it says, "And the Lord added to their number daily those who were being saved."

First Symbol of Jesus' Relationship to the Church:
Building on a Foundation

Let me show you three symbols in the Bible that describe Jesus' inseparable relationship to the church. First, 1 Peter 2:5–6 compares the church to a building established on a firm foundation: "...you also, like living stones, are being built into a spiritual house to be a holy priesthood, offering spiritual sacrifices acceptable to God through Jesus Christ...a chosen and precious cornerstone..." If a building is separated from its foundation, it collapses.

Second Symbol of Jesus' Relationship to the Church:
The Head and the Body

The second analogy is Ephesians 5:23, that says, "...Christ is the head of the church, his body, of which he is the Savior." The head and the body are inseparable. We're to be the visible body of Christ on earth, His hands and feet, to do His will.

Third Symbol of Jesus' Relationship to the Church:
Groom and Bride

My third and favorite analogy is a groom who loves his bride, Ephesians 5: "Husbands, love your wives, just as Christ loved the church and gave himself up for her to make her holy, cleansing her by the washing with water through the word, and to present her to himself as a radiant church, without stain or wrinkle or any other blemish, but holy and blameless" (vv. 25–27).

Now the groom normally loves the bride and focuses on her positive traits, overlooks her negative traits. And the Bible says Christ is the groom who loves the bride, and He sees the church as washed and pure and cleansed by His blood. John 3:29 says, "The bride belongs to the bridegroom. The friend who attends the bridegroom waits and listens for him, and is full of joy when he hears the bridegroom's voice."

I had a wedding here years ago in which the groom really loved the bride, and it was a good thing, because when she was coming down the aisle, she was so overcome with emotion she came down bawling. I don't mean just shedding tears; she was sobbing out loud. And when she got near the front, it was not a pretty sight. Her face was contorted and there were tears that streamed dark mascara down her cheeks, and the black droplets were dripping on her white dress, staining it. I looked at the groom and he was weeping too, and I understood why. I could not get this girl to settle down, and so I hurried through the ceremony, but when I said to the groom, "You may kiss the bride," instead of taking her veil and lifting it back over her head, he took the veil and pulled it out and scooted up underneath it and kissed her briefly, and then scooted back and put the veil back down over her face. But that groom loved his bride, and they went on to a fun honeymoon and a meaningful life together, because he saw beyond the tears and the stains for who she really was.

Christ the groom loves the bride and sees us without stain or wrinkle or blemish, and, one day, the bridegroom is going to return for the bride and the church is going to rise to meet Him. The Bible says, " . . . the Lord himself will come down from heaven, with a loud command, with the voice of the archangel and with the trumpet call of God, and the dead in Christ will rise first. After that, we who are still alive and are left will be caught up together with them in the clouds to meet the Lord in the air. And so we will be with the Lord forever" (1 Thess. 4:16–17). And you know what the first thing the Bible says the groom is going to do for the bride? First thing, He will wipe away all tears from our eyes. I think when that day comes, we're going to be so overwhelmed with gratitude and joy we're going to be sobbing, but the groom will wipe away all tears from our eyes, and so shall we be with the Lord forever. I love the church, because it's the bride of Christ, waiting for that wedding ceremony.

Reason #2: Because I Love the People in the Church

I also love the church because I love the people in the church. Jesus said, "Blessed are you, Simon… I'm going to give you the keys to the Kingdom" (Mt. 16:17a, 19a, preacher's paraphrase). Simon Peter? A very flawed man, and yet Jesus loved him and trusted him with a vital role in the church. Wouldn't the first-century comedians have had a field day with Simon Peter? Such a hypocrite, one day walking on water and the next minute he's up to his neck drowning. One day he claims Jesus is the Messiah, and the next minute he's countering Jesus' statement that He's going to die. One minute he says he'd die for Jesus, the next minute he's denying he even knows Him. One day he takes a stand, including the Gentiles in the church, and a few days later he is prejudiced against them. But Jesus told Simon Peter, "I'm going to give you the keys to the Kingdom." A key is for opening the door, and, in Acts 2, it's Simon Peter who preaches the first sermon in Jerusalem, opening the door for thousands of Jewish people to become Christian. Acts 10, it's Simon Peter who speaks the Gospel to a Roman centurion named Cornelius, opening the door for the Gentiles to come into the Kingdom.

In fact, Jesus went a step further and promised Simon Peter that whatever he bound on earth would be bound in heaven; whatever he loosed on earth would be loosed in heaven. Acts 3, Peter and John met a lame man at the temple, and Peter said, "In the name of Jesus, get up and walk" (v. 6b, preacher's paraphrase), and the "chains" that bound that man's legs were loosed, and he immediately began to walk and leap and praise God. Acts 5 records a man named Ananias who lied about the amount that he was giving to the church and God struck him dead, as a reminder the church is supposed to be a place of truthfulness. …[T]hree hours later, Ananias' wife Sapphira repeated the same lie, and Peter said to her, "Look! The feet of the men who buried your husband are at the door, and they will carry you out also" (v. 9b), and she died. What he bound on earth was bound in heaven. Simon Peter was far from perfect, and yet Jesus loved him and gave him a key role in the early church.

Now church people aren't perfect, but I'm going to tell you what: some of the best people in the world are in the church. Now I will admit I've met some people who are not Christian that I've liked better than some people in the church, but the church is made up of imperfect people who aspire to grow to be like Christ. That perfect model results in higher values, higher compassion, better attitudes, than most people in the world.

Let's say you're traveling in an unfamiliar city late at night and you're about out of gas, so you pull off the expressway to a service station: station closed. You drive around the block, and you realize you're in a rough section of town...and you run out of gas. Your family's in the car, 11:30 at night. Your heart is pounding, and you see three guys coming through the darkness down the sidewalk, right at you. Would you feel better if they were carrying in their hand a wine bottle, or a Bible? If they had just come from the bar, or if they had just come from a Bible study? Chances are, if you saw them carrying a Bible, you'd breathe a sigh of relief and realize they're probably not out to do you bodily harm. You might even ask them to help you. Now that's no guarantee, but the odds are in your favor. Some of the best people in the world are in the church. They're the salt of the earth.

Several weeks ago, I was at the Cove, the Billy Graham Training Center in Asheville, North Carolina, and behind the speaker, there was a picture of Billy Graham, Cliff Barrows—his song leader—and George Beverly Shea. Now it's incredible that these guys started out together in evangelism years ago, and they're still together. Billy Graham is, I think, 92 years old, and Cliff Barrows is 91. George Beverly Shea is 101 years old, and he still drives a car, and he still sings sometimes. But when people say to me, "Oh, the church is full of hypocrites," what about Billy Graham? What about Cliff Barrows? What about George Beverly Shea? What about Coach John Wooden? What about Mother Teresa? What about Butch Dabney? What about Sarah King? What about hundreds of other people who have been genuine believers all their lives?

There are elders in this church who give 50 percent of their incomes away. There are scores of couples in this church who have adopted little children of other races, children with disabilities, even though they have several biological children. There is a couple in this church, I read in the newspaper, who quit their jobs in their forties, and moved to Montana to become house parents at a ranch for troubled children. There are couples in my ministry who just donate three days a month to come and serve ministers who come to a retreat. They valet their cars; they carry their luggage; they shuttle them back and forth to the airport. No pay, just service. There's a husband in this church whose wife has had Alzheimer's for ten years. She's still in her sixties, but he loves her and bathes her and cares for her tenderly, even though she cannot reciprocate a second of love. "I made a promise to God," he said. His story's not in the newspaper. There's a wonderful woman in this church who's had over 200 major operations in her life, but she still gives glory to God and trusts in Him. There are wonderful, selfless, compassionate people in the church.

And you know what I miss most about Southeast Christian Church? I've been gone for three years now, and I don't miss the meetings, I don't miss fundraising, I don't miss preaching. I preach more now than I ever did when I was here. I just don't have to write new sermons; I just put a new title on the old sermon and preach it. What I miss most are the casual friendships that I had here with people that I'd walk by every Sunday, or see regularly at some dinner or something. I don't see those people, and I miss that part of the church. For three years, I've been a man without a church, and there is a spiritual void in my life because of that. I still go to church every weekend, I still do my devotions, but there's something missing. You know what it's like? It's kind of like when you're hungry and you just eat a salad…and you know something's not right inside. So I made a conscious effort; next year, I'm just going to speak two weekends a month and be here two weekends a month, so I can be more involved—because I need the church. I love the people in the church. I see that the Small Groups Ministry is promoting a group connection, an opportunity for you to try a small group for just seven weeks to see what it's like. I just encourage you to try that. You'll meet, I think, some of the best people in the world, and it will enhance your life.

Reason #3: Because of Its Positive Influence

I also love the church because I love its positive influence. Jesus said, "I'm going to build my church on this truth, that I am the Messiah. I am going to use people like Simon Peter, who is imperfect" [preacher's interpolation of Scripture found in Mt. 16:18a],…"and the gates of Hades will not overcome it." (Mt. 16:18b). When I first started studying this Scripture, I prepared an entire point on the durability of the church. We're a part of something that, though Satan has attacked it and people try to stamp it out, it has continued for two thousand years, and that's amazing. But when Jesus said, "The gates of Hades will not stop the church," the imagery is not one of the church defending itself, but one of the church being on the offense. Gates are defensive weapons. The only gates I could think of we'd all identify with would be the gates outside the Valhalla Country Club Golf Course, off Shelbyville Road. Now that's not the gates of hell; that's the gates to paradise in golf. But you understand the analogy. If I say, "The gates of Valhalla are not going to overcome me," you don't think of those gates hitting me. You think, "He's going to go in there and play, even though he's not a member." I'm going to overcome those gates. Now, Jesus said, "I'll build my church and the gates of hell will not stop it." The church was on the offense. Jesus commissioned them to go into all the world with the truth that He was the Messiah, that He died for the sins of humankind, that He arose from the dead–giving us the power to do that too. We had hope of life after death.

So the Christians didn't huddle in the upper room every Sunday and rejoice that they were saved. We can summarize Acts 2 on what happened.:

They went out on the streets of Jerusalem, and Simon Peter stood up and said, "You men of Israel, listen to this. Jesus of Nazareth was a man accredited by God with miracles, wonders, and signs, but you, with wicked hands, have crucified and slain Him. But God has raised him from the dead, and now God has made this Jesus, whom you crucified, both Lord and Christ," and three thousand people repented and were baptized and were added to the church.

And the religious elite were furious with them and they constructed a gate to stop them. And they said, "You can no longer cross this line. You can't speak about Jesus in the streets of Jerusalem anymore." But the disciples said, "We've got to obey God, not humans." And they kept preaching the truth.

Acts 4 says there were five thousand people in the church, and early historians estimate that, within a few years, there were over a hundred thousand believers in the Jerusalem church[3].

And ever since that time, when the church has proclaimed this truth about Christ, it has had an incredible influence in the culture. The Roman world had its gates; Caesar said, "We are a multicultural society. We believe that there are many gods, and you Christians cannot go around saying that there is only one true God and one way to Him, through Jesus Christ." But they did it anyway, and Nero began to persecute them–nail them to the cross and burn them, throw them to the wild beasts in the arena and tear them apart. But the blood of the martyrs became the seed of the church, and by 350 A.D., Christianity was the state religion in Rome.

England had gates that protected slavery. Slavery was foundational to their economy, but William Wilberforce and other Christians said, "We're going to demolish those gates." And even though there were some in the church who owned slaves, it was the influence of godly people like Wilberforce that crashed the gates of that evil.

Today, the Chinese government has done just about everything it can to stop the church, because it sees it as a threat to the Communist system. But there are now over one hundred million Christians in China, most of them meeting in house churches. There are more Christians in China, maybe, than in any nation in the world, and the gates of Communism cannot stop it.

Now the United States of America was originally established as a country with no gates, no religious boundaries, freedom of religion. This nation was not intended to be a theocracy, but it was firmly founded on Judeo-Christian principles. President John Adams, second president, said, "The general principles on which the fathers achieved independence were the general principles of Christianity."[1] And think about the influence of the church in America, where there are few gates to stop it. It was the church that started 106 of the first 108 colleges in this country, beginning with Yale and Harvard.

Or, look around our community. Who's established most of the hospitals here? Not the Atheist Society, but the Baptists, the Methodists, Norton—started by the Episcopalians, St. Mary's and Elizabeth—by the Catholics: the *church*. The church has funded most of the inner-city missions, like Wayside Mission that ministers to the homeless. The church started most orphanages and homes for the elderly, like Christian Church Homes of Kentucky. Who constantly visits with and conducts services for those in prison? The church. Who establishes crisis pregnancy centers to help women in desperation? The church. Who teaches the moral values that undergird ethics in business? The church. Who taught many of us older people, long before the civil rights movement, to sing, "Red and yellow, black and white, they are precious in His sight. Jesus loves the little children of the world"? It was the church. When Hurricane Katrina ripped the Gulf Coast, who was there first with the most practical help? Who sent the most money without scraping any off the top? Who's still there today? The church.

But in spite of that positive influence in this nation, there are some influential politicians now suggesting we are not a Christian nation and there must be stricter boundaries on the church. President George Washington warned in his farewell address, "Of all the dispositions and habits which lead to political prosperity, religion and morality are indispensable supports. In vain would that man claim the tribute of patriotism, who should labor to subvert these great pillars." But now those in authority are saying, "Don't bring your Bible in here. Don't post those Ten Commandments here. Don't put your manger scene here. Don't pray in Jesus' name here. Don't say, 'Merry Christmas' here." And what we need are Christians who will have the courage of those early disciples, who will say, "We've got to obey God, not human rules, and the gates of hell will not stop us."

Last month, I visited Central Christian Church in Las Vegas, Nevada. Do you know we've got a church in Las Vegas that has twelve thousand people every weekend? They started a church that has over six thousand. We're helping here at Southeast to support a young man who interned here, Vince Antonucci. They're now starting a church right on the Strip. That Central Church had a baptism Sunday like we've had here. In April, they had over a thousand baptisms. It may be called "Sin City," but the Bible says, "**where sin increased**, grace **increased** all the more"(Romans 5:20) " ...and the gates of Hades will not overcome it" (Matt. 16:18).

I want you to think for a moment about the positive influence of Southeast Christian Church over the last 47 years. I'm hesitant about this next section, because I know it's going to sound like I'm bragging, but I want to give glory for what God has done here. When Joshua led the children of Israel across the dry ground of the Jordan River, when he got to the other side, God said to him, "Joshua, I want you to build a monument here of 12 stones." And then Joshua said:

"In the future when your descendants ask their fathers, 'What do these stones mean?' tell them,... 'The LORD your God did to the Jordan just what he had done to the Red Sea when he dried it up before us until we had crossed over. He did this so that all the peoples of the earth might know that the hand of the LORD is powerful and so that you might always fear the LORD your God'"(Josh. 4:21, 23b–24).

Southeast Christian Church is in a wonderful season right now, and I would that you would look to the future. But at the same time, let's remember how the powerful hand of God has blessed this place in the past. I wonder how many people are going to heaven because of the outreach of this church, how many people have been saved here? I'm going to ask you to stand up if you came to know the Lord here. I know a number of you got saved elsewhere, but if you came to know the Lord here and you were baptized here, and you were saved because of the ministry of this church, would you stand up right now? Thank you. Let's never forget that's our primary task: to make an eternal difference. Our primary task is to seek and save the lost.

But how do you measure the number of marriages that have been saved, the number of children kept off drugs or out of jail, how many benevolence organizations would not exist if it weren't for this church? Without this church, there would not be a Lifebridge Benevolence Ministry caring for the needy. There probably would be no Christian Academy of Louisville, no Country Lake Camp, no Wings of Refuge Ministry to abused women, no ROCK—which seeks to knock down the strongholds of pornography. Without this church, there would be no *Southeast Outlook* newspaper, no Crisis Pregnancy Center, no Necole's Place providing help to single women in the inner city. There'd be no National Medical Missions Conference, no Easter Passion. There'd be no Hopeful Hearts Adoption Agency providing aid to thousands of orphans in Ukraine. Without Southeast, there'd be no Touched Twice Medical Center in south Louisville, no City on a Hill Christian Production Studio, no Southeast Leadership Conference, no Living Word radio ministry, no four thousand AIDS tests in Kenya, no medical clinic in the suburbs of Kabul (Afghanistan), no Hikes Point Christian Church, no Fern Creek Christian Church, no Mosaic Christian Church in Baltimore (Maryland), no satellite church in southern Indiana. There wouldn't be scores of young preachers and missionaries who were nurtured in this church and are taking the Gospel around the world. Bates Memorial Baptist Church in Smoketown wouldn't have a new sanctuary. There wouldn't have been a $480,000 offering for victims of 9/11, no

$896,000 offering for victims of the tsunami in Asia, no $711,000 offering for victims of Hurricane Katrina. I wish I had time to tell you about the influence of this church. Now I know…I know God could have raised up other places to get the same things done, but the fact is, He used this church. And frankly, I don't see that kind of thing happening at that group meeting at Starbucks

I just got back, last Friday, from preaching in South Korea. You'd be interested in knowing the Christian church is doing well in Korea. We've got 400 churches there, and people are vibrant, excited about the future. They had a Christian convention, and I was the guest speaker. Now I was apprehensive about it, because I had to speak through a translator and that's kind of tedious, and I knew that it would be laborious at times. But I went in to the first service–two thousand people jammed into this little convention center–and the service was a whole lot more Pentecostal than I had anticipated. I mean, Asian speakers are so forceful, and the people shouting, "Amen!" and praying all together. I know I don't go over very well in that kind of setting. I wrote a note to Don Waddell, my administrative assistant. I said, "I think I'm in trouble." And I scooted that note to him, and then I thought, "You know, I've just got to be myself. I've just got to be myself." And I saw Don write, "Just…"–and I knew what he was going to say: "Just be yourself." He passed the note back over, and I read it. It said, "Just pep it up a little."

Well, I couldn't "pep it up a little," and it was just phrase by phrase through a translator, and I was teaching through Genesis 2 and 3 about the fall of humanity. There weren't many "amens," and when I got finished, a half-hour sermon was over an hour, and I thought, "Well, I've really bombed out." But a woman came up to me afterward, a young woman, and she handed me a note that said, "Thank you for your precious preach. That was so touched for to me." I preached three more times, and they were patient. And at the end, we had an invitation, and 27 came to accept Christ, and 25 came saying they wanted to preach and go into mission work. And I thought, "You know, we're dealing with folks with such a powerful word here that transcends worship styles and cultures and languages and generations. It is incredible." But I can't tell you how many of those preachers would come up to me, and in broken English they would say, "Thank you for Southeast Church. We've looked on the Internet," or, "We read the book." "We visited your church, and we want to do here what happened in Kentucky." I didn't know that, and I guarantee you didn't know that, halfway around the world– and this community doesn't know that. And you know, maybe that's the way it ought to be, because Jesus said, "You're to be the salt of the earth." And you never get up from the table and say, "That was great salt, don't you think?" No, nobody knows; it just does its job. But that's the influence of the church.

Now I know my time is up, but I haven't preached for a year so I'm going to—would you give me five more minutes? Whether you're going to give them, I'm going to take them, because I want to show you another church that I love. I showed you this picture seven or eight years ago, but I've been showing this picture to a lot of preachers and they say that it helps them, and I hope that it'll help you.

[Projection of a black and white photo]

This is a picture of a class from First Christian Church in Meadville, Pennsylvania; it was my home church for a while. And it's not a very impressive picture; there's not a college graduate in this picture, 1941. The only college graduate's the preacher, but you would think, "What difference could these people make in our world? This is Meadville, Pennsylvania, which is not exactly the garden spot of the world." I showed this picture one place, and a young man came up to me and said, "I grew up in Meadville. I was in eighth grade…," he said, "before I understood that the Lord's Prayer was not 'deliver us from Meadville.'"

But before you ridicule these people as nobodies, let me tell you about some of the people. On the front row is Sue Anderson; she was the church organist. She and her husband Homer, a mailman, just came to church faithfully. Now their daughter, Donna, is very active in Team Expansion, helping send missionaries all over the globe. Her daughter is a missionary, and her son, Tim Cole, is in charge of all the new church plants in the state of Virginia for Christian churches. On the far right is Stanley Betray; he and his wife Mabel, up there on the front row, shortly after this picture was taken, went to Atlanta Christian College, studied missions, and they spent 30 years of their lives as missionaries to Tokyo, Japan. In the middle are Edgar and Eva Pressey, very unglamorous people. They're holding—Eva's holding in her arms a little baby named Arnold. Arnold Pressey. When he was a little boy, he was a holy terror. My dad taught fifth grade Sunday school class when Arnold was in there, and he'd come home and say, "Arnold is going to wind up in the penitentiary. You can write it down." Arnold Pressey is a preacher in North Carolina today. On the back row is Mr. Ward; Mr. Ward was kind of a stern elder, kind of legalistic. His daughter Dorothy, however, became a missionary to Alaska, and he has a son-in-law who's a preacher, and three grandsons in ministry.

On the front row are my mother and father, and they're holding my older sister, Rosanne, who grew up to be a great Bible teacher. My mom and dad had six children. My dad had a rough upbringing—did not know the Lord. Met my mother, gave his life to Christ, and never looked back. And he loved the church. Worked in a factory all his life, scraped to get by, but he tithed to the church from the very beginning, gave 10 percent to the church. When I was in seventh grade, they started a new church in the little hometown where we lived—35 people—and my dad loved that church.

First one there, last one to leave. One of our early preachers skipped town, leaving a lot of unpaid bills. My dad didn't want the church to have a bad reputation in the community, so he went to the bank, borrowed $2,500 of his own money, paid off all the preacher's bills, and took a second job working in a saw mill to pay it back. I have a brother who's a preacher; I have two sisters married to preachers, another sister married to an elder in the church. My parents have five grandsons in ministry.

On the back row is D.P. Schaefer, the preacher. D.P. Schaefer's son, Raymond Schaefer, became the two-term governor of the state of Pennsylvania, and served on President Nixon's cabinet for a while. I show people this picture, and they say, "Wow, that was a great church." Well, maybe so, but we sure didn't know it at the time—it was pretty stagnant. Shortly after this picture was taken, D.P. Schaefer was asked to resign, since nothing seemed to be happening. He went to his grave thinking he hadn't done much in ministry, but look at it 60 years later. Don't ridicule these people. Don't apologize for them until your record is equal to theirs.

But folks, when somebody looks at Southeast Christian Church 60 years from now, what are they going to say about the influence of this church? There is nothing, nothing like the Gospel of Christ that changes lives and directions of cultures from generation to generation. So, Southeast Church, don't you grow weary in doing good. In due season, you'll reap a harvest if you don't give up.

I'm going to pray, and then we're going to offer songs of invitation. If you have never accepted Christ, what a great day to do that, and the Lord'll add you to His church. But may I say a word to some of you, who may pridefully have come to this church for a long time and you've never become a part? Or, maybe you're dabbling in two or three places. Every sheep needs a fold. Every individual believer needs a body to which they're accountable. Can I challenge you today to step out quickly and say, "Okay, I'm ready"? Make a commitment to the church, and maybe by coming, you'll lead somebody who needs to come to Christ. Let's pray.

Thank You, Father, that Jesus loved the church. Thank You that He loves us. Even though we've got some stains and some wrinkles, He doesn't even see them. We've been cleansed by the washing of water through the Word. May we be the church that is a worthy bride for the coming groom. We pray in Christ's name, Amen.

Gene Appel

Gene Appel is senior pastor of Eastside Christian Church, a multi-site church in California and Minnesota. Gene began his ministry as a 20-year-old intern at Eastside. After moving on to pastor two of the largest churches in the nation–Central Christian Church, Las Vegas, Nevada, and Willow Creek Community Church, South Barrington, Illinois–he returned in 2008 to lead Eastside into its next dynamic chapter. Since that time Eastside has become one of the fastest-growing churches in America. Following in the footsteps of his late father, a pastor and Christian leader, Gene sensed God's call on his life to ministry at an early age. He received a BA degree in Preaching Ministry from Lincoln Christian University in Lincoln, Illinois, and did additional graduate work at Lincoln Christian Seminary and Hope International University, which conferred upon him an honorary DD. Gene has coached church leaders from around the world on how to lead churches through healthy change.

Gene has preached his sermon "Building Bridges" at the North American Christian Convention and churches all over the country. The first time was in August of 2014 at Eastside Christian Church. He uses the NIV, except as noted. In the sermon, he takes a scriptural look at the 2,000-year tendency in the church to build walls instead of bridges to people who are different from us. Without sacrificing truth, he makes a compelling case that calls the church to extend the gospel to all–no matter what race, background, religion, or lifestyle they come from.

"Building Bridges"

Acts 10

Introduction

Years ago, when Bobby Kennedy was furiously fighting for the Democratic nomination for president in 1968, on one unusually hot and humid spring day in New York City, he spent *five* hours crisscrossing streets in some of the poorest neighborhoods of Spanish Harlem. By the time the tour was over, Kennedy was caked with dirt and soaked in perspiration. His guide couldn't help but wonder why this privileged son, this affluent guy from an affluent family, came to the ghetto so often. So he asked him, "Why are you doing this?" And Bobby Kennedy replied, "Because I found out something I never knew. I found out that my world was not the real world."

"I found out that my world was not the real world…"

I grew up in a predominantly white, middle-class, Midwest, conservative, small town pastor's home… And after moving away and living in Las Vegas for over 18 years, Chicago for five, and now southern California for nearly six years,…I've discovered something I never knew in my growing up years…that my world was not the real world… At least, the world I grew up in was just a very small narrow slice of the real world.

In the town I grew up in, I really didn't ever have to confront my feelings about people who were different from me—religiously, racially, socially, economically, politically, sexually, spiritually—because I didn't know very many people who were different from me. I didn't have to confront my feelings about racial issues, because I didn't have any close relationships with someone of another race. I didn't have to confront my feelings about people who followed other major world religions, because I never encountered any. I never had to deal with my feelings toward homosexuals, because in the little town I grew up in I didn't know any—at least, I didn't think I did… Homosexuality wasn't something in my little world in Lincoln, Illinois. It was somewhere "out there." And I found out it was out there…in Las Vegas!

Those years in Las Vegas were so good for me, and redefined my life and ministry, because I really had to wrestle in a new way with what Jesus' words meant when he said [Project: Matthew 19:19 "Love your neighbor as yourself."] That was a lot easier to do in my hometown, because most of my neighbors were a lot like me. But in Vegas that became a new challenge for me, because Jesus didn't put any qualifiers on that statement.

Jesus didn't say, "Love your neighbor if he dresses like you, if she believes like you do, if your neighbor doesn't ever cheat on his wife, or if your neighbor lives a lifestyle just like yours." He just said, "Love your neighbor as yourself." Period. There's no qualifier…no prerequisite. There's no asterisk: "Oh, except those who have different political leanings from yours, except those who have a different ethnic heritage from yours, except those who follow a different God from the one you follow, except those who are addicted and strung out, except those who are gay." Jesus says, "Just treat them, even if they are different from you, with love."

This weekend I want us to wrestle with an event in the Bible that forces us to deal with our own ethnic, moral, political, generational, and religious pride that sometimes keeps us distant from people who are different from us…sometimes far from God.

You see, I spend much more time than I would like to admit with one of *these* in my eye. [Show a plank.] I can be one of those kinds of people Jesus talked about when he said you love to judge and see the *speck* in the eye of others, while you have one of *these* in your own eye. And I'll bet if you're honest about it, you would have to acknowledge that you spend a fair amount of time with one of these in your eyes too and deal with similar issues with pride and prejudice that create a distance between you and others. I find that I possess this dark, depraved, instinctive nature to take the plank in my eye and use it to build a wall between me and those who are different from me...

Our Instinctive Nature to Build Walls

And that's why I am so challenged, and convicted, and inspired by an event recorded for us in Acts 10, where we see a side of the apostle Peter that's uncomfortable, that we're not used to seeing... Even though Peter was handpicked by Jesus to be a leader, an apostle... Even though he had been there when the words rolled off Jesus' lips, "Go into all the world and make disciples of all nations (all ethnic groups, all kinds of people)" (Mt. 28:19, preacher's paraphrase). Even though Peter had stood up on the day the church began in Acts 2 and confidently communicated that "Everyone who calls on the name of the Lord will be saved" (v. 21),...Peter was a deeply prejudiced and self-righteous individual. He had one of these planks in his eye that he'd been building a wall with.

The fact is Peter was deeply prejudiced against anybody who wasn't a Jew. He was brought up in an atmosphere that had led him to believe that people who weren't Jews were less than human: That if you accidentally brushed up against a non-Jew in public, you needed to rush home to wash off the contamination. That you shouldn't help a Gentile woman in a time of childbirth, because it would only bring another Gentile into the world. And never have a Gentile into your home, nor go into a home of a Gentile... because it will defile you.

In the first ten years of church history, there's no record of anyone communicating the good news about amazing grace through Jesus to a single Gentile. And that was comfortable for Peter. That felt safe to Peter.

You see, all of us have this instinctive dark nature that Peter had—to develop these planks in our eyes that we in turn use to build walls. For some, it's the wall you build between yourself and people of different skin colors or nationalities...whether black or Latino or Asian or Arab or Jew or Eastern European. For some, it's political liberals that you can't tolerate,...and for others it's political conservatives who make your blood boil. For some, it's the body-pierced, tattoo-covered student who dresses so differently than you do; or the graying senior who seems so out of touch with a world of iPhones, text messaging, and online communities. Or, maybe it's the neighbor who doesn't believe like you do; the partying, womanizing guy down the block who lives a lifestyle so opposite from yours. For some it's the person of a different religious school of thought...the follower of Islam, Mormonism, Buddhism, Hinduism, Judaism, New Age kind of beliefs. For some, it's the person who is HIV infected...

I'll never forget watching a softball game in the bleachers at a local park in Las Vegas and I couldn't help but eavesdrop on the conversation of some of the other spectators sitting near me... (I know I'm probably the only one who has ever done that). These people were kind of reliving their life-cycle of the past couple of weeks in their lives. And basically, it was get up, go to work, go party after work, find someone to sleep with, go to bed late; get up, go to work, go party, find someone else to sleep with, etc. Now as I'm listening to this, do you know what my reaction was? I didn't find my heart breaking and saying, "Oh, if only these people knew how valuable they were to God." I didn't find myself remembering that I could be in the same cycle—searching for meaning and coming up empty—if it were not for the work of God's grace in my life. Instead, I found myself thinking, "Whoa! I'm sure thankful I'm not like *them.*"

And I leaned over to a friend and said, "You're not going to believe the conversation these people are having next to me." And here's what I said—Gene Appel, Senior Pastor of Eastside—word for word, "They are a bunch of sleaze-balls!" And right then my friend said, "You know, every time I'm around people like this I think, 'This is where Jesus would be. These are the kinds of people He would be spending time with and loving.'"

And right there I put my face in my hands and said, "God, what is the matter with me? I stand up week after week and tell people how much you love them and the extent you have gone to love them,...and I'm not loving very well right now."

You know, from time to time we've all heard of a church leader who had to resign for what is described as a "moral failure," and that usually refers to a sexual sin or a financial sin. But I've never heard of a church leader who had to leave a church because of a "lack of love." For some reason, we don't categorize a "lack of love" as a "moral failure." In the average church, if it's discovered the pastor has had an affair, there's a scandal, and there's gossip, and it's a horrendous thing. But the truth is Gene Appel can live next to his neighbors day after day, week after week, year after year, and never do a loving thing for them...

And you can do the same thing, and there won't be any scandal. There won't be any little whisperings at church about our moral failure, because I think most of us aren't haunted by a failure to love. But I'll tell you who is... God is!

A few years before Barbara and I left Las Vegas, we moved into a neighborhood that forced us to deal with our own natural inclination to take our planks and build walls and isolate others. Across the street from us was a Jewish family. And right next to us, was just your typical Las Vegas heathen family. Very far and distant from God. Two Mercedes in the driveway. He was an attorney, and she was a topless dancer in a Las Vegas show! And our kids played with their kids every day. Now what do you do with that? You see, something I've learned over the years and something Peter has to discover…is that while we have this instinctive nature to take our planks and build walls with them, there is….

A Universal Need in This World for Us to Take Our Planks and Build *Bridges* with Them

In Acts 10, we encounter a man who was not a Jew, not a part of Peter's ethnic group, who was not an insider, who was not a part of Peter's clique, and his name is Cornelius. He was a military guy…who oversaw a regiment of Italian soldiers…and he lived in a town on the Mediterranean Sea called Caesarea. Though he was not a Christian, though he didn't know about Jesus, he had an awareness of God, he prayed to God; and he gave generously to under-resourced people. And if Cornelius had died, somebody probably would have stood up at the funeral and said, "If anybody is in heaven, it would be Cornelius, because he was such a good guy." But Cornelius and his family were spiritually lost…

If they weren't, there would be no need for this chapter in the Bible, and no need for God to ask Peter to build a bridge to him. And the only thing sadder than the fact that Cornelius was lost is that up to this point nobody cared whether or not he was lost.

Peter certainly didn't, because Cornelius wasn't like him… Cornelius wasn't one of his people. But one day God gives Cornelius a vision… He sees an angel of God, and the angel instructs Cornelius to send some of his soldiers to get a guy named Peter who was staying in the house of Simon the Tanner in a town called Joppa. So he does that…

Now Peter has no idea God is about to do some quadruple by-pass surgery on his heart for people who are different from him. God is just so good at taking things we have resisted all our lives and just bringing us face to face with them.

In our neighborhood, God brought us face to face with these people who were different from us… And we started getting to know them– especially the Jewish family across the street and the family disinterested in God next door. Our kids started playing together. They were in our house. Our kids were in theirs. They would go on vacation and ask us to get their newspaper and mail while they were gone… (Let me tell you, there were some interesting subscriptions in that stack of mail.) We would do birthday parties together in each other's homes. Let me tell you, we met a lot of surgically enhanced people! …And you know what we discovered about our eclectic neighbors that we were gradually getting to know?… We started to like them. They started mattering to us. In fact, we loved them… It was if God were saying, "Do you get it? Do you get it? I want you to be a bridge builder to them…"

And that's what God is wondering about Peter… "Do you get it? Do you get it?" The next day, while Cornelius' guys are en route, Peter goes up on the roof to pray; he's hungry, and he starts dreaming about food. And he sees this large sheet like a parachute being lowered from heaven with all kinds of food items a good kosher Jew would never eat… And then Peter hears a voice say the words, "Get up, Peter. Kill and eat" (Acts 10:13). "…Go ahead, have that ham sandwich… Enjoy bacon with your eggs in the morning. Have a pork chop for dinner." That must have felt like fingernails on a chalkboard to Peter, because he was very proud of his diet. He had followed a long list of dietary restrictions his whole life. And so, in this vision God puts all kinds of forbidden animals on the sheet and says, "Kill and eat." Breaking out of this comfort zone was painful for Peter.

I love his response [Project: Verse 14, "Surely not, Lord! I have never eaten anything impure or unclean."]

Oh, nice move, Peter!… Just tell God what to do… And can you hear the self-righteous pride in his voice?… "Oh, I've never done anything like that!… I'd never eat the things on that sheet, Lord." He just didn't get it that God was all about tearing down these walls and building bridges. So God gives him the same vision a second time to see if he gets it. And then God gives him the same vision a third time.

And then the text says [Project: vv. 19–20, "While Peter was still thinking about the vision, the Spirit said to him, 'Simon, three men are looking for you. So get up and go downstairs. Do not hesitate to go with them, for I have sent them.'"]

As Peter was heading downstairs I'll bet he was thinking, "Oh, no! They're going to be Gentiles. I just know it." God is just so good at taking things we've resisted all of our lives and just bringing us face to face with them. Peter goes down and learns that these guys at the door have been sent by this guy he's never met named Cornelius. And Peter does something unheard of in that day… I don't know if we can appreciate the magnitude of this… He invites these guys on the other side of the wall to come into the house to be his guests.

Can you imagine the reaction of the Jewish neighbors as they see these non-Jews go next door? A husband is out front washing his chariot in the driveway and the wife's planting flowers, and they remark to each other, "Did you see who just went into the house next door? There goes the neighborhood. Before long they will all be moving in everywhere."

Peter had carried this plank in his eye too long, and it was blinding him of how valuable these people were to God and the extent He had gone to in order to love them and build a bridge to them.

When Barbara and I got married, I had [Project photo] this antique children's bank…a cast iron little bank I had had since I was a child, where you put a penny or nickel in a little man's hand, pull a lever, and it turns and dumps it in the bank. The paint was rubbed off in a number of spots, there were cracks in the cast iron, but I had always had it prominently displayed on a shelf in my bedroom for many years,...a shelf where I intended to continue displaying it for many more years... But Barbara thought it was an eye-sore...and wasn't as convinced as I was that it enhanced the beauty of our home. She wanted to display it in the closet...or, better yet, try to eliminate it at a garage sale or something.

But I said to her, "Honey, I just have a feeling that to some people that bank is worth a lot more than you think it is."

And she would say things like, "Dream on. You'd be fortunate to get $5 for it and you ought to feel guilty about asking that much."

I said, "But honey, it's an antique! People collect this stuff. It could be worth a significant amount to someone."

Well, finally, I convinced her, rather than to just give it away, to go to an antique store and see what they might give us for it. So she walks in and says, "My husband insists that this bank of his is worth something. And I wondered what you might give us for it?"

The collector looked it over and said, "I'll give you $120 for it." Now five minutes earlier she would have been ecstatic to get $5 for it at a garage sale. But now that there's a collector that will give her $120 for it, do you think she's going take it?... Not a chance!

She calls me at my office and says, "Honey, maybe you're right... Our bank might be worth a lot more than what we thought it was!" – Now it's "*our* bank." And so, we went to the library and found some collector magazines and got in touch with some collectors. We called a collector in Washington, D.C., who asked us to overnight him some pictures. When he saw the pictures, he offered to overnight us a cashier's check for $2,000 for this bank.

Now do you think my wife was going to take $2,000 for this bank that weeks earlier she would have been glad to give away just to get it out of the house?... Not in a millions years! To make a long story short, we eventually sold this old beat-up children's bank that Barbara thought was worthless to a collector in Pennsylvania for $4,000! (Aren't you happy for us???... Rejoice with those who rejoice!)

All of a sudden, we were looking through all of our closets, "What other junk do we have around here that we could sell?!" True story: I recently went online and saw that this identical bank to what we had, recently sold for $52,000... So you can see how brilliant we were to sell it.

Now I told you that to remind you of something we all know... Value is determined by what someone is willing to pay for an item, right? It wasn't the value that Barbara placed on the bank that determined its value. It doesn't matter what an appraisal says your house is worth. Value's determined by what someone is willing to pay for something.

Here's the value of all people... Here's the value of every single human being you've ever laid eyes on. No matter who they are, [Project: 1 Corinthians 6:20 (NLT) says, "For God bought you with a high price."] It's a costly kind of love.

With the plank in our eye, we can look at people and say, "You're not even garage sale material." God looks at them and says, "I'll take a plank, and let my only son die on it to build a bridge to you. I'll give my only son to be pierced for your transgressions and crushed for your iniquities. The punishment that will bring you peace will be on His shoulders. By His wounds you can be healed. That's how valuable you are. I'll build a costly bridge to you." And some of you who wonder how valuable you are to God need to hear that... You really matter to Him.

The Costly Process of Becoming a Bridge Builder

You see, friends, bridges tend to be enormously expensive and tremendously difficult to build.

The next day, Peter travels back to Caesarea with these guys Cornelius sent. I wonder what he was thinking as he traveled with these guys?... Remember, he hadn't spent time with people not like him. I wonder if he wasn't thinking, "Hey, these guys aren't so bad. They're normal. We actually have things in common. They're real human beings and interesting to talk to... I've been missing out on this all my life." And when they arrive at the house, Cornelius, his relatives, and close friends are all gathered there. And Peter is faced with a defining decision... Would he enter the house of Cornelius? Again, remember, no Jew would ever consider stepping across that line...and building that bridge... They were wall builders. Once he did, everything would change...

So Peter is faced with building one of the most costly bridges he has ever built... It will cost him his pride...self-righteousness...his prejudice... It will cost him his reputation in many circles... Fully aware of the price he would pay, Peter...walks through the door and builds a bridge... What a moment!

And he finds himself in a situation that many of our African American, and Latino, and Asian, and Arab friends find themselves in here... He's in the minority for the first time of his life. [Project: Verse 25, "As Peter entered the house, Cornelius met him and fell at his feet in reverence."] Peter could have really played this up... "Yes, yes, bless you my son... Get on your knees and bow down at the feet of the reverend, apostle, pastor, doctor Peter as he powers up over you." But to his credit, he didn't do that [Project: verse 26, Peter made him get up. "Stand up," he said, "I am only a man myself."]

I really like that... "I'm just a guy like you... I'm just struggling and growing in life, like you... I don't have it all together."

It reminds me of something Tony Evans, the great African American pastor in Dallas, says–I love this–"No matter what ship we came over on, we're all in the same boat now." It's as if Peter is recognizing, "Hey Cornelius we're just in the same boat." We're both in need of God's grace. Well, there's this fantastic conversation that takes place... Cornelius shares with Peter all about his vision from God and the instructions to send for Peter. And the lights go on for Peter, [Project: vv. 34–35 (GNT), "...Peter began to speak: 'I now realize that it is true that God treats everyone on the same basis. Whoever fears him and does what is right is acceptable to him, no matter what race he belongs to.'"]

In your soul, have you come to that realization yet–that God treats everyone on the same basis? Do you treat everyone on the same basis, no matter what lifestyle, or group, or background, or race, or political party he or she belongs to?

Peter goes on and shares with these people he wouldn't have even eaten with a few days earlier about the bridge Jesus Christ built across the chasm of sin that separated all of us, no matter who we are, from the God who made us. And an amazing thing started to happen. They started to believe that message. They started walking across that bridge and trusting what Jesus Christ did on a cross for them. And God's power, God the Holy Spirit, showed up in a supernatural way and they started speaking in languages they had never learned.

Peter looks at that, remembers his own experience in Acts 2 when he and the other apostles had this supernatural experience of speaking in languages they had never learned and he says, [Project: vv. 47-48... "Can anyone keep these people from being baptized with water? They have received the Holy Spirit just as we have." So he ordered that they be baptized in the name of Jesus Christ. Then they asked Peter to stay with them for a few days.]

This was the first Gentile baptism service ever. There had never been a Gentile baptism before, that we know of. And then they asked Peter to stay a few extra days with them... What an experience that must have been. For the first time in his life he has a ham sandwich, sweet pickles, and shrimp cocktail...

Now here's my take on this story of the conversion of Cornelius... There's actually two conversions going on here... There's the conversion of Cornelius, but the bigger conversion is Peter himself. While Cornelius and his family were discovering a costly bridge that God had built to them through His son, Peter was learning to build a costly bridge to people who were different from him...in honor of the God who had built a bridge to him.

Strangely, as Barbara and I got to know these people who were so different from us...we found ourselves beginning to love them. And we found ourselves with a renewed awareness of what was hanging in the balance for their lives spiritually. And so, we just started praying every day that God would somehow use us in their lives… We knew if anything were to happen, it would be a long-term project… We thought it would be at least five years before we could even get them in the door of the church for the first time. But after a little over a year of being neighbors, 9/11 happened… And, you remember, the next weekend churches all across the country were packed… There was nothing else to do… All sporting events were cancelled; no airplanes were flying…

And after our 9 o'clock service that morning, Barbara came into my office in tears…and she said, "You'll never guess who I just sat with this morning." I said, "Who?" She said their names and I couldn't believe it. It was the attorney and topless dancer from next door. I said, "What?" Well, we hadn't talked to them that week, and we didn't know that the best man who stood up with them in their wedding had been killed in the collapse of the World Trade Center…and they sensed a need for God, and didn't know where to turn, and we were the only church they knew. That morning I had asked people who had lost people they cared about to stand…and I said, "Now reach out and put your hand on them and let's pray for them." What I didn't know was that my neighbors were there; they were standing. Barbara is reaching out with her hands on them and praying for them… Tears are coming down their faces… I couldn't believe it.

Well, later that morning, after the 11 o'clock service, I was just making my way through the hallways trying to talk to and touch as many people as possible…and I run into my Jewish neighbor from across the street. Her name's Stacey and she had tears in her eyes and she came up and gave me a big hug and she said, "Oh, Gene, you have no idea what being here today has meant to me." And that was a catalyst for some great spiritual progress in their lives.

When we left Las Vegas, we had so many difficult good-byes. It was so hard to say good-bye to our church family who meant everything to us, to our oldest son who stayed to finish college; to Barbara's family… But something that took us by complete surprise was that our most difficult good-bye was to our neighbors who we used to think we didn't have anything in common with,…but who God used to force us to look at the plank in our eye, and take it out and build a bridge to them.

Conclusion

Friends, God's dream for His church…has always been a bridge-building kind of dream—where, in honor of His son who died on a plank to build a bridge to us, we take the plank out of our eyes that we used to build walls with…and…we use it to build bridges.

I'm going to ask our band and worship team to come out right now… and while they're doing that, I want to ask you to just take your plank…

just hold it in your hand… And I want to ask you to just look at it and wrestle with this question:… What is the plank in your eye right now? Who are you labeling, slam-dunking; just writing-off? Who are you pridefully lording your spirituality over? Who have you secretly condemned? What's the plank in your eye? Do you have it in mind? Can you name it? Can you call it for what it is?… There's no other way to say it… When we have a wall-building mentality, when we make demeaning comments about people, against people,…it's sin. It's wrong.

That doesn't mean you can't have sincere disagreements and can't stand for truth… We are to speak the truth in love. It just means it's wrong to demean them, because, when we demean any person, we are demeaning the very God in whose image they are made.

Today is an opportunity to confess and acknowledge that sin, that plank in our eye. And I want to invite you to do something very courageous right now… Take something to write with…and I'm going to ask you to name the plank in your eye and write it down on that piece of wood. Maybe it's a particular group of people–those who belong to a certain political party, those who belong to a certain religious group, those of a certain ethnic group, those who live a certain lifestyle–and you'll just want to write down that name. (No one will look.)

Maybe it's a particular person…and it's so hard for you to love this person. Yet this is someone God couldn't bear the thought of spending eternity without, so He gave His son to build a bridge to them. But you wouldn't give the time of day to them. You have contempt for them. Is there a particular person you need to write down that's your plank in the eye?

Or, maybe you'll want to write down the emotion or the attitude that prevents you from removing the plank…maybe it's ego, maybe it's pride, maybe it's hate, maybe it's anger, maybe it's an unforgiving spirit; maybe it's a lack of love.

You know my fear is that after a teaching like this all of us could sit here and say, "Yep, that's the plank in my eye… It's wrong… It's sin." But then we leave here without taking it out of our eye, without making a commitment to get inside out and start building bridges.

Sometimes it's helpful to us if there's kind of an actual activity we can do to take the plank out…that we associate with saying, "I'm naming this for what it is and I'm going to follow Jesus and take the plank out."

In just a few moments, we're going to have a time of worship and response… It's a time to actually do business and take the plank out…a time for us to say, "Do I mean business with this or not?… Will I go out of my comfort zone or not?"

So let me just identify some ways you could actually respond and do something in this time of worship and response…

Some of you, in an act of breaking this habit, may just want to risk some splinters and take your plank and break it in two...and we'll hear the sound of planks breaking all over the room.

Some of you may want to take the plank and remove it... And as a symbol of laying it on the altar of surrender, you just bring it forward and place it on the edge of the stage and say, "I'm leaving that behind. I'm letting it go. I'm done with that... I'm taking the plank out of my eye." Wouldn't that be something, if people just from wherever they were sitting felt a nudge of the Holy Spirit and actually obeyed it and came here to do that?...

Some of you may want to take the plank with you and keep it in a pocket or a purse to remind you each day of your proclivity to build walls, and let God use it to convict you to build bridges whenever it starts to display itself.

Some have someone in mind, a specific person, and maybe when you get home you will want to humble yourself and personally take it to them and say, "I'm so sorry... I've carried this... I haven't loved you like I should and I'm taking the plank out of my eye." And maybe you could just have some conversations of reconciliation and grace.

Let's stand together... You can blow these next few moments off... You can say that's way outside of my comfort zone...or, you could just open yourself to the activity of God in your life and worship and respond.

Laura Buffington

Laura Buffington is a graduate of Milligan College and Emmanuel Christian Seminary. She has been on staff at South Brook Christian Church in Miamisburg, Ohio, since 2003. Laura has served as the Creative Director, Spiritual Formation Pastor, and as a Teaching Pastor.

This sermon was a part of a sermon series called "Scandal," highlighting the stories of Scripture that show God's working in the midst of headline-worthy, scandal-filled lives. As the sermon was taught, Pastor Buffington sat at a dinner table onstage, moving around and playing the different roles in the story. The hope is that it might bring the dynamics of the story to life and to help the church see how they are still present around all our tables. The sermon was preached at South Brook, using the NIV, in July of 2014.

"Notorious Woman Crashes Party"

Luke 7:36–50

We are spending this summer with the salacious, scandalous stories of the Bible. We've talked about people who are used to tell the story of God's working in the world even though they are drunkards, adulterers, murderers, prostitutes, and womanizers. We've looked at the way they have responded in the aftermath of their scandals—how sometimes the scandal has defined them, and, sometimes, it's become a source of eventual strength.

As we've seen, especially in the Old Testament, it was a rough-and-tumble world, and God had to use people with sharp edges. And sometimes, the sin of people has helped make the story ring true. It's helped us see God's goodness at work instead of Moses, or Noah, or David, or Rahab's. God used broken people because that's all there is.

But maybe you've wondered, as we've made our way through: *What about their sin?* After all, when we encounter Scripture, and the Gospel of Jesus, and—for many of us—when we've heard from the church, we hear that sin matters, that sin keeps us from God, that the best news we have is that Jesus covers our sins on the cross and overcomes death a few days later at the empty grave. What does God think of the fact that Noah got drunk? What does God think about David's committing adultery and having the husband killed? What does God think about Rahab's making money as a prostitute?

We wonder about this because we wonder about our own sin. What does God think of the ways we fall short? What does God think of the wrongs we've done and the wrongs done around us?

So today, let's talk about the time God had dinner with sin.

Being people is hard. We are prone to awkwardness. Just watch people try to high-five—there's like a 5 percent success rate.

This week, at the convention, all day long, every encounter felt like a test about whether we were hugging friends, hand shaking, waving at friends. Even when we both hugged, sometimes we both went left. We're just people, and we do weird things.

Ever been to an awkward dinner party? I'm pretty sure every dinner party has some level of awkwardness. Maybe it's low-level awkwardness, where there are just a few too many…silences—that moment when nobody can think of anything to say at exactly the same time. So we go through our default communicational files—let's talk about the weather, or movies, or roller coasters. Maybe you've even heard the rule—whenever there's silence, don't think about Abraham Lincoln. The next awkward silence you're in, you won't be able to stop thinking about Abraham Lincoln.

Those things happen. But then there's *high-level* awkward. Ever been to a dinner party filled with subtext? Where there's some crazy relational dynamic that nobody's talking about but everybody's working around? Where at least half of the people around the table think every little thing that's said is really about something else? Somebody says something about how the corn tastes good, but it gets interpreted as a slam on who your sister married? Maybe you call that dinner party "Thanksgiving." Or, every family meal ever.

Dinner parties have a way of bringing out the "people" in people. You know what I mean? We only have the food to protect us. We're not trying to accomplish anything; we're not active; we're just trapped around the table, and salads are a lousy defense against personal offenses. I'm convinced that awkward dinner parties are the reason coffee shops are so popular. You can connect with people, but it only has to last as long as one cup, not four courses. Coffee shops are easier than meals. So are bars. They're a quick way to connect, but a quick way to escape. Not like dinner parties. If there's dinner involved, and you're not strategically placed around the table, you could find yourself a conversational hostage where there's no escape. Somebody's just talking, or just fighting, or just not talking.

In today's story, Jesus finds himself hostage at a super awkward dinner party. When one of the Pharisees invited Jesus to have dinner with him, Jesus went to the Pharisee's house and reclined at the table.

We should note already, this is awkward. You may remember Pharisees as being social enemies of Jesus. They are the Jewish leaders of the day. Many of them are prone to legalism, not just for themselves, but for the "good" of other people. At this point in Luke's Gospel, Jesus has already had some good fights with Pharisees. They've been mad at him already for his dinner habits. He had a way of eating around tables with sinners, and they didn't like that. They didn't like that he had been healing people and feeding people on the Sabbath, when they were busy all day keeping their Sabbath rules. They also got mad at him for talking about forgiveness. When you're the one in charge of getting people to keep rules, you don't like forgiveness.

But Jesus is eating at this house anyway—maybe because he said no the last time, so he had to go this time. Who knows? If I were Jesus, I probably would have come up with something better to do. I would have stayed home that night and done laundry or whittled some lawn art—whatever Jesus might have done with free time. But he accepts this invitation and:

> A woman in that town who lived a sinful life learned that Jesus was eating at the Pharisee's house, so she came there with an alabaster jar of perfume. As she stood behind him at his feet weeping, she began to wet his feet with her tears. Then she wiped them with her hair, kissed them and poured perfume on them. When the Pharisee who had invited him saw this, he said to himself, "If this man were a prophet, he would know who is touching him and what kind of woman she is—that she is a sinner." (Lk. 7:37–39)

"A sinner"—not like him, the Pharisee who can't even remember the last time he sinned. She, on the other hand, is famous for sinning. Nobody even remembers her name, she's answered to "Sinner" for so long. Get ready, because Jesus is about to do something brilliant—he knows this Pharisee likes counting sins, so he's got a story:

> Jesus answered him, "Simon, I have something to tell you."

> "Tell me, teacher," he said [*sarcastically,* probably—it doesn't say that but it's implied in the font].

> "Two people owed money to a certain moneylender. One owed him five hundred denarii, and the other fifty. Neither of them had the money to pay him back, so he forgave the debts of both. Now which of them will love him more?"

> Simon replied, "I suppose the one who had the bigger debt forgiven."

> "You have judged correctly," Jesus said. (vv. 40–43)

> And then, Jesus starts talking about manners

> Then he turned toward the woman and said to Simon, "Do you see this woman? [*SEE* her? Of course, she wasn't invited. She's crashing the party and she's not subtle. Of course, they see her. But maybe Jesus is asking if they've ever really looked at her. No, really, do you *see* her?] I came into your house. You did not give me any

water for my feet, but she wet my feet with her tears and wiped them with her hair. You did not give me a kiss, but this woman, from the time I entered, has not stopped kissing my feet. You did not put oil on my head, but she has poured perfume on my feet. Therefore, I tell you, her many sins have been forgiven–as her great love has shown. But whoever has been forgiven little loves little."

Then Jesus said to her, "Your sins are forgiven."

The other guests began to say among themselves, "Who is this who even forgives sins?"

Jesus said to the woman, "Your faith has saved you; go in peace." (vv. 44–50)

Now, before we get further into this story, you may recognize this story and how much it resembles another–there's similar accounts of a woman anointing Jesus during dinner. Both Matthew and Mark tell stories like this. However, the stories they tell are identical to each other and this one is different in several ways. It happens in a different city. The response of Jesus and the people is different. Also, in the other story, the focus of the story seems to be on the woman getting Jesus ready for the cross, as a kind of anointing. In this story, the focus is really on forgiveness. So the chances are that something like this happened twice in the life of Jesus.

So let's look around the table a bit, because this awkward story has a lot to tell us about us. We have a lot in common with everybody around this table.

Let's start with the Sinful Woman. We know very little about her. Because of the confusion that happens sometimes, people sometimes think this story is about Mary Magdalene. In the other story about a woman anointing Jesus, that woman is called Mary, but no Magdalene. In this one, she has no name, so we can't be sure who she is. Really, we can't be completely sure of what her Regular, Famous, Notorious Sin is. For reasons that may tell us more about us than her, people usually think she's guilty of some kind of sexual sin. In some ways, that makes sense. After all, because of the world they live in, women are often particularly shamed for sexual sin, generally more than men. If you remember the story about the woman caught in adultery, she certainly didn't sin alone, yet she's the only one brought to Jesus, while the man gets to run away. In their world, the honor of men was protected at all costs, where women were particularly shamed for sexual behavior.

It's probably at least a little fair to say that our world isn't that different. We have a lot of names for women who we know are having sex–more names than we give to men. We have a lot of expectations and a lot of shame that we put on women about their bodies. At the very least, we could agree that our world wrestles with battles between sexes and shifts the blame from one to the other all the time. So it's not surprising that people have assumed her Sin that's earned her this name, instead of her own, is sexual in nature.

We do get another clue from the story about the kind of woman she's become. Whether her main sin problem is sex or not, any woman in this world who let her hair down has given up any pretense of purity. Women were expected to keep their hair tied up and covered. For women, and to some degree, men, long hair let free would have been a sign of openness to sexual encounters. That's one of the reasons Paul has to spend so much time on hair and head coverings in his letters to the churches. She is so shamed that she doesn't even bother anymore, even in the home of a Pharisee who would have been appalled at the sight of her long hair. Interesting though—this wild, loose, let-down, devil-may-care hair is the same thing she uses to wipe the feet of Jesus.

Here's the thing about this sinner: she's honest. Who knows what she felt about her sin before she walks into this party? Maybe she was some kind of victim, who resorted to sin as a way to survive. Maybe her sin started with something small that just gave her some quiet, secret thrill. Maybe she loved whatever sin she happened to be caught up in that day, or for life. There's a line from a song I can hear playing as she walks in: "Sometimes you feel a little closer to heaven when you raise a little hell." Maybe that's how her sin made her feel. We don't know.

What we do know is that, at the sight of Jesus, she weeps. She kisses his feet! I don't even like to see feet. In fact, I'm pretty excited for winter to return so people will stop posting their feet all over the Internet. "Here's my feet at the beach! Here's my feet by a lake! Here's my feet on a trip to the Science Museum!" They're everywhere. And we don't need to see them.

She weeps. She kisses his feet. She covers him with expensive perfume that couldn't have come easily to a woman with her reputation. She breaks all the rules of fine dinner parties to interrupt this table and give a heartfelt, heart-compelled welcome to Jesus, when he's not even in her home.

Maybe it's better that we don't know her name. Maybe it's better that we can only speculate on her kind of sin—because, She could be Us. What if her sin wasn't sex? What if her sin was greed? Or gossip? Or self-centeredness? What if her sin was gluttony—of anything? There are all kinds of things that could keep any of us out of a law-keeper's party.

But this woman, this *sinful* woman, can't leave Jesus to the professional faith people; she wants to welcome him. She wants to bring all of who she is, let-down hair and all, and leave it at his feet. And for that kind of honesty, boldness, and for those tears, she gets forgiveness.

It's worth noting that she doesn't take this forgiveness for granted. She doesn't approach Jesus casually. She isn't all: "Thanks, Jesus for being so cool about my sin." Something about who he is breaks down who she has become. But we'll get to him in a minute.

Let's move around the seating chart.

In this corner, weighing 200 pounds of self-righteousness, is Simon the Pharisee. That's really all we know of him. The Pharisees were trained in the Old Testament law. We know from other interactions with Jesus that some of them had a way of emphasizing the external keeping of the law without letting the law affect their heart and their internal operations. Jesus accuses them of behaving like whitewashed tombs: clean on the outside, and filled with death inside. Their tendency to count and calculate sin created an atmosphere of fear. Everybody had to be nervous around them—those Pharisees were always accusing. I imagine they would have loved sending e-mails.

They might have had people over for dinner, but life around that sort of Pharisee wouldn't have been much of a party. Even just in this story, we can tell that Simon lets Jesus recline around the table, but it's a superficial welcome at best. As Jesus points out, Simon neglects to do any of the things that would have marked a good host. He lets Jesus in the house, but that's it. He doesn't take his coat, offer him water, show him around. Why would he, a keeper of the law, offer a genuine welcome for this guy who has shown such blatant disrespect for his way of seeing the world?

We're tough on the Pharisees from this point in history. But we sit in this chair more than we want to admit. You know that bit about how "You might be a redneck if...?" This is like that, without any of the fun...

If you've ever stood beside someone and thought about how much better you are than him or her, you might be a Pharisee.

If you've ever stood beside a judgmental person and thought about how great it was that you aren't like them—congratulations, you just became one of them.

If you've ever pretended to do the right thing when you were secretly doing the wrong thing, you might be a Pharisee.

If you've ever counted up or kept score of somebody else's wrongs, you might be a Pharisee.

If you've ever seen the flaws in someone long before you've seen any potential, you might be a Pharisee.

If you've ever replaced a person's name with another label, like "Sinner" or "Liberal" or "Poor," you might be a Pharisee.

If you've ever said the phrase, "You can't say that at church," only to repeat the same thing the next day somewhere else, you might be a Pharisee.

If you've ever given the appearance of welcoming Jesus into your life, or your home, without any sign of tears, or honesty, but only the most superficial, mechanical "hello," just so other people could see that you were good with Jesus, you might be a Pharisee.

If you've ever thought that you were too pure to share a table with a sinner, you might be a Pharisee. If you've ever thought you were too smart to share a table with a Pharisee, you're already at one.

There's a good chance you're like *her,* but you probably have your days when you're like *him* too. I know I do. There isn't just one sinner at this table with Jesus, there are two. As Jesus points out in so many ways, the Pharisees have their sins; they just hide them better. They keep their hair up, like you're supposed to. But they have forgotten to weep. They have missed the party.

And if you've ever spent time calculating sin instead of being honest about it, you've missed the party too.

If you've ever refused the forgiveness of Jesus because you didn't think you had that much to be sorry for, you might be a Pharisee.

And if you've ever spent too much time calling out the Sinner around the table, or posting about the sinners on Facebook, or if you've ever been glad that someday people will get what they deserve, you're missing the party too.

Let's get to Jesus.

One way to look at this story is to see Jesus as the guest of two sinners. We get to see the way the Pharisee only *pretends* to welcome Jesus, while the Sinful woman welcomes Jesus with her whole heart and life. But in many ways, Jesus is the real Host at this table. He is the one, after all, who's God in the flesh. He *made* the table. If we can get our minds around the fact that Jesus is somehow God *and* man–the Christ, the Savior, who for this moment is as real as any other guy around the table–then we are seeing exactly how the Host of the whole Life party welcomes and responds to sinners.

After all, it's his credibility on the line at this awkward party. Everyone there, and maybe a few of us here, are wondering exactly who he is. Is he a prophet? Simon thinks he must not be since he lets this Sinner get close to him. The Sinner thinks he must be. Who is this Jesus who acts like forgiveness has something to do with him? That's what they're all wondering. Again, it looks like the scandal is a loose-haired woman crashing the party, but Jesus himself is the real scandal. And if he's God, then God must also be a killer party host.

If we want to know what God thinks of sin, this party shows us all of it. Something in Jesus' face, something in his words, his countenance, the way his mouth moves, his eyes look, his feet walk, his body reclines; something in the way he eats and drinks; something in the way he is around the table lets this woman know that he is the right place to bring everything she is. And all those same somethings let the Pharisee know that there is danger ahead. That his world is about to crumble. That his calculations were off. Something about grace turns this whole party around.

And here's the thing: *we are her.* We are the sinners without names. We are the ones with long lists of ways we have all fallen short. If you still feel like the part you're playing with your life is this part, you need to follow this woman in honesty and bravery. Tell the truth about your life to someone: to God in prayer; to a friend over dinner. But tell it. Cry if you need to. This story reminds us that grace isn't some blanket covering, but it is the very real exchange of honest confession for real forgiveness. You only get there when you tell the truth.

Try to see in Jesus what this woman saw. Something in his very presence let her know that "Sin" wasn't her name. Something in his words and his life told her she could be someone new. Something in his face let her know that she could come to the table without shame. Get to know his words and his life.

If you find yourself, more often than you want, playing the part of the Pharisee—keeping lists of wrongs and rights, sizing each other up, pushing people away—you also need to know the life and words of Jesus. Give up your categories of sin that put some on the scandalous list and some on the acceptable list. Pray honest prayers. Serve and love people who are not like you so you can know that we can all be close to God. Ask yourself honestly if the welcome you've given to Jesus is real in your life, if it's taken ahold of your whole self.

We all go through seasons of our lives when we are the guests at this party. But our real life starts when we realize that we also get to be the hosts at the table—that we are called to not only accept the invitation to be close to Jesus but to represent him at tables all over the place. We are the ones who get to give her a name. We are the ones who get to free him up. We are the ones who get to give grace a body, and a face, and words.

Eugene Cho says the church is full of people who just keep on acting like guests when they should be hosts. We know some of you still feel like "Sin" is your name. We know some of you are still standing outside trying to decide if this party is worth crashing. We even know that most of us will go through moments and seasons of our lives when the Pharisee inside us will win. But Jesus' way around the table is eventually supposed to be ours.

Paul gives us the analogy: the church is supposed to be the body of Jesus. Not that we need people washing our feet or crying at us, but we need to point them in his direction. We need to welcome them. We need to demonstrate forgiveness—not in a way that makes everybody think sin is awesome, but in a way that shows them who they can be.

If you are here, and I know some of you are, and you're honest about the sin that's part of you, and you're gracious towards the sin that's part of everybody else, then you need to throw more parties. You may need to start being a host. You may need to serve or lead, or open your home.

You may need to start some spiritual conversations with people. Take joy in being able to welcome people towards Jesus. It may still be awkward, but it will be worth it.

I don't think it's any coincidence that Jesus' last memories with his followers had to do with meals. This meal thing is a really big part of how I understand the life of the church. I don't think it's at all surprising that Jesus asked us to remember him through time around a table. I hope when we come here, we know that this is all about sinners crashing and hosting a God-party. I hope we know that this is about forgiveness. This is about extending invitations. This is about a table that's met for years, that meets all over the world, that can grow to fit the room, and can be set with whatever we have.

In many ways, Communion is an awkward dinner party. We sit here with people we don't know—maybe a few we don't like. We may have some hesitations about what it all means, about whether we want to get too close. And the things that keep us apart around tables can keep us apart here. And they can keep us far away from God. Jesus brings us all to the table. This "following Jesus" thing is a thing we should be in together.

I finished working on this message and it started pouring down rain, the power went out, and I was left in the dark just thinking about Jesus around this table. And I don't know—I just started rhyming. Here's some words about me and Communion and, hopefully, *you* and Communion:

> I showed up at this table as just a kid who wanted in.
> I've taken this cup and this bread after nights and days that shouldn't have been.
> I've been around some tables that filled their cups with real wines.
> I've been around some tables with friends who get dangerous walking all kinds of lines.
> Once on the beach, we set this table in sand.
> We broke Pop-Tarts which were His body and the blood came out of a can.
> I've stayed here at this table with griefs and pains to bear.
> There are days I carry nothing to the table and nothing I can share.
> But with every taste, with every drink, I start to finally see,
> It's not about what I bring, but what God says: "take and eat.
> Here is love baked in the sun, grace grown on a vine.
> As real in your hands as the truth that you, my Beloved, are mine."

LeRoy Lawson

LeRoy Lawson's long career has spanned six decades, with a double focus on education and pastoral ministry. Ordained in 1959, the year he planted Tigard (Oregon) Christian Church, he subsequently served churches in Tennessee, Indiana, and Arizona, the longest being with Central Christian Church in Mesa, Arizona (1979–1999). In addition, he was a high school teacher (1962–1964), a professor of English and Humanities and Vice President of Milligan College, Tennessee (1965-1973), and professor at Emmanuel Christian Seminary (2012–2016). From 1990–2003 Lawson was president of Hope International University (California), the first nine years in conjunction with his ministry in Arizona. He has worked as International Consultant for CMF International from 2004 to the present. His formal education includes a BA from Northwest Christian University (Oregon) and Cascade College (Oregon–theology and English), a MA in Teaching from Reed College (Oregon) and a PhD in English from Vanderbilt University (Tennessee). For 56 years he has been married to Joy Whitney Lawson, with whom he takes pride in a large family of biological and "Velcro" children, grandchildren, and great-grandchildren.

"Ebenezer and Me" was preached for the opening convocation of Emmanuel Christian Seminary's 2013 fall semester, using the NRSV. The sermon draws a parallel between the world of the Old Testament and our own world, one filled with wars and injustices and the need for hope-filled believers and the blessing of God.

"Ebenezer and Me"

Come, thou Fount of every blessing, tune my heart to sing thy grace;
streams of mercy, never ceasing, call for songs of loudest praise.
Teach me some melodious sonnet, sung by flaming tongues above.
Praise the mount! I'm fixed upon it, mount of thy redeeming love.
Here I raise mine Ebenezer, hither by thy help I'm come;
and I hope, by thy good pleasure, safely to arrive at home.
Jesus sought me when a stranger, wandering from the fold of God;
he, to rescue me from danger, interposed his precious blood.[1]

Some of you have been to Israel. When you returned home, many images of the Holy Land were etched in your memory–the beautiful grounds at the Garden Tomb, the gnarled trees on the Mount of Olives, the deep blue of the Sea of Galilee, the crowds and smells and clamor of Jerusalem, the passionate praying at the Wailing Wall, the surprisingly modern Church of the Nativity, the panoramic view from the top of Masada.

Whenever I remember our trips to the Holy Land, I think of rocks. The Galilee is fertile, but Judea is a dry and barren land. Rocks are everywhere, the primary product. Most are quite nondescript, each one pretty much like the next: covered with dust and decidedly unappealing—which is why tour guides exhort their busloads of visitors to take one home as a souvenir... Take a handful...

But some rocks aren't just rocks. They are chosen to be transformed. They become building blocks for houses and temples or paving stones for Israel's roads. Still others, unfortunately, serve as missiles hurled at the enemy in the country's never-ending civil war.

But a few are called to loftier purposes—like the stone called *Ebenezer*.

Earlier in this service, we sang "Come Thou Fount." It took me back to my home church, where we sang it often. Mostly, I didn't know what I was singing. I didn't know what a "fount of blessing" was, hadn't lived long enough to understand "grace," wasn't sure about those "flaming tongues above." But the biggest puzzle was this thing called *Ebenezer*. Probably a sword, I thought, since it was raised and help is associated with it—like King Arthur's *Excalibur*. (A sword would be more dramatic, sometimes even more deadly, than throwing rocks.) Outside of church, the only Ebenezer I'd ever heard of was Mr. Scrooge in Dickens' *A Christmas Carol*. I was pretty certain we weren't singing about him!

Then, I learned the story. It's in the early chapters of 1 Samuel. The Israelites are at war with their perpetual enemies, the Philistines—and the Philistines are pummeling them. In desperation, the Israelites even send for the Ark of the Lord. Surely, they reason, "Its presence in the camp will guarantee our victory, 'cause where the Ark is, there is God." These people are, after all, God's people. With God in their midst, what can mere mortals do against them?

It turns out they could do a lot. In the very next battle, with the Ark prominently on display, the fighting is ferocious. Thirty thousand Israelite soldiers die on the battlefield and, humiliatingly, the Philistines even make off with the Ark. It not only hasn't protected them; it couldn't even save itself. What will become of God's people now?

But their defeat isn't the whole story. (In the Scriptures, when it seems all is lost, you want to keep reading. Defeat is not the end of the story.) There is, inevitably, yet another engagement, and this time their judge Samuel leads them in a supreme effort at Mizpah; the balance shifts in their favor. The Israelites win the day.

It's time to celebrate. With grateful heart, Samuel chooses a rock, a rock like so many other rocks. But this one he names "Ebenezer." (That's how we pronounce it in English.) It's a made-up name from a couple of

Hebrew words, words for "stone" and "help." With this special name, he memorializes this special victory: "Then Samuel took a stone and set it up between Mizpah and Jeshanah, and named it Ebenezer; for he said, "Thus far the LORD has helped us" (1 Sam. 7:12). A commonplace rock, dignified by special words, becomes a complex symbol of gratitude, humility, and hope.

I'd like to talk a bit about each of these words—but first this observation. Are you impressed with what Samuel doesn't do? He's just achieved something great, a stunning victory. Self-congratulations are in order, or at least so you'd think. That's what they do on the football field. Watch the ridiculous victory-strutting at the goal line. Or, listen elsewhere to the self-congratulatory speeches in winner's circles, or stand along the route of the parade of champions in New York: "Look what we just did! Hurrah for us!" Frank Sinatra's song caught the pride of so many when he boasted, "...and, what's more, I did it my way."

When our daughter Kim was about four, she was sitting on the kitchen counter helping her mother bake a cake. She was stirring. Flour was flying everywhere. Her mother wanted to help her—and save her kitchen. But Kim stopped her: "I'd rather do it my selfish," she told her mother.

That's the right word, when it's all about you and you are under the delusion that you can go it alone, that you are sufficient, that the victory cup belongs to you only.

This is exactly what Samuel doesn't do; he doesn't boast. He knows better. He hasn't done it himself. It isn't about his brilliant generalship or the overwhelming might of his troops. No, the wise man says, "Thus far the LORD has helped us." He and his hosts have not fought alone, and he's humble enough to acknowledge the help.

"Thus far..." Do you catch the hint of hope in Samuel's brief statement? *Thus far*—and the implication, the conviction, is...: "The One who brought us this far will take us farther."

Can you forgive my bringing up another old song from my home church?

(May I say something parenthetically here? Pay attention to the songs and hymns and spiritual songs you are singing in your youth. They're the ones you will be drawing on in your old age. What the rising generation calls music is expressed in a musical tongue that's foreign to you. So you stand mute as they sing, and reminisce of how you loved to sing, back then, back when you were young. The songs of your youth are written in your musical native tongue. They abide.)

Back to that song I was starting to tell you about. It was called "Stand Up for Jesus." Here are the words:

Stand up, stand up for Jesus, ye soldiers of the cross;
Lift high His royal banner, it must not suffer loss.

> From victory unto victory His army shall He lead,
> Till every foe is vanquished, and Christ is Lord indeed.[2]

The tune is militaristic, and the words even more so. The politically correct among us would not promote it today, and I'm not promoting it either. What I am suggesting, though, is that we hear again that wonderful phrase, "From victory unto victory…" There's hope in those words, isn't there? We learn from our failures—and Samuel's people have had plenty of lessons to learn before Mizpah—but hope grows out of victory, somebody's victory, our own or others we belong to, or the One sent from God, to lead us from Christ's victory to our victories. Humility keeps everything in perspective. We acknowledge that we have benefited from a strength not our own. *Thus far* the Lord has helped us. And the Lord will help us again. From victory unto victory.

That theme has been picked up in a more recent chorus that says, so simply, "He didn't bring us this far to leave us now," Thus far…and farther. Victory. And then victory.

It should be said here, also, that for as long as Samuel lived, the Hebrews were not defeated again. The Scripture doesn't tell us whether he planted any more Ebenezers. Perhaps the impact of one was enough. He wouldn't forget.

Humility. Hope. Now for a closer look at gratitude, which is really want I want to talk about. A book from my summer reading was one of the triggers for this meditation. The author is Associate Justice of the Supreme Court Sonia Sotomayor. When President Obama appointed her, he ignited a raging controversy—but he had the votes, and she's on the bench. I reacted critically at first when I saw she had published her personal story. I wasn't certain a sitting justice should talk this much about herself. (I felt the same way when Associate Justice Clarence Thomas previously published his in 2008.) My idealism would prefer our most exalted jurors to be faceless deciders, perched high and lifted above us mere mortals, disembodied intellectuals who have studied all sides of an issue and then dispassionately, objectively come to a decision uninfluenced by their personal histories or political persuasion. Dream on.

The reality is that all nine justices of any Supreme Court are political appointees whose weighty opinions derive from their reading of the law *and* the living of their lives. Justice Sotomayor is female, American of Puerto Rican descent, Catholic, Democrat, an outspoken advocate of the poor. She is a confident proponent of whatever position she holds. She lives life large. Her title signals gratitude: *My Beloved World,* she calls it.

She didn't choose the title carelessly. You must know her whole story before you can grasp why she calls her world "beloved." Her alcoholic father died when Sonia was but a girl. Her widowed mother worked at several jobs in order somehow to hold her family together. Their home was a housing project in the Bronx. If you were a betting person, you wouldn't have placed your money on Sonia, a poor little girl from a broken home hanging on to the outermost edge of American society. But she defied the odds, rising from nowhere, gaining the best education her country has to offer. She eventually practiced law as a public prosecutor and later became a private corporate attorney. Her brilliance did not escape the attention of people in power. She was appointed to the bench of federal courts and ultimately to the Supreme Court. Her story is inspiring.

Learning about Justice Sotomayor's amazing odyssey made me proud to be an American. This is still, despite all the obstacles we put in the way, a land of opportunity. It has been for her, and it is for me, a "Beloved World." Her story is chock full of heartache and disappointment and reversals, but also of opportunities and friendships and family love and community service. And through it all she continues to give thanks. She is acquainted with Ebenezer. "Thus far the LORD has led us."

And ours is not the only such country where Ebenezer can be found. Another summer book was Nelson Mandela's even more improbable life story. Its setting is racist, apartheid-cursed South Africa. It's about a poor African cattle boy, son of a big man in the Chosa tribe. Nelson's mother was one of his father's four wives; both his mother and his father were illiterate, but his mother was a believer, so Nelson received a Methodist education—and he never stopped learning. His whole lifetime was one of struggle against almost insuperable odds: a struggle for his bread, for his learning, for his dignity, for his people's freedom. The white Afrikaner-dominated nation steadily, inexorably tightened the screws on the much larger native population. No room on Afrikaner soil for black feet; no room in Afrikaner schools for black children. No room in white hospitals for black sick people. No room for Nelson Mandela.

You know the end of the story. That cattle boy rose to top leadership in the fight to liberate native Africans from virtual slavery to the white minority. He was such an effective leader that eventually the Afrikaners did find room for this black boy. His place was prison. They kept him there for 27 years.

But now Ebenezer enters the story. The Lord had brought him thus far—and then further. At long last the election was held, at long last black hands cast ballots, and this time the native Africans won. And Nelson, like a latter-day Samuel, led the new government—a government of the people and by the people and for *all* the people of South Africa—as the first freely elected native African president. And the old man who wrote his autobiography looks back over the long struggle—and gives thanks.

This book, *Long Walk to Freedom,* is hard to read. That's not so because Mandela is not a good storyteller nor because the book is so thick (625 packed pages), but because the suffering inflicted on South Africa's native population almost defies belief. It's too much like reading about the Nazi Holocaust all over again; only the gas chambers are missing. Or, reading about our own civil rights struggle.

We were recently reminded of our complicity in writing the awful history of race relations in America when our own president, the first black American president, visited South Africa this summer. He stood in Mandela's cell on Robben Island; he peered out through the barred window in the little cell that had been Mandela's home for 17 years.

But I wanted to talk about Sonia Sotomayor and Nelson Mandela because I had first read about Samuel and his Ebenezer. Both of these writers impressed me with their gratitude, their humility, and their hopefulness. Both could have given up—surely wanted to give up—in the face of their repeated, harsh emotional beatings. But they didn't. Instead, they gave thanks for their opportunities, prayed for strength to carry on, refused to wallow in self-pity, and defeated the temptation to get even. They could have let past defeats spell for them a future of anger or despair. Instead, they saw the potential victory in their defeats and, choosing to keep on keeping on, and trusting in a strength not their own, they let humility and hope and gratitude lead them from personal victory to political and professional victory. Thus far the Lord has led them. They are acquainted with Ebenezer.

I'm speaking this morning to young men and women who also don't know what tomorrow will bring. One thing I can promise you for certain: you will face trouble. When I sat where you sit, things looked pretty good for me. I had a beautiful wife and, still in my twenties, three lively, lovely children. I enjoyed job security, and my vocation was deeply satisfying. My parents were still living—all four of them if I count the step-parents. I couldn't have guessed then what lay ahead. I knew my parents would die, of course; that's the natural course of things. But to bury one of those beautiful children? I had no idea. And that job security? Well, I did have that, but could not have dreamed that the country's great recession would take a family business down with it. When my head was in the books in those early years, I hadn't calculated what it would be like to see friends desert, or critics take delight in calumny, or feel the embarrassment of a government in chaos and confusion and moral bankruptcy, or see my own best plans end in failure. Yes, there have been Philistines in my past. And they've won many a battle.

So why am I still in this business? It has to do with Ebenezer, with the conviction that God has led thus far—and that God will not desert now.

Many years ago, when I was only a little older than the average seminary student today, Cookie Helsabeck here at Emmanuel asked me some probing questions about my prayer life. She often probed, this good friend: "What do you pray about? How do you pray?" Rather personal questions, I thought, but that was Cookie's way and Cookie was always seeking spiritual insight. She deserved an answer. I answered her truthfully, "Mostly, I just give thanks." Even as a young man I was overwhelmed with the sense of inhabiting a life I wasn't entirely in charge of, the direction of which was not completely in my own hands. I was the beneficiary of undeserved blessings. It seemed presumptuous to let petitions dominate my prayers. Praise and thanksgiving seemed the proper key for my songs.

You are aware of that famous injunction of the Apostle Paul, contained in some final instructions to his friends in Thessalonica: "Rejoice always, pray without ceasing, give thanks in all circumstances; for this is the will of God in Christ Jesus for you" (1 Thess. 5:16–18).

What he exhorts believers to do seems to me to be normal Christian behavior, tying rejoicing and praying and thanksgiving together in a bundle that builds Christian character. Unfortunately, unless guarded against, the pursuit of higher education can instead be a direct route to carping, preying spelled with an "e," and resenting. Early in my own academic career I discovered that there is no automatic correlation between academic achievement and real job satisfaction. Often we academicians appear to be the chief of whiners. What sometimes distinguishes us is not our joy of living so much as our articulate worrying and carping.

The antidote to that poison is thanksgiving. This subject looms so large with me because I not only have the normal human propensity to find fault and complain, but my "schizophrenic" professional life has outfitted me beautifully to major in judging others, to wield a curled lip and a quick barb.

I am *a preacher,* which means I have studied how one should live before a holy God. This study has given me an arsenal of weapons for discovering and disclosing and zapping the sins of others in the name of God. I am a good judge.

That's only half my problem. The other half is that I am an English teacher. The preacher in me knows what you shouldn't do, and the English teacher in me knows how you shouldn't say it.

In other words, I have been professionally trained to criticize, to find fault–in you. To pick nits, to argue for my own righteous positions, and skewer the weaknesses in yours. My academic preparation helped me with argumentation, with demonstration, with persuasion. It did not make me a better person. It did not teach me to give thanks in all things, to pray without ceasing, to praise God from whom all blessings flow.

For the life of me, I had to turn elsewhere.

That's why Ebenezer now means so much–stone of help, reminding that the Lord has led us thus far and, as we serve in humility and with gratitude, will lead us forward. We have reason to hope.

Bob Mink

Bob Mink was in ministry for 44 years as a youth minister, minister, and pastor. In 2014, after 30 years as the senior pastor, he stepped down from the church he planted. A graduate of Cincinnati Christian University, he also has graduate degrees from Eastern Baptist Theological Seminary (MDiv and DMin), Princeton Theological Seminary (ThM), and Temple University (MA). All his ministries were characterized by young people's choosing ministry as a vocation. Mink is the author of *A Pastor and the People: An Inside Look through Letters*[1] and *Questioning Jesus: Considering His Responses.*[2] He writes a weekly blog at bobmmink.com.

"This Is Jesus Angry" was preached on March 9, 2014, and is a message from a nine-week series entitled "This Is Jesus" that was preached leading up to Easter at Discovery Christian Church, Morena Valley, California. Mink uses the NIV. Other messages in the series included "This Is Jesus at a Wedding," "This Is Jesus Welcoming Children," and the Easter Sunday message: "This Is Jesus Dealing with Doubt." Throughout his ministry, Pastor Bob always preached a series leading up to Easter focused on Jesus.

"This Is Jesus Angry"

No matter how well we think we know someone, there is always the possibility they may say or do something that surprises us. Unfortunately, sometimes what a person we know says or does that surprises us disappoints us. As a matter of fact, when a parent is disciplining a child, we will often hear them say, "What you did really disappoints me." On the other hand, and much to be preferred, sometimes what a person we know does or says that surprises us makes us feel good about them. I don't know about other husbands, but I love it when I do or say something that surprises my wife and she says, "I'm proud of you."

During His ministry, Jesus regularly did things that surprised people. In this message, we're going to look at a situation in which He was angry. And at first, that may surprise some. But as we consider the situation, I think it only will make us think more highly of Him. Listen to Mark 3:1–6:

> Another time he went into the synagogue, and a man with a shriveled hand was there. Some of them were looking for a reason to accuse Jesus, so they watched him closely to see if he would heal him on the Sabbath. Jesus said to the man with the shriveled hand, "Stand up in front of everyone." Then Jesus asked them, "Which is lawful on the Sabbath: to do good or to do evil, to save life or

to kill?" But they remained silent. He looked around at them in anger and, deeply distressed at their stubborn hearts, said to the man, "Stretch out your hand." He stretched it out, and his hand was completely restored. Then the Pharisees went out and began to plot with the Herodians how they might kill Jesus.

Let's Begin by Meeting the Players

First, and obviously, Jesus is in this account. He is at a synagogue on the Sabbath (Saturday). And while not exactly the same, for the Jewish people in Jesus' day, going to the synagogue on Saturday to worship was similar to going to church on Sunday for Christians today. Luke 4:16 tells us that in Nazareth, where Jesus had been brought up, it was His custom to go to the synagogue on the Sabbath day.

It's telling and important for us to know that during His life, Jesus made a practice of going to worship with His fellow Jews to worship God on a weekly basis. And His practice is a good example and encouragement for us today in terms of our weekly gathering with His followers to worship. Coming together today for worship is, in many ways, exactly what Jesus did during His life and ministry on earth.

A second player we need to note is a man with a shriveled hand who was also at the synagogue. We do not know if his hand was this way from birth or the result of an accident; only that his hand was deformed in some way. There is an early tradition that he was a plasterer or mason and could not work due to not being able to use both hands. And, as far as we know, this man was present at the synagogue to worship.

Third, Jesus' critics were there. And Mark does not tell us immediately who these critics were. Verse 2 simply says, "Some of them were looking for a reason to accuse Jesus, so they watched him closely to see if he would heal him on the Sabbath." It isn't until the episode is over that Mark tells us in verse 6, "Then the Pharisees went out and began to plot with the Herodians how they might kill Jesus." We'll return to this in a moment, but the Pharisees were the religious leaders of the day, who were obsessed with following the letter of the law.

Finally, there were other Jewish worshipers there. The verses do not explicitly say it, but we can safely assume there were others in addition to Jesus, the man with the withered hand, and the Pharisees.

Perhaps you noted when we read the verses how before His exchange with His critics and healing the man, in verse 3, Jesus told the man he was going to heal, "Stand up in front of everyone." Jesus not only wanted to heal this man, He wanted to use the occasion to teach both His critics as well as the others who had come to synagogue that day.

Let's Think about Some Right and Wrong Reasons to Go to Church

The place of worship in which this healing took place was not the temple in Jerusalem, but a local synagogue; in many ways similar to a church today. The temple in Jerusalem was the center of worship for the great feast days, but throughout the Holy Land and beyond were local places of worship–synagogues–for the Jewish people. And the primary day of worship for the Jews was the Sabbath, Saturday. As you may remember, that is what the fourth commandment is about. Exodus 20:8 says, "Remember the Sabbath day by keeping it holy."

The Pharisees, the critics of Jesus, were there for the wrong reason. On this Saturday, the Pharisees did not go to synagogue to worship God. Remember, the Pharisees were the religious leaders of the day who were obsessed with following the letter of the law.

What we need to understand is that keeping the Sabbath was the most important practice of the Jewish people in Jesus' time. And while it included going to synagogue for worship, it included much more than just going to synagogue for worship. Part of keeping the Sabbath day holy as required in the fourth commandment included not working on the Sabbath. And the Pharisees believed and taught that healing was work. That's why they were there "looking for a reason to accuse Jesus." They were watching Him to see if He would heal this man with a shriveled hand. That's a wrong reason to go to synagogue: to watch Jesus to see if they could accuse Him.

There are, of course, wrong reasons to go to church today. For example, it's still wrong to go to church to watch others and to criticize them. Through the years I have been amazed at the amount of criticism offered by some about others who come to church. I'll never forget one Easter Sunday a person who had not been in church for some time came up to me and told me how disappointed he was that we allowed adulterers in our church. And, of course, he had someone in mind and had come to see if that person was in church that day. With tongue in cheek, I said to him, "Next week, I'll put up a sign that says, 'No adulterers, please.'"

I have been taken aback at times by the intensity and nastiness of the way some people have criticized the way others have dressed for church. Let me say as gently as I can, it is not your business what people wear or don't wear to church. And hopefully no one here this morning came just to criticize the friendliness or the music or the preaching or the coffee in the cafe.

There are other wrong reasons to go to church than just to see who is there or to criticize people who are there. Church is not a place to come to make contacts to promote your business. And with that thought in mind, I want to say a word about our policy of discouraging young people from bringing their fundraising products to show at church. Now we support our children and youth in terms of their sports and clubs and activities and the need to sell things to raise funds, but Sunday morning church isn't the place to do so. And can you imagine what it would be like here if all our young people who were doing fundraisers brought their stuff to sell? It reminds me a little bit of the better-known incident in the New Testament when Jesus got angry: when He chased the moneychangers out of the temple.

There are, of course, good and right reasons for going to church. A secondary reason is to see and fellowship with friends. That is totally appropriate and is not the same as coming to make contacts and promote your business. One of the highlights for me on Sundays is seeing so many friends and having the opportunity to catch up.

Another reason to come to church is to serve. There are so many ways to serve the Lord and others on Sunday mornings. And for most who serve, it only enhances the primary reason we come to church.

But the primary reason we come to church is to worship God—to meet with Him, to praise Him, to sing about and to Him, to hear from Him, to be challenged and encouraged, to remember what He has done for us, to thank Him, and to honor Him through our giving. We come with the expectation that God will meet us and welcome us into His presence. And we come open and wanting Him to do something in our hearts and souls. We come seeking to know His will so we can learn and grow.

Let's Think, Finally, about Appropriate and Inappropriate Anger

As we have seen, Jesus' critics were there to watch Him. At this point, Jesus had only been publicly teaching for a short time, but these religious leaders were already put off and threatened by Him. They were hoping Jesus would heal the man with the shriveled hand so they could accuse Him of breaking the Sabbath. To them, healing was work, and work was not allowed on the Sabbath.

Jesus went along with their plan. To make sure everyone was on the same page, so to speak, the first thing He did was call the man with the shriveled hand up in front of everyone. And then, He asked a question in verse 4, "Which is lawful on the Sabbath: to do good or to do evil, to save life or to kill?" But they remained silent. It was a question they could not answer. *Of course* it was lawful to do good on the Sabbath day! Given the opportunity, not to do good was in essence to do evil.

We come in verse 5 to the primary thing I want us to see about Jesus today, "He looked at them in anger and, deeply distressed at their stubborn hearts, said to the man, 'Stretch out your hand.' He stretched it out, and his hand was completely restored." Some are probably surprised at Jesus' anger, because they have always pictured Him as meek and gentle. And He is, but that does not mean He could never be angry.

In the introduction of today's talk, I suggested, "No matter how well we think we know someone, there is always the possibility they may say or do something that surprises us." And I said what that person does that surprises us sometimes disappoints us, but sometimes it makes us feel good about them. If Jesus' getting angry with these critics surprises you, I hope it makes you feel good about Him. Jesus was angry with them because of their "stubborn hearts." Another translation says Jesus "was saddened by their hard hearts" (NLT). They didn't care about the man with a shriveled hand. They had no interest in him; they only saw the opportunity to accuse Jesus. Hard and stubborn hearts are more than just calloused and cruel; they are the opposite of a humble heart that is open to submitting to and cooperating with God.

What about the fact that Jesus was angry? Isn't anger bad? Isn't it sinful? Obviously, if *Jesus* was angry, it is not always bad and sinful.

The Bible does teach us that anger is dangerous and warns us about inappropriate anger. In Ephesians 4:26, the Apostle Paul quotes the Old Testament admonition, "In your anger do not sin," warning us that, when angry, we are more susceptible to sin. And in 1 Corinthians, the Apostle Paul tells us, "[Love] is not easily angered" (13:5).

When we are angry, our emotions are on edge and we are less restrained and more likely to say or do something we normally would not do or say. One of the reasons some may struggle with Jesus' being angry is because we usually think of anger as something that is bad; we associate it with immaturity and selfishness. And it often is; and most of us know that because we have seen it in others—or, more importantly, we have seen it in ourselves.

One of the reasons some anger is inappropriate is because it often tries to hurt the perceived source of the anger. In our anger, we try to get even. And when we do that, we often deeply hurt people whom we love.

Inappropriate anger can destroy our wider Christian testimony. One pastor suggests, "It is hard to believe a person is really a Christian when you see him honking his horn and shaking his fist at someone. It is hard to believe a person is a real Christian when in anger he uses language and says things not befitting a Christian; or when he behaves at work in ways that a Christian should not behave."

But as we said a moment ago, if *Jesus* was angry, it is not always bad and sinful. Ephesians 4:26 warns, "In your anger do not sin," but it does not say anger is sin. First Corinthians 13:5 says, "[Love] is not easily angered," but it does not say, "Love never gets angry." The Bible discourages anger and warns us about anger, but it does not totally forbid anger. Anger is not in the same category as lying, stealing, using the Lord's name in vain, getting drunk, and other such sins. Jesus' anger was perfectly appropriate, right, and godly—and, I think, for two reasons that also would make our anger appropriate, right, and godly.

First, because of why He was angry; or, we might say because of what it was that made Him angry. There is a place for righteous anger. There are some things about which we *should* get mad. But I find it so instructive to note all the times in Jesus' ministry when He didn't get angry when most of us would have. Jesus became angry at the right things. And we can too as long as our anger is directed at the right things.

The other reason Jesus' anger was appropriate, right, and godly was because of what His anger led Him to do, as well as what it did not result in. I'm saying anger is okay if we are angry for the right reason, and anger is okay as long as it results in our doing the right thing and not the wrong thing. Jesus gives us the example. Anger can motivate us and give us energy to make a positive difference.

Conclusion

Let's be honest: some of us have an anger problem, don't we? (I do, and I am aware of it and making progress.) Some of us get angry for the wrong reasons and our anger results in our saying and doing the wrong things. Our anger is hurtful and destructive—often regarding the people we are closest to; and, beyond that, it mars our Christian testimony.

And there are probably some who have the opposite problem: you never get angry or disgusted or moved by anything, no matter how bad it is. You need a greater sense of justice and compassion, as well as commitment and resolve for the Lord and the things of God.

And going back to the Pharisees, if we will be honest, some of us don't always come to church for the right reasons. Some come to criticize and keep an eye on people and things, or other wrong reasons. And I challenge all of us to recommit to coming to church first and primarily to meet with God to worship Him, and secondarily to fellowship with His people.

Glen Elliott

Glen Elliott is the Lead Pastor of Pantano Christian Church in Tucson, Arizona. It's a church he loves and has been at for 18 years. Glen holds two degrees from Pacific Christian College (BA '77, MA '82). He spends a significant amount of time mentoring, teaching, and encouraging leaders. He has traveled all over the world doing pioneering church, relief, and development work in places such as Ukraine, Kosovo, India, and most recently Cuba. He speaks Russian and loves the diversity of cultures. Glen cares deeply about racial unity and about the church truly making a difference both locally and globally.

This sermon is from the 2015 series at Pantano called "A Beautiful Mess." The sermon was based off some key issues found in the letter of 1 Corinthians, and was preached May 17. Pastor Elliott uses the TNIV. First Corinthians is a letter that guides followers of Jesus how to navigate the challenges of living in a messed-up culture. This series was particularly directed to let the audience know that the church is made up of *people*–all of whom are loved by God while being messed up, broken, and sinning.

"A Beautiful Mess: Got It Together?"

We are continuing our series called "A Beautiful Mess." We are looking at the book, or letter, in the New Testament called 1 Corinthians. The church in Corinth is a church that is beautiful to God and a mess at the same time. One of their messes or problems is that they feel compelled to have it all together and expect their leaders to also do likewise.

That is a powerful temptation that we all face. There is no one here who doesn't face this temptation, even me. The temptation is to put on a public façade of having it all together. It is our social face. It is our Facebook image. We simply want to look good for others. Can you imagine going to a job interview or meeting someone for the first time and saying: "Hi, I'm Glen Elliott and I'm a mess and rarely have it all together"? That's not the socially accepted way to present yourself.

It's the pride thing we talked about last weekend. Pride is at the root of all our messes. (You can watch that online from last week.) There is a powerful social need to put on a façade. It goes deeper. More than just a façade, we do want to have it all together. We work hard at it or feel guilty if we don't. And if we don't, we experience shame and try to hide our weaknesses.

And that social face we carry into our faith world as well. We put on what I call the "church face." We want others to think that, when it comes to faith, we have it all or mostly together. Part of that comes from a mistaken view of faith. For many of us, we hold this belief that faith is for the purpose of putting our lives all together. If we have a real strong faith, then God will fix our problems and we'll get our act together. If we don't have it all together, then there must be something wrong with our faith.

Church is famous as a place where you should look like you have it together. Having it all together, after all, would make Jesus look good, right? In the last 18 months, I've had three conversations with people who have visited our church. I often ask new folks who visit how they found out about Pantano. Each of these folks said they were searching for God, had driven by our church, and decided to visit. But after they pulled into the parking lot, they got scared—showing up at a new place, and at a church of all places. Each of the three said they sat in their car to watch the people who were coming onto our church campus. I asked why. They said they wanted to see if the people coming were normal people or if they were people who looked like they had it all together. In other words, as hurting people who had messes in their lives, they were wondering if they would fit in here and be welcomed. The question people have is this: Is this a place where people are real and don't have it all together!? The church has a reputation as being a place where folks are expected to have it all together.

What does it look like to have it together? Confident. Organized. Disciplined. Self-sufficient. Healthy. In shape. Great job. Plenty of money. Happy family. Great marriage. Successful. Well-behaved kids. Happy life. Problems all managed and under control. No stress or worry... How are you measuring up?

There is a huge cost to trying to have it all together. It is really hard work. You must try to control everything in your life—not just yourself, but all the people you interact with. Or, you try to play it safe and thereby keep your messed-up self hidden. Or, we refuse to take any risks where we might fail or be exposed. Or, you just try to hide the messes and you have to run a continual PR program. To avoid the shame problem, we have determined that not having it together must be avoided...somehow. All this is exhausting. And futile!

That brings us to our series, "A Beautiful Mess," and 1 Corinthians. The Apostle Paul wrote to a church he started in a city called Corinth. The church was in a culture that rejected brokenness and weakness. One of the highest values in that city was human accomplishment and perfection. It was highly valued, using our phrase, to "have it all together." And good leaders had to have it all together.

But here's the cold, hard, spiritual truth. I'll speak in first person because that is the most honest way to address this. Maybe you can identify too. I am a sinner. I mess up daily. I disappoint God. I disappoint myself. I have spiritual, emotional and social weaknesses. I struggle with a number of issues inside, and most of you will never know about most of them. I hurt.

I'm lonely. I struggle with being competent. I see areas of my character that are not yet right. There are temptations that never go away, and, on occasion, I give in to those temptations. Pain will always be a part of my life. I know that I'll never have it together in this life, yet I work really, really hard to have it all together. But I am broken. In fact, that's how I've come to summarize my life: I am broken.

It was just about eight years ago that I, finally, not only realized I was broken, but also that I could admit I was a broken mess. That turned out to be one of the most freeing times of my life. It took me far too long to come to that place of freedom. And in the last few months I came to a newer admission that I could and must embrace. I will *never* have it all together! That was one more step in my spiritual journey. I will always suffer under my weaknesses and brokenness. I'll be a sinner until I "graduate" and go to heaven. The spiritual struggles and emotional turmoil are forever with me. Suffering is a promise and "togetherness" is a myth. Let me say it again. Togetherness is a myth. What do I do with that reality and truth? What will you do with it?

I find some terrific help in understanding this in Paul's first letter to the Corinthians. Here's what I love about this letter that he wrote. Over and over Paul admits that he is a beautiful mess! Paul is writing to a church that has bought the cultural value of having it together. But he takes the honest approach. Paul admits and embraces his weakness and brokenness. He even says that God will not remove his brokenness and weaknesses. So here's what I've learned from God through Paul in the Bible. Here's what I want to challenge you with today...

[Project: "You can try to hold it together or hold on to the One who holds you together."]

Paul knows the church expects him to have it together and act like he has it together. Great leaders, after all, have it all together. By the way, we still believe that today. We expect our athletes, politicians and public servants, clergy and priests, teachers and professors, and business leaders to have it all together. But listen to what he says in 1 Corinthians 2:1–5:

> And so it was with me, brothers and sisters. When I came to you, I did not come with eloquence or human wisdom as I proclaimed to you the testimony about God. For I resolved to know nothing while I was with you except Jesus Christ and him crucified. I came to you in weakness with great fear and trembling. My message and my preaching were not with wise and persuasive words, but with a demonstration of the Spirit's power, so that your faith might not rest on human wisdom, but on God's power.

That doesn't sound like a guy whom God used to *literally* change the world! That doesn't sound like the guy who took a tiny persecuted church and spread it all over the Western world. He was a poor speaker who was weak and afraid, and he admits it! He didn't have it together, and didn't put on a church face.

But here's the key. In admitting he was weak and inadequate, it forced him to rely on the power of God and not on his abilities. God was able to use Paul because he did not have confidence in himself but totally relied on the truth of the message about God and the power of God through the Spirit of God. In his weakness, he had to cling to the One who is strong and true. And that brings us to another key truth. We only find God in our weaknesses.

Paul is not embarrassed about his messed-up life. Rather, he embraces his brokenness and weakness. He embraces that he does *not* have it together. Let me be clear. I'm not saying it is okay to sin. Sin damages us, our relationship with God, and others. But the fact is we *all* sin and have weaknesses. We have to be honest and vulnerable about admitting that. Paul admits to us all that he was a weak, broken, messed-up man. He struggled with all kinds of issues. He wasn't competent in all aspects of his vocation. He suffered greatly. He faced some temptations that never went away. He was not thought highly of by lots of people. His self-described life would be considered a mess by most people. We can't miss that or ignore that.

Imagine if Paul submitted a resume based on what he writes about himself in the New Testament. Imagine if he applied to be the Lead Pastor at our church or a manager of a company? I'm confident that we would not even give him an interview based on the fact that he freely admits that he just doesn't have it together.

Let me go to the second letter we have that Paul wrote to the Corinthian church. It gives us the clearest picture of how Paul not only embraced his weakness, but how, in doing so, God used that as a strength. Let's read 2 Corinthians 12:7b–10...

[Project: Therefore, in order to keep me from becoming conceited, I was given a thorn in my flesh, a messenger of Satan, to torment me. Three times I pleaded with the Lord to take it away from me. But he said to me, "My grace is sufficient for you, for my power is made perfect in weakness." Therefore I will boast all the more gladly about my weaknesses, so that Christ's power may rest on me. That is why, for Christ's sake, I delight in weaknesses, in insults, in hardships, in persecutions, in difficulties. For when I am weak, then I am strong.]

There is lots of speculation as to what the "thorn" in his flesh was. Some kind of physical ailment? A continual sinful temptation? It doesn't really matter. It was painful. It caused him suffering. It would not go away. And it was a gift from God to keep his pride in check. (We are back to the issue of pride again!) God was, in effect, saying to Paul,

[Project: "You can try to hold it together or hold on to the One who holds you together."]

It was in this that Paul found "It!" He found how to really have it together. And it wasn't by having it together. He found *It* by not having "it" together. The blessing of brokenness is that it helps us see and experience God's grace. It is not about my keeping it together but my allowing God to hold me together through the weakness, pain, and brokenness. God never promised to protect us from brokenness. He did promise that his grace is sufficient for us to be able to go through our brokenness. When we are weak, we find our strength. That strength is God alone. His love is perfect and never fails. He has the ability to guide us through the struggles. That's why I suggest: You can try to hold it together or hold on to the One who holds you together.

Don't miss what Paul does in verses 9 and 10. Paul says he "boasts" and "delights" in his weaknesses. He celebrates his weakness, hardship, and brokenness. That's key! It is not something that can be avoided, anyway. So understand that in our brokenness, we find God. And that's the whole point. When we are weak, we find God. In our brokenness, we find a God not of our making (who will make us happy or whatever) but the true God. For God is best experienced in the messes! Our life is a beautiful mess! The church is a beautiful mess.

When life is falling apart and far from being together, it is often only then that we discover something that can only be found when we are being broken—our hidden idolatry and false gods that we have come to depend on. For me, my main god and hidden idol is self-sufficiency: "I can do it myself!" And, more often than not, I can—but at a price. From an early age, I was forced to be independent. I learned the skills well. For me, the god of self-sufficiency was my main way to "hold it all together." No one can do that better than I can!

What is your god and path to try to hold life together? I don't know what yours might be, but you have hidden idols and gods too. And the *only* way to discover them, I believe, is through the desperateness of being broken. It is then that we see what we have depended on for happiness and fulfillment. But we fight being broken, and work hard to get it all together. And we miss God as we (the "we" is pride) try to hold it all together.

Two things happen when we fight against our weaknesses and brokenness. We miss the work and power of God. God does his best work in our weakness. We box God out as we try to keep it together. Second, we miss the experiences of real love and grace from God and others. When we put up the façade and try to be strong, we don't allow others to love us unconditionally. We miss the best things in life by failing to embrace and live in our weakness and struggle. So we have a choice: You can try to hold it together or hold on to the One who holds you together.

Here are ways about how to respond to your continual struggle, weaknesses, sin, and brokenness. First, admit you don't have it all together; that's where it has to start. Some of you have never been able to do this. Decide you can embrace and even celebrate your weakness, struggle, and brokenness. That is both an admission and a decision.

Second, in your brokenness, look to see the grace or gift God might have for you *in* the mess. The gift may be the uncovering of a god or idol that robs us of a better life. Or, the gift may be encountering God in a deeper way. For sure, the gift will be that we can relax and find joy as we quit trying to hold it all together by ourselves. But if we don't look, we won't find the gift God has.

There are so many benefits to this. We can truly relax. We can find joy. Our vulnerability allows us to be real, thus approachable. This is vital in our efforts to kill pride, which we talked about last week. Most of all, it drives us to hold on to Jesus, the One who holds us together.

Finally, we rarely deal with our brokenness alone. We need others. It is then that we put down the church face or social façade. It is then that we can begin to experience the grace of God through others. Let me make a strong statement that I am confident to be true. You will never be able to embrace your brokenness apart from the spiritual community of a small group. That group may be as small as one other person. It is in a group where you can confess your weakness that you find help, encouragement, and accountability to face the weakness. You can only really embrace your brokenness with others, not alone. That's why I urge you to join or start a small group. We have folks at our "Next Step" that can help you. Go to guest services and they'll direct you there after any service.

Pantano Christian Church, be real. You don't have to have it all together. You don't! You won't. We are sinners. We are broken. We are weak. We need a Savior. We need forgiveness. We need God's grace. We need each other. Our only hope for our brokenness is Jesus.

Mark Scott

Mark Scott presently serves as Professor of Preaching and New Testament and Director of the Preaching Department at Ozark Christian College (Joplin, Missouri). Previously, Mark served as the Exposition and Leadership Pastor at Mountainview Community Christian Church in Highlands Ranch, Colorado (2011–2014). Before that, he served as Academic Dean at Ozark Christian College, where he taught New Testament and Preaching from 1983 to 2011. Mark graduated from Ozark Christian College, Lincoln Christian Seminary, and has a DMin from Denver Seminary.

This sermon was preached in the Ozark Christian College Chapel Service on Nov. 3, 2015. It was the second sermon of a four-part chapel sermon series on "Kingdom Footprints." It is submitted because it is from the entire second chapter of Acts (a crucial chapter in the Stone-Campbell heritage) and because the third movement of the sermon deals with whether or not Acts 2:37–47 is exemplary for the church today (i.e., apostolic precedent–although he does not use that language in the actual message). Scott uses the ESV in this sermon. The introduction to the sermon is a brief video from the 21 students in his fall Expository Preaching Class. They had to make the following statement: "Hi, I'm _____, and a sermon that changed my life was_____."

"Kingdom Preaching"

Acts 2

[Sermon followed a video from the Expository Preaching Class, Fall, 2015.]

Give it up for my Expository Preaching Class this fall. Those are 21 fine students, and they are good preachers too. We're having a good time together this fall. I can tell you this–their preaching is changing my life, and their collective testimony is that preaching can still change lives today.

This I know: preaching about the kingdom of God radically rearranges peoples' worlds. When the government of God collides with the kingdoms of this world, all kinds of hell and heaven break loose. It was certainly that way on the day of Pentecost, wasn't it?

We've been talking to you from the Elisha narratives in 2 Kings about *Kingdom previews.* Now we are talking with you about Kingdom snapshots or footprints from the early chapters of Acts. President Proctor spoke about "Kingdom Prayer" from Acts 1 last week. I am to talk with you about

"Kingdom Preaching" from Acts 2 this week–and, for a preaching professor, that's about as good as it gets.

Let's say this, and then we'll get down to it: Acts is more about the *ecclesia* than the *basileia*. "Church" appears about 114 times in the New Testament, and 23 times in Acts. "Kingdom" appears 162 times in the NT, and only 8 times in Acts. But...where the word *kingdom* appears is instructive (1:3, 6; 8:12; 14:22; 19:8; 20:25; 28:23, 31)–mostly in the big ethnic and geographical shifts areas. I don't personally believe that *ecclesia* and *basileia* are synonyms, but, after Acts 2, they are sure interwoven.

Think of it this way. Let's say that you set up a camera and interviewed people on the streets of Jerusalem on the Day of Pentecost: "Tell us of a sermon that changed your life." It might go something like this: "Hi, I'm Levi, and a sermon that changed my life was Peter's on Joel 2." Or, "Hi, I'm Mary, and a sermon that changed my life was Peter's on Joel 2." Or, "Hi, I'm Naomi, and a sermon that changed my life was Peter's on Joel 2." They would all say the same thing, because it was what you could call the first "official" gospel or Kingdom sermon. You see, Acts 2 is a new page in the story; not a new book–the story of God's promise to Israel continues–but a new chapter. But there is something new here too. You see the fuller reign of God can now be experienced. And we might as well get down to what that is.

Kingdom Preaching Has Something to Do with the Holy Spirit (Acts 2:1–21)

Moses certainly longed for this day. Do you remember Numbers 11:16–30? God took the Spirit from Moses and put it on 70 elders. Well, two guys were tardy to the meeting. Eldad and Medad had remained at the camp, but they were prophesying. People complained. Moses said, "Would that all the LORD's people were prophets, and that the LORD would put his Spirit on [everyone]" (v. 29b). Well, that day has arrived. The prophets longed for this day. Ezekiel had predicted that God's people would get a new spirit and not have a heart of stone (Ezek. 11:19). Well, that day had arrived. And Jesus longed for this day. He said to the apostles that he had been *with* them, but there was coming a time when he would be *in* them (Jn. 14:17). Just a little left of our text, in one of the resurrection appearances, Jesus breathed on the disciples in prophetic symbolism and said, "Receive the Holy Spirit" (Jn. 20:22). But they could not have received it then because of John 7:38–39!! But...the next time, they heard "wind" (breath)–or, more accurately, a sound like wind. They knew, "This is it!!" That day had arrived.

Let's read Acts 2:1–4.

[Project: When the day of Pentecost arrived, they were all together in one place. And suddenly there came from heaven a sound like a mighty rushing wind, and it filled the entire house where they were sitting. And divided tongues as of fire appeared to them and rested on each one of them. And they were all filled with the Holy Spirit and began to speak in other tongues as the Spirit gave them utterance.]

Several signs of theophanies are present–sound like wind, tongues as fire, and inspired speech. The tongues (*glossa*) and languages (dialects) are for the purpose of people's (from all over the Roman world, vv. 5–11) understanding the message. I'll be honest–the tongues in Corinthians make me wonder if they are something other than known human languages. But here, I'm pretty sure that's the case–and maybe in Acts 10 and 19 as well.

Anyway, you know how the text goes–some were amazed and some mocked (12–13). Peter says that they are not filled with *gleukos* because it's too early. Darn, Peter, can't you do better than that? Why not say, "We abide by the *OCC Student Handbook,* and we don't touch the stuff." "It's too early"–what an answer. Ha! But I will tell you this–the apostles are drunk on the Spirit of God (just like Paul says in Eph. 5:18).

Then Peter takes his text from Joel 2:28–32. How can a rather "early" prophet telling his people about a locust plague have anything for us? Well, maybe more than you think. Joel tells his people that God will send his Spirit, so they had better "rend their heart[s]" (Joel 2:13). And, indeed, the preaching of Jesus Christ brought about this very thing: When the people heard this, they were cut to the heart and said to Peter and the other apostles, "Brothers, what shall we do?" And the apostle told them "Repent and be baptized, every one of you, in the name of Jesus Christ for the forgiveness of your sins. And you will receive the gift of the Holy Spirit" (Acts 2:37-38).

Well, when the Spirit comes, gender and age won't be big deals. Holy Spirit phenomena will break out. Cosmic signs (perhaps figuratively understood and giving way to literal understanding someday) will announce that God is beginning to bring in the end, that he is rearranging the way things are in the world. And best of all–if you call on the *name* of the Lord you will be saved (2:21, 38; then chapters 3–5 emphasize the echo effect of the "name of the Lord").

So how about it? What about the Holy Spirit? Is he the *Forgotten God,* as Francis Chan says? Chan says that if he were Satan, he would try to get people to just ignore the Holy Spirit.[1] Can you explain your life without the Holy Spirit?[2] Is he the shy member of the Trinity?

Do you understand part of our heritage? Could I convince you to take a field trip to Paris, Kentucky? There you will see beautiful green grass, nice fences, and a little church building. Try to imagine twenty thousand people out there—some listening to a Methodist preacher on one stump, some listening to a Baptist preacher on another stump, and some listening to a Presbyterian preacher on another stump. Holy Spirit phenomena were taking place that are hard to quantify. While the Campbells weren't sure about it, Barton W. Stone thought it was a genuine movement of the Spirit of God. Those are some of our roots.

Do you understand the college where you are studying? When Brother Seth Wilson started the college, he wanted more teaching in three areas—hermeneutics, apologetics, and positive teaching on the Holy Spirit. Do you think it was an accident that Don DeWelt taught here for 27 years and traveled the country lecturing on the power of the Holy Spirit? When I was a student here in the 1970s, there was a lot of controversy about the Holy Spirit. One day, classes were cancelled and we all came to the chapel for some special teaching on the Holy Spirit. The charismatic movement was making big inroads in those days, and Brother Wilson just wanted us to think rightly about the Holy Spirit. So we could have the right spirit, I remember Brother Wilson reading several of Paul's prayers from the epistles to set the mood for our study.

If we are going to talk about kingdom preaching, then we must talk about the Holy Spirit. A poem that captures this for me was from Boyce Mouton. It's entitled, "Mary Had a Little Pig."

> Mary had a little pig, and it was white as snow,
> That is, when it had had a bath, as you, of course, might know.
> And Mary had an awful time to keep that piggy clean,
> For he was just the dirtiest pig that one had ever seen.
> Washing him she'd scrub him, till he'd squirm and squeal,
> As if he wanted her to know it was an unfair deal.
> And then in the green backyard he'd play from morning until night,
> Unless he'd happen to slip right out and lose himself from sight.
> Now Mary thought and wondered much what she could ever do,
> And then she figured out a plan that she carried through.
> She took him to the doctor, who put the pig to sleep,
> And then he took his heart right out, but not of course to keep.
> And then he took a little lamb, and took its heart out too,
> And put it in the little pig, before the piggy knew.
> And when the piggy did awake, he had no more desire
> To wallow in the mud and forever in the mire.
> So, you see boys and girls, we need a new heart too,
> Just like the little piggy did, the old will never do.[3]

When Boyce Mouton shared this with some junior high boys, one responded, "Hey mister, whatever happened to the lamb?" Boyce quickly changed the tune and the tone of the moment and said, "That's heavy too, for 'he was wounded for our transgressions, he was bruised for our iniquities: the chastisement [of us all] was [laid on] him, and [by] his stripes we are healed'" (Isa. 53:5, KJV). Kingdom preaching has something to do with the Holy Spirit.

Kingdom Preaching Has Something to Do with Announcing the Jesus Story (2:22–36)

Consider Acts 2:22, "Men of Israel, hear these words: Jesus of Nazareth, a man attested to you by God with mighty works and wonders and signs that God did through him in your midst, as you yourselves know…" That's it. The Kingdom is about Jesus. The Kingdom *is* Jesus. His three-year ministry is compressed into one verse. The miracles of Jesus are evidences that God is setting the world right. The miracles of Jesus are God's effort to start saving the world even before Jesus gets to Golgotha. The miracles of Jesus are God's previews of coming attractions. They let us consider a future world for just a brief moment.

But look at this. His three-year ministry gets one verse, but his death, burial, resurrection, and ascension/exaltation get *14* verses. You tell me where the accent is. You tell me where the best of the good news is located. All his teachings and all his miracles matter, but the key is the crucifixion and resurrection. With a skillful use of two supporting texts from the Psalms (Ps. 16 and 110), Peter draws a distinction between King David and the King who is the true Son of David. It may have looked as if humankind was running the Kingdom. But alas, not so. You are not allowed to run the Kingdom unless you can come back from the grave. Peter makes it very clear that, in contrast to David's body, which is in the tomb to that day, Jesus' body wasn't in the grave long enough to decompose or become corrupt.

Joel Gregory tells the story of Mr. Corruption and Mr. Tomb having a conversation the day that Jesus died. It's 3:00 p.m. on Friday afternoon and Mr. Corruption says to Mr. Tomb, "Do you have him secure? Are you holding him?" Mr. Tomb says, "Yes, I've got him. No worries." Friday evening Mr. Corruption says to Mr. Tomb, "Are you still holding him so I can do my work?" Mr. Tomb, "Well, yes, I've got him. I think you can go to work now." Saturday morning Mr. Corruption says to Mr. Tomb, "Do you still have him?" Mr. Tomb, "Well, yes, I've got him, but you might want to get busy." Saturday afternoon Mr. Corruption says to Mr. Tomb, "Are you still holding him so I can do my work?" Mr. Tomb, "Listen, I am trying to hold him, but something funny is going on in here. I think if you are going to do something, you'd best be at it." Saturday evening Mr. Corruption says to Mr. Tomb, "Do you still have him?" Mr. Tomb, "Hey, I'm not exactly sure what's going on, but I think if you are going to do something you'd better do it, because I'm not too sure I can hold him anymore." Sunday morning Mr. Corruption said to Mr. Tomb, "Do you still have him?" Mr. Tomb said,

"You're too late, I couldn't hold him anymore."[1] That's what we believe.

I need to tell you that kingdom preaching in the NT is primarily announcement. Yes, the early missionaries *reasoned* in the synagogues and *dialogued* with the people. But primarily preaching in Acts is this: God has come in Jesus Christ to set the world right. Humankind killed Jesus, but God raised him from the dead. We are witnesses of this so we urge you to believe this. Peter brings them to the point of conviction. He brackets the middle move of the sermon (vv. 23 & 36). Look at verse 36, "Let all the house of Israel therefore know for certain that God has made him both Lord and Christ, this Jesus whom you crucified." There's the punch of the announcement.

Finally, Kingdom Preaching Has Something to Do with a New Community (2:37–47)

The sermon worked. The people were convicted and asked what to do. Peter told them what to do (2:38). He pled with them to accept the call of God in Christ (vv. 39–40), and three thousand were baptized and became a new community for God (v. 41).

I know of few things as beautiful as Christian conversion. When someone turns to Christ and trusts him for salvation, repents of sin, and is baptized for the forgiveness of sins and the gift of the Holy Spirit, it is a living dramatization of God's remaking the world. It is one more step toward a new creation. It is a microcosm of what God is trying to do in the whole universe (Rom. 8:18–27; Rev. 21–22). This is God's forever family living in community before we get to the new heaven and new earth.

We got to see Susan this last spring. We hadn't seen her in years. We were headed to speak at the Mississippi State Convention and stopped in Arkansas to see some dear friends named Arfston. They said that they had a surprise for us that evening. A little later Susan came walking in. We had no idea she lived in the area. Susan came into our church in Illinois many years ago. I'll never forget that day. We had prepared for her baptism. We were waiting to get into the baptistry while the congregation was finishing their song. She said, "Now listen, when we get in there you put me all the way under. Do you understand?" I thought, "Trust me, Susan, I will get you all the way under if I have to stand on you." But I appreciated her earnestness to get in this new community.

I just talked to Ryan on the phone. Ryan was baptized into Christ in our Denver ministry, but he had to go to prison for some past crimes and poor choices. I would go visit him in the Denver Detention Center. Then we moved back to Joplin. Ryan had about an 18-month prison sentence. But he's out and living with his folks in Arizona. Oh, my goodness. He has been healed. Kind, humble, gracious, forgiving, and grateful that God let him go through that experience so that he could get his life permanently fixed. He is so grateful to be part of this new community.

I could argue that Acts 2:42–47 is one of the greatest *church paragraphs* in the New Testament. There is not one imperative. It's all indicative. So how could it be a model for us? Let me make two responses: (1) Luke contextualizes it with seeming approval. (2) The things they did are commanded elsewhere in the NT. They taught, shared meals and money, observed the Lord's table, prayed, worked miracles, sold possessions so they could take good care of one another, and they grew numerically like crazy. Sometimes, when people talk about restoring the church in the NT, they talk about which church you want to restore–because they all had flaws (Corinth, Thessalonica, etc.). In my opinion, that all but misses the point. We are talking about restoring an ideal–not an individual church. This paragraph describes the church at its best. And you can feel it, can't you? Some days, church is really church, and you want to say, "God, this is so good–shoot me and take me to heaven right now." Kingdom preaching has something to do with a new community.

This Kingdom preaching changed the lives of three thousand people. Here is Charles Koller's outline of Acts 2:

(1) This is That.

(2) This is Who.

(3) This is How.

I like that so much. I guess I am trying to say something similar. *Big Idea:* Kingdom preaching is empowered by the Spirit, announces the Jesus story, and produces a new community.

James Booth was the founder of the Salvation Army. He had the book of Acts memorized. In his declining years he lost his sight. But when people would come visit him, he would ask for a copy of the Scriptures to be brought to him. He would have them open it to the book of Acts and place his hand on the text. He would ask the person where his hand was. They would tell him, and he would begin to quote from that place and just quote for a while. When he would get tired, he would close the Bible, pat it with his hand, and say, "O Lord, do it again. O Lord, do it again." Maybe, just maybe, he can do it again through you.

SECTION THREE

CHRISTIAN CHURCH
(DISCIPLES OF CHRIST)

Orientation to Preaching in the Christian Church (Disciples of Christ), 1968–2018

by Casey Sigmon and Richard Voelz

For Disciples, 1968 would be the year the "Movement," after many failed attempts, restructured itself as a denomination. With restructure came the opportunity for the loosely knit collection of agencies and congregations to covenant together and find a way to speak as one Church. So, as Disciples' restructure loomed on the horizon, leading scholars and ministers took up the task of describing various aspects of the faith and life of what would become the Christian Church (Disciples of Christ). This resulted in three volumes popularly known as *The Panel of Scholar Reports.* Within those three volumes published in 1963, William West described the context of preaching at the dawn of the 1960s: a world where Communism threatened, where "racial strife has engulfed all nations in new dimensions of depth," and where mental illness impacted thousands.[1] West summarized the context for preachers as "a world of anxiety" and corresponding "ontological loneliness" awaiting the gospel of Jesus Christ.[2]

At a time when the United States as a nation struggled over racial integration, women's rights, and the many cultural changes that bespoke our differences, over this period the Disciples of Christ claimed a theological and organizational identity that would enfold previously unauthorized voices into the life of this body. Rather than remaining separate but equal, the ministries of minority communities such as the National Convocation of the Christian Church (African American Disciples), the Central Pastoral office for Hispanic Ministries, and North American Pacific/Asian Disciples (NAPAD) covenanted with predominately white Disciples to form a General Assembly in pursuit of that vision.

How striking, then, that in the years following restructure, the identity statement that emerged for the Disciples' would proclaim: "We are Disciples of Christ, a movement for wholeness in a fragmented world. As part of the one body of Christ, we welcome all to the Lord's table as God has welcomed us."[3] As even the early sermons in this collection will show, this identity statement has had a long trajectory in Disciples' preaching.

1968 also provides a fitting starting point for these five decades of preaching in the Disciples tradition, for it was only three years prior to the landmark work of Fred Craddock. Craddock's *As One Without Authority* and the inductive method helped begin something of a renaissance of mainline denominational preaching in the United States. We cannot begin to talk about the last 50 years of preaching in the U.S., much less among the Stone-Campbell Movement, without mentioning Professor Craddock's influence and his clarion call to turn to the listener in preparation for and delivery of the sermon.

A qualitative analysis of sermons 20 years after restructure revealed some growing edges for preaching in the Disciple's tradition. Joseph E. Faulkner sought out sermons preached during 1988 for content analysis. He ended up with a pool of 206 sermons, though lamentably 99 percent of the preachers were white and only 7 percent were women. The glimpse of themes and sources of authority consulted in this pool of sermons demonstrate both "an almost Marcionic approach to the bulk of the Bible"—meaning the Hebrew Bible—as well as "scant attention" paid "to issues of social justice, racism, feminisms, and other such contemporary concerns."[4] Faulkner also lamented the haphazard use of illustrations that seem inorganic to the preacher and listeners. Perhaps Craddock's vision had not quite fully taken root in some quarters of Disciples' preaching.

If we partner Faulkner's analysis with an essay published only one year prior, we witness a striking incongruity. In "'*Vox Populi Vox Dei*': Toward a Definition of Preaching," Neal Kentch argues that the definitive nature of preaching in the Disciples' tradition is as an interpretive act. Preaching "mediates between the community and its scripture by rendering these scriptures intelligible in terms of the community's experience and by rendering the community's experience intelligible in terms of its scripture."[5] Thus, context is central to the preaching act, according to Kentch. While Kentch writes a prescriptive essay for the essence of Disciples preaching, Faulkner offers a descriptive picture of the reality of Disciples preaching at the end of the 1980s, a reality where preaching doctrine was more important than interpretive mediation between Scripture and experience.

A few years later, Joseph Jeter would write with concern about the state of preaching among Disciples. Jeter highlighted several factors that had led to what he believed was a slow unraveling of the tradition. First, he charged that contemporary biblical criticism offered little benefit for preaching in the eyes of many Disciples preachers, and they studied less for week-to-week preaching, rather than more. Second, the church of the 1960s and 1970s de-emphasized preaching, and seminaries followed suit, resulting in a vacuum of excellent preaching among what then were considered "great pulpits" filled by "pulpit princes."[6] Third, and related, the demands of ministry had changed, such that study and sermon preparation suffered. Finally, Disciples preaching lacked the kind of sermons that engaged and inspired congregations for the pressing concerns of the time.

Jeter's tone is unquestionably hesitant about the state of preaching at that time, but he pointed to what he saw as unfolding good news for Disciples preaching. Congregations were beginning to demand better preaching, ministers were prioritizing practices that led to good preaching, great preaching was no longer recognized to exist only in urban "steeple" churches by white males, and the Bible was once again taking a prominent place in the pulpit (keeping in mind that Jeter wrote in 1992, the same year the *Revised Common Lectionary* was published in its current form).[7]

By 2000, Ronald J. Allen pointedly asked: What remains distinctive about the Disciples of Christ preaching tradition now that it is on the whole assimilated into the American mainline? Most of what Allen outlines as seven characteristics of Disciples preaching is present in the sermons gathered here from 1968 into today—most notably, the theme of unity in diversity, the importance of the Table and the liturgical setting for preaching, and articulation of a hopeful social vision based on the realm of God.[8]

With all this in mind, we turn our attention to the preachers and sermons included in this collection. Considering the previous collections of sermons by W.T. Moore and Hunter Beckelhymer, no doubt readers will notice that the collection of preachers here represents a much wider diversity.[9] The current collection includes women, persons of color, voices from racial-ethnic communities, and those who identify as LGBTQAI. Present as well are individuals from every aspect of life within the Disciples: local church ministers, seminary professors, regional ministers, and leaders of general ministry units. Every effort has been made to reflect as many as possible of the voices that have been preaching among the Christian Church (Disciples of Christ) over the past 50 years, despite having only 13 sermons in which to do so. And, still, this collection misses some voices. Disciples worship each week in a multitude of languages, and preachers come from a wide variety of backgrounds. While a blessing for the wider church, we lament the difficulty this range of diversity presents in assembling representative preaching from our tradition. Thankfully, we are a people of grace and welcome, as well as a people committed to the long, steady work of healing and wholeness.

Fred Craddock, who is discussed in the Introduction to this volume, was representative of the great tradition of teachers of preaching in the Christian Church (Disciples of Christ). As he clearly demonstrates, the axiom that those who "cannot do, teach" does not hold for Disciples professors of preaching. Harry Baker Adams, Hunter Beckelhymer, Susan Bond, Mike Graves, Robert Howard, Joseph Jeter, Pablo Jiménez, Leander Keck, Lance Pape, Dwight Stevenson, Frank Thomas, Mary Donovan Turner, Richard White, Joseph Webb, and Don Wismar do not have sermons here; however, their influence surely infiltrates many of these sermons.

The sermons collected here are contiguous with the common characteristics of Disciples preaching from the past 50 years outlined above, as well as themes emerging from the institutional life of the Christian Church (Disciples of Christ). Still, there are some different themes that arise, indicative of more recent concerns—including the realities of mainline denominational decline (Morales and Davison), pluralism and secularism (Morales), reinterpretation of classic theological topoi such as the atonement and Christology (Harris and Penwell), inclusion of those whom we might find as "other," women's empowerment (Carpenter), and preaching in the context of the liturgical year (Harris).

The sermons are all quite different, illustrating the breadth and depth of preaching at work among the Christian Church (Disciples of Christ) over the past 50 years. Readers will find in these sermons theological formulations and language that are reflective of their times and will not represent the thought of all Disciples. Several of the sermons display opposing viewpoints–for instance, the different theological understandings of the death of Jesus. And there are some difficult issues that Disciples have carefully considered over these years that do not appear here. This of course demonstrates principles long at work among the Stone-Campbell Movement: we are people who appreciate thoughtful faith and we value "unity, not uniformity."

Finally, it is an odd task to lift up sermons, events in time and place that usher in the ministry of the Living Word, and print them here–divorced from the people whose lives were on the heart of the pastor who spoke, out of line with the headlines that week that troubled their minds. As mentioned above, Disciples preaching has been deeply reflective on context and has sought to interpret faith for the church with theological and contextual acumen. Indeed, Ron Allen has brought forward the image of the preacher as "interpreter of the gospel" as an image of utmost importance, rising from and appropriate for Disciples preachers.[10] And yet, these sermons are here, time capsules of moments and places of the church in pursuit of the gospel of Jesus Christ.

Mary Louise Rowand

The vast majority of preachers were male in the Disciples in 1968. Mary Louise Rowand (1918–2008), a European American, was one of a small but vibrant number of Disciples women preachers in 1968, the outset of restructure. Her sermon contains typical themes of the period.

Mary Louise Rowand graduated from Fairmount State University and attended Brite Divinity School. Married to E.C. Rowand, a Disciples minister, she served "as an un-official co-minister to her husband," including 1953–1978 at Central Christian Church (Disciples of Christ), Dallas, Texas.[1] Ordained in 1965, she was a leader in opening doors for women, serving as president of International Christian Women's Fellowship and advocating for women in many other roles.

The biblical text for this sermon, preached in 1968 at Central Christian Church in Dallas, is Revelation 2:8–11, especially 2:10c. Rev. Rowand uses the KJV. The preacher makes a prophetic analogy between the sin of Smyrna and the sin of Dallas. The preacher assumes the church is part-and-parcel of the larger culture, but failing in its social responsibility. The printed version of the sermon below preserves much of the oral quality of the sermon: e.g., when the preacher does not explicitly state the subject of a verb, as in, "Heard about a preacher the other day, never mind who…"

"Three-Letter Words Can Be Worse"

Revelation 2:2–22

Heard a preacher the other day, never mind who, say that his church was working out very happily. He had just about succeeded, after all these years as pastor, in weeding out the undesirables. I wonder who he meant. Which of the sheep does the shepherd take pains to "accidentally" lose? Which of its members does he think the body of Christ would be better off without?[2]

The extreme rights? The extreme lefts? Churches are full of them, and they're one of the real crosses for preachers, alright. Every day of the world. But we carry it gladly, trying to get to Jesus' great prayer that we will all be one someday.

Or, does he mean the people who always want to run everything? Criticize constantly, grumble. Or, is it some of the secularized laity, whose terms of measurement for the church are the same as those of the world and who define the office of the minister, not as a spokesperson of God, but just another practitioner of a trade—with a daily, over-busy program like any business downtown.

But if the church can't put up with them, who will?

Maybe it's the "haters" of this and that? The alcoholics, homosexuals, drug addicts, the lonely? Is Christ's love to come to them only through a friendly bartender or taxi driver? The "blind," the "deaf," and the halt–not physically, but those you have to eternally explain things to three or four times, wait on them, pick up after them, do it for them. How reluctant we are, and I don't mean just preachers, to give freely what we have freely received. How reluctant we are to mediate the love of God Almighty to whatever needy and unpromising miscellany God sees fit to send our way.

"Surely, inasmuch as we have weeded out one of the least of these, we have weeded out Christ."[3]

In the Scripture this morning, that little verse, "Be [ye] faithful unto death" (2:10c), is one of those embarrassingly demanding texts that we would avoid if we could. It's so utterly demanding that we usually leave it right there where it is–the letter to Smyrna. It's safe in Smyrna, for Smyrna is dead. Not there anymore.

Except that Dallas is Smyrna too, we could go on avoiding it. Except that it speaks of the vast gulf between our "is" and "ought," between the vast demands of life in Smyrna and the life we have lived in the church. This haunts me: the agonizing awareness that Christendom is not yet Christ's, and the church has a lot of lesser gods. Not forever and for always does it haunt very many of us. We have learned to upholster the sharp edges of these demands, to give these embarrassing ones a comfortable interpretation. We have required, and we have built a very satisfying religion. We can even defend it.

Dr. Van Harvey out at Southern Methodist University said it this way:

You can see the Enemy at prayer every Sunday at 11 a.m. Injustice and indifference made possible for many people because of their "Christian belief." Walk around any white, Protestant church within driving distance of this campus…(and would you think about the churches that surround SMU)…on Sunday and see silk-shrouded women drive up in big cars, and young businessmen-on-the-make, with gold money clips shaped in the form of Texas, playing at church, tasting the sermon, mumbling the hymns, thanking God for Dallas, praying for victory in Vietnam, and go out on Monday and complain about property values declining where Negroes are moving in. Worrying about the integration of the schools. Racial crises and tensions rising daily, and they utter banalities about love, decry violence, buy revolvers, petition their police for greater protection, and support a church that retreats to some kind of inner religiosity in which a man's chief and only worry is about something he calls his soul, his private relation to God."[4]

He made me mad when I heard these words, and I went backstage and copied down what he said, and I've been thinking about it... Do we refuse to see that we are on the front line facing the Enemy, and not safely at headquarters in the rear?

That text, "Be...faithful unto death," is hard. It takes a lot to be faithful in that way. So, to give us strength, we sometimes say, "God will take care of you." We usually hear that text in an affirming way. But what if we consider it as a threat? What if God *should* actually "take care of" us?

To be faithful unto death never meant: "*Believe* certain statements through life till you die. Just know the words and sit around believing them." It has always meant what it meant in Smyrna: the Son of God says, "Do what I say; be what I am; go where I send; live as I lived, and die as I died."

When these words were written, Domitian was emperor of the Romans. It was the law to address him as "our Lord and our God." Statues of his entire family stood across the country with the captions "We are your gods," enforced by six-foot Pretorian guards. Domitian may have thought he was God, but he was still afraid of death and a knife. Stone mirrors set in palace walls. Knife blows come from the rear in Rome when you are emperor. Nero had been "reborn," but the church refused to lick the spittle. Death was beginning to drop among the churches and Smyrna was next. We might paraphrase John's point here: "Live so that your devotion defies death."

Our comfortable Christianity, a far cry from such a text. Domitian has not died. Look around you. We have new idols: speed limits of 70 miles per hour on the highway, plenty of sex, and size. (If it's bigger, it's got to be better). That which rules your life is your god. What rules your life? I sometimes wonder if the Son of God has any troops in that Smyrna which is Dallas.

The church is a fifth-rate power. Really, a sort of fifth wheel bolted on behind, while we ride on business, government, home, and school. Business is first. Politics or public life, or status, or relaxation, comes ahead of *worship*.

"And the country club and golfing bills are higher every month than their stewardship," says a respected Highland Park minister. The children in one of our large, nearby churches were polled recently to see how many different postures of prayer they'd seen their parents in at home. Most of the children said they had never seen their parents praying except in the church services—and very few even said grace at meals.

So the church holds its little group meetings, and begs you to come to them; limps along on half-staffed educational channels, knowing what miracles could take place with more people, time, and money; has its discussions about what evangelism would be if we were evangelists. Hence: we come when we like; give when we please; do what we wish; say what we choose; and go where we have no business.

We are the half-born ones to whom Jesus cries, "Why call ye me, Lord,...and do not the things [I command you]?" (Lk. 6:46).

But we have a chance here. A chance to recapture the Spirit, and relive the fidelity of the church at Smyrna. This church can be *His* church. Our church. For, I see you these days breaking your bonds to the dull and commonplace. You are no longer running away from people with needs you don't understand, problems you don't want to know about, and that you can't help anyway. You have demonstrated that you will endure hard preaching of a hard gospel. You show an eagerness for new light. I think you are ready for the next generation "Reformation" in Christianity: the stripping away of the superficial.

Today's kids come equipped with X-ray eyes. They can judge what is vital and what is just trimming in the show window. Long before they're eight, they know that three-quarters of the earth is covered with revolt, poverty, and illiteracy. There are still some who believe that the power of the gospel of Jesus as the Christ can deal with these. Only trouble is, they like the prophet but not the priest. They like Christ, but they don't like his church. Tennyson's lines come to me:

Ah, what shall I be at fifty
should Nature keep me alive,
If I find the world so bitter
When I am but twenty-five?[5]

But I have hope. I have hope because you're beginning to ask *why.* "Why?" can be such a bad word. A dirty word. Four-letter words are not the worst words. The really bad words today are three-letter words. Powerful words–like *sex.* Terrible words–like *God.* And *why* is a truly dreadful word: "*Why* do we have to do this and this and this when this goes on here?" "*Why* is there meat and fruit and liquor and ice for you and not for them...?"

When somebody asks, "Why?" it's already too late to hide. "Why?" is the switch that lights up the end of the world.

We need to get one truth right here. You *and* I can't stand to be guilty. You know how it is–the fault is never ours. Last week on vacation, there I was, riding along in the car, with the map spread out on my knees, and, I sent E.C. down the wrong road. When we discovered it, we were way off the route–and, then you should have heard me, "That was the poorest marked thing I've ever seen. What's the matter with the highway department? E.C., this map's wrong!"

Why didn't I just admit that I was the guilty one and it was all my fault? You all could add your own experiences right here–at home this week, the little everyday things. We're like this in big things, too. Can't stand to be guilty.

Dr. Carlyle Marney is the greatest Southern Baptist preacher I know. I've heard him in that big marble pulpit in North Carolina. He says we've used Judas enough in these churches of ours; that we are all a company of betrayers. We forget those terrible words that follow the account of Judas' sneaking out the side door: "then all the disciples forsook him and fled" (Mt. 26:56b). *All the disciples.* Jesus said, "He that dippeth his hand with me in the dish...shall betray me" (Mt. 26:23). They all had their hands in that dish.[6]

It's as old as Exodus. Israel always had two goats: one unblemished kid on the altar, and the other who bore all our guilt away—and they'd lead that one off into the wilderness.

This same dread reality keeps demanding new Judases. We can't stand to be the guilty ones. We keep trying to justify ourselves. Carlyle Marney goes on to ask:

Who taught field hands they had no time to wash, and didn't need to marry to have children? Who taught field hands their sanitation wasn't a problem in the fields? Who taught field hands that fat-back and weevily flour and dandelion greens was good enough? Who created hate? And what church of God Almighty is saying these are our people; we shaped them economically, geographically, spiritually, and physically.[7]

Carlyle Marney said it, and I'm thinking about it.

I thought about it when I travelled not five miles from these very walls of ours, with a busload of church women, and stood inside shacks of one-room, where the smell was suffocating of rotting food, rancid mattresses, dead rats, and stale odors of human life. Eight people lived in each one, or more. Everything went on in that one room. I looked at the roaches and the toilet bowl in the corner without a seat, and I remembered that this is the sort of place in which most people live, in most of the world, for most of the time. This, or something worse. And this fact made it my home, too.

Not is a scary three-letter word. "When ye have *not* done it unto the least of these, ye have *not* done it unto me!" (Mt. 25:45, preacher's paraphrase). You and I can disagree violently on how this "taking care of the least of these" comes to pass, but we've spent too much time arguing on which is Caesar's and which is Christ's. I'm to the place that I don't care how you carry out Christ's instructions; but, for his sake, let's do it!

Let's not "be...faithful unto death," just sitting around believing the words that he said. That's not what he meant. Not in Smyrna. And not in Dallas.

Poverty and black-and-white America are not our only problems! I see the very best of our young people coming into maturity (nine million will turn 20 this year)...for all the world like kids fresh from a dizzying rollercoaster ride, with everything blurred, nothing clear, with no positive standards, with everything in doubt.

God is over 30 years old. Decency is dirty feet. Love is something you need penicillin for. Wars we don't want, and we elect our presidents with bullets in the violent States of America. There are those who think the next funeral procession will be for our Republic itself; and the "American Dream" will roll up Pennsylvania Avenue behind the roll of drums.

I am sick to death of hearing about the "sickness of the church." We have to get rid of this "old-time image" that church is, where the preacher warns you to "be good" and "be Christian." Too many have no understanding of what being a good Christian really is. Being nice and not doing anything wrong—not sufficient. We're not doing *enough* of something right. How can you argue with second-hand doubt?

We don't know the Scriptures. Most of us just have a little "grab-bag of Bible verses." Not your fault—the blame falls on a culture which has isolated the church from common everyday life, and has secularized education. Christianity is not just a little pleasant weekend diversion. He's the Lord of all, or he's not the Lord a'tall! Perhaps the gospel has to become "bad news" before it can become "good news." Not a disease, but a dis-ease.

The very fact that we can get disturbed is proof of the presence of the grace of God prodding us to search for a *better* way, and to stop being so preoccupied with sweeping the little minor sins off the front steps of the sanctuary, and paying no attention to the huge corporate sins climbin' in through every backdoor and window of pride, prejudice, and power.

I made one of E.C.'s hospital calls for him the other week. I visited a man who doesn't go to church. Comes very rarely. He is one of those for whom "the banquet is set every week, and at the Lord's invitation." But like the song: "I have fields and commitments that cost a pretty sum. / Pray have me excused, I cannot come."[8]

He was glad to see me. We like each other. "Mrs. Rowand," he said, "why is that we have to lie with our toes pointing to the ceiling, before we think of what we're on this earth for?"

There he lay. I didn't know if he would be talking or not. A bottle hung upside down over his bed, food and drink seeping quietly through the needle strapped to his hand. We could hear the sounds outside his door: those insistent calls in hospital corridors for a faceless horde, doctors and dames of mercy, and visitors hurrying up and down. And then he said, "There's one out there. For him, no lock on the door. I know he lurks somewhere. I've never seen him, but lots of my friends have. Know his habit though. He comes without warning."

And I thought, "Dear God, life is more than an *intermission* between two dates on a tombstone. Born 1918, died 1968! 'Be...faithful unto death'—

we're not even faithful unto life!" Glad tidings of great joy "unto you is born this day in the city of David" (Lk. 2:11a)! How many of you know true joyfulness? Even the "haves," with more money than God, can walk into a house where no love is. "Live life. Don't let life live you."

And we're right back to the first and last word: you have to *know* the Savior. Jesus Christ is not available for casual acquaintance. You can't really know somebody by nodding to them politely once a week. Every Sunday of the world, you and I come to this Table. Jesus told us to do it each time we meet: to remember him. When you remember Jesus, what do *you remember?* During communion time, what do you think about?

- Listen to those four verbs he used: he took bread, he blessed it, he broke it, and gave it to them. To me, every week, he takes us (we're the "world," the stuff of life); he blesses us (he says, "I love you"); he breaks us (our little selfishnesses, pettiness, all our sins); and gives us back ("now, use it"). Incredible!

- The one he takes from us Jesus as he was on this earth—not the same as he gives back to us in his resurrected form. *Renewal.* You're supposed to be changed, made different.

- We'll leave here today in a few minutes. When we go out that door, Dallas won't be any different from when we came in. God won't be any different. But you could be. And God working through you could change Dallas.

David Kagiwada

Although born in the United States, David Kagiwada was sent with his parents to a concentration camp for people of Japanese descent, in Arizona during World War II, leaving him with a lifelong commitment to fighting injustice wherever it struck. After realizing his Christian faith was central to his life, he attended seminary, was ordained, and committed to helping reconcile different Asian groups and helping Disciples utilize the gifts of Asian Americans in the church. Rev. Kagiwada was the first convener of Asian American Disciples (now North American Pacific/Asian Disciples). He also encouraged the denomination to recognize the gifts of women. He served as pastor of San Lorenzo Community Church (UCC), California, where this sermon was preached. His later ministry as senior pastor at Crestview Christian Church, Indianapolis, was cut short by his untimely death in 1985. The sermon incorporates typical Disciple influences, focusing on Jesus and the importance of unity amid God's intentional diversity. The supersessionist implication in the middle section, during which he treats ancient Judaism as closed-minded and Christianity as overcoming separations, reminds us the sermon is dated, yet is a helpful example of Kagiwada's ability to speak accessibly to people about issues that could be divisive in 1977, the year he preached this sermon. He uses the NIV.

"Uniting Our Diversities"

Genesis 1:1–5; Ephesians 2:11–18; Luke 3:15–17, 21–22

As I listened to the Old Testament lesson with imagination, I imaged the creation as the process by which God took the void and then began to make differentiations.

First God separated

the heavens and the earth,

then the light and the dark,

the dry land and the sea,

day and night,

plants, those bearing seed and those with seeds inside,

animals: birds of the air, animals on the ground, the fish of the sea,

then humankind: male and female.

The process of creation is the process of differentiating, separating, identifying the variety and multiplicity of creation.

The biblical story halts this process on the seventh day, but if we are open to the idea of a continuing creation–that the world is continuing to grow and to change moment by moment, day by day, year by year–then we could project this dividing and differentiating process ad infinitum. Diversity, multiplicity, differences would be infinite and endless.

To appreciate difference is to celebrate the wonder of creation. God's creation was one which brought about diversity, and with it uniqueness, and that is good. I'm glad that all of you are not alike. If you possessed a quality that I disliked, then I could not stand a single one of you.

If you all possessed a quality that I liked, then that could be too much of a good thing. When it comes to eating chicken, my wife likes dark meat and I like light meat, so we get along fine. The nursery rhyme says, "Jack Sprat could eat no fat; his wife could eat no lean. So together, don't you see, they licked the platter clean!" There is complementary value in differences.

But then, if we are to be realistic, we would have to admit that differences are not always the source of benefit and harmony. According to Genesis 11, which tells the story of the Tower of Babel, differences in tongues become the basis of misunderstanding and lack of communication. Very often, differences, or the inability to accept or resolve differences, become the curse of life. Differences divide and separate people. Differences become the basis for some people's feeling superior to others, and others' feeling inferior. Each culture develops stories of "We're the Best." White people have white supremacy stories. Black people have black supremacy stories. We yellow people have our yellow supremacy stories. The one that I recall from my childhood is how God made humankind. After shaping a human being, God put it into the oven. The first try was underdone–too light; that was the white folks. The second try was overdone–the black people. And, you guessed it; the third try was just right–the yellow people.

In the beginning, differences were meant to be good and to bless, not meant to be bad and to curse; but, so often in the world of our experience, that is not the case. Differences separate, divide, create walls of suspicion and hostility. "They" are not our kind of people.

II

It is interesting, then, to read in the New Testament lesson that the work of Christ is one in which the separations and divisions of the world are overcome. The New Testament lesson refers to the separation of the "circumcised" and the "uncircumcised." This refers to the division of Jew and Gentile as "us" and "them." The Old Testament people of God saw themselves as separated from the rest of God's creation. They were separated based on physical requirements (circumcision), dietary requirements (kosher food), ritual requirements (observance of the Sabbath). A people who were called to be a blessing to all people developed a superiority complex ("We are God's chosen people") and said to everybody else, "Nuts to you." But in Christ, God was acting to overcome these separations–to create unity, oneness, togetherness, community in the midst of the differences and separations of the world. "But now in Christ Jesus you who once were far away have been brought near by the blood of Christ" (Eph. 2:13). The separated are made one. The barriers which divided are overcome.

In the spirit of Christ, God works to restore the harmony, the unity, the balance of all creation, so that the differentiated and separated people can come together. This is not to say that everybody becomes the same, uniform–but there is a spirit of unity, interdependence, community.

This is no easy thing. It is in the cross that this coming together is made possible. The cross suggests that there are misunderstandings to be endured, burdens to be borne, sufferings to be endured. To bear the cross is to be willing to accept some of the "guff" of the world in order that channels might be opened, bridges built.

The Gospels suggest that we participate in this work of the cross. When we are baptized with water, we are declaring ourselves to be Christ's people. In this baptism, we are opening ourselves up to what the gospel calls the baptism of fire: "His winnowing fork is in his hand to clear his threshing floor" (Lk. 3:17a). This is not just an open and all-accepting politeness where everything goes, but it is saying that some things have to be swept off the floor if the house is to be set in order. The wheat is gathered into the barn; the chaff is burned. Under the leading of God's Spirit, there may be some of our pet ideas, habits, and possessions that must go. That is what is involved in this coming together.

III

All of us have a lot of problems with people who are different from us–differing outlooks, different values, different habits. We tend to look for people who are like us rather than different from us. The different, whether it be of age or sex or outlook or race or culture, can be threatening. We find security in similarity. But if anything is real about our world, it is the reality of differences. We can't go and hide out. We must live in a global community, and we have to deal with difference.

We need to deal with differences in our community as we face the matter of deciding its future. What is needed is not necessarily unanimity (thinking all alike), though that might simplify the problems. But what we need is unity–feeling together, feeling oneness in an open and free exchange of ideas, so that whatever we decide is decided on the basis of all feeling that they have been heard. This is unity. So often, decisions are made on the basis of plurality or majority vote, with the minority feeling like losers.

God created differences, but it is not God's will that differences lead to separation. Rather, through Christ, it is God's work to overcome the separations that people feel in the world, which begins with overcoming the separations that we might feel toward God–the source of our being in the universe. Then, God calls us to reconcile the separations that we might feel toward other people. How do we join in this work?

By trying to understand views and ways and people who are different from us. By putting ourselves into settings that might be very different, to see how we react, and trying to understand our own feelings in strange settings. By praying for the unity of all creation–in the name of God's Spirit.

Norman Reed

Norman Reed, a native of Indianapolis, Indiana, is a graduate of Shortridge High School, Purdue University, and Christian Theological Seminary. He was the pastor of Alameda Christian Church, Nashville, Tennessee, for 24 years. He also served as manager of Greenwood Cemetery in Nashville, and is past Moderator of the Christian Church in Tennessee. Rev. Reed currently serves as an Elder at Light of the World Christian Church, Indianapolis, Indiana. He is married to the former May F. Lindsey and father of Lynnette F. Reed (deceased) and attorney Norman L. Reed.

Dr. Reed, an African American preacher, gave this sermon on January 23, 1994, at Alameda Christian Church on what he considered "a normal Sunday." He uses the NKJV. This sermon follows his efforts to preach sermons from time to time "that highlighted what I consider important tenets of Disciple 'polity,' hoping to help parishioners and visitors better understand the Christian Church (Disciples of Christ) and the gospel." In step with Disciple influences, this sermon on Christian unity reminds us of our Disciples history and stresses our attachment to Scripture, even as it admits the difficulty of being one body amidst all our differences. Dr. Reed's focus on the love of God affirms our ability to be one church.

"Can We Be One?"

1 Corinthians 12:12–25

Ask just about any "die hard" member of the Christian Church (Disciples of Christ) and they will tell you that "Christian Unity is our Polar Star." Look at any ecumenical movement and the odds are you will find the Disciples of Christ there. Christian Unity is in our ecclesiastical DNA.

From the very beginning of the Stone-Campbell Movement, Christian unity has been promoted as the will of God for His church. It is recorded in the *Declaration and Address,* a founding document of the Disciples of Christ, authored by Thomas Campbell: "The Church of Christ upon earth is essentially, intentionally and constitutionally one."[1] The Disciples' founding parents adopted this tenet after a thorough reading of the New Testament. The essential unity of the church is a theme that frequently appears in the apostle Paul's writings. Chapter twelve of First Corinthians gives a classic view of the apostle's understanding of unity in the church.

We read in 1 Corinthians 12:12, "For as the body is one and has many members, but all the members of that one body, being many, are one body, so also is Christ." The apostle's favorite image of the church is the body of Christ. Again, in Ephesians 1:22–23 he writes, "He put all things under His feet, and gave Him to be head over all things to the church, which is His body..."

The church is the new incarnation. Just as God was in Christ Jesus revealing Himself to the world, He is now revealing Himself to the world through the church–the body of Christ. The church, the body of Christ, bound together in Christian unity. Christian unity as articulated in Ephesians 4:4–6, "There is one body and one Spirit, just as you [are] called in one hope of your calling; one Lord, one faith, one baptism; one God and Father of all, who is above all, and through all, and in you all."

Jesus prayed to the Father that His disciples, hence the church, might be one. "Now I am no longer in the world, but these [His disciples] are in the world, and I come to You, Holy Father, keep through Your name those whom You have given Me, that they may be one as We are [one]" (Jn. 17:11). Yes, we, the church, are called to be one as the Son and the Father are one. The witness of the New Testament is that the church of Jesus Christ upon the earth is intended to be and constituted to be a united movement.

One might look at the church of Christ upon the earth today and ask the question, "Preacher, can we be one?" Dozens of denominations, mega-congregations trying to be mini-denominations, super-ego pastors seeking to be ecclesiastical czars, and a pervasive spirit of individualism throughout many cultures–can there be a unified church? Eleven o'clock on Sunday morning is still the most segregated hour of the week. Can we be one?

An infinite spectrum of personalities, distorted and exaggerated ethnic differences and fears, an ever-widening economic gulf between the haves and the have-nots, and divisive political and governmental policies causing social schisms everywhere, and yet Jesus still calls for His body, the church, to be one. Can we be one?

How can we be one when parts of the body don't want to be around other parts of the body? Perhaps that was part of the problem in the church at Corinth that Paul was trying to address in the twelfth chapter of 1 Corinthians. We read in verse 15, "If the foot should say, 'Because I am not a hand, I am not part of the body,' is it therefore not part of the body?"

Some parts don't seem to like other parts. In verse 21, the apostle declares, "[T]he eye cannot say to the hand, 'I have no need of you': nor again the head to the feet, 'I have no need of you.'" In other words, the neurosurgeon cannot say to the day laborer, "I have no need of you": nor can the Methodist say to the Presbyterian, "I have no need of you." If the church of Christ upon the earth is to be all that God wants it to be, all believers must work together.

Have you met or known someone who wishes a certain part of their body were different? One says, "My toes are too crooked." Another complains, "My nose is too flat." And yet another sighs, "My lips are too thick." Plastic surgeons and pharmaceutical companies have accumulated fortunes from people who wanted to change their "God-given" appearance. It cannot be healthy for a person to dislike part of their body. After all, God made you like that. Could it be that we are at our healthiest when we learn to be content with how we are made? Likewise, is the church, the body of Christ, healthiest when the members are content with where God has placed them in the "body" and with whom they have been placed?

Paul argues that God has placed the members in His church just as He wants them. First Corinthians 12:18 says, "God has set the members, each one of them, in the body [*the church*] just as He pleased." And I believe He has placed those "members" in the church so that their gifts and talents complement each other. He has put the members together and so constructed the church that the members should work together as a unit to accomplish the work of the ministry. The question remains, "Can we be one?"

With all of these splintered parts, how can we be one? May I suggest that we may become one through the ties that bind us together? Remember the old hymn of the church which says, "Blest be the tie that binds our hearts in Christian love; / The fellowship of kindred minds is like to that above."[2]

I want to suggest three ties that can bind us Christians together and make us one. First is the love of God. One of the basic tenets of Christianity is the truth expressed in John 3:16, "For God so loved the world…He gave His only begotten Son, that whoever believes in Him should not perish but have [eternal] life." We are all beloved creations of God. Knowing that we are loved by the Creator God should inspire us to love Him and one another.

Secondly, we are made one through the blood and sacrifice of Jesus Christ. Listen to the apostle's proclamation in Galatians 4:4–6, "[W]hen the fullness of the time had come, God sent forth His Son, born of a woman, born under the law, to redeem those who were under the law, that we might receive the adoption as sons [and daughters]. And because you are sons [and daughters], God has sent forth the Spirit of His Son into your hearts, crying, 'Abba Father!'" What an awesome thought! God so dearly wants you to be a part of His holy family that He allowed His Son—only begotten Son—to be sacrificed that you/we might believe in Jesus and be adopted into God's family.

Thirdly, we can be one because we are bound together by the power of the Holy Spirit. First Corinthians 12:13 says, "[B]y one Spirit we were all baptized into the body—whether Jews or Greeks, whether slaves or free—and all have been made to drink into one Spirit." The Holy Spirit is at work in us teaching us that we might know and realize the common ground amongst all believers, and would be believers, which should bring all peoples together as one—even as the Father and the Son are one. I believe that the Holy Spirit will enable us to experience "the fellowship of kindred minds" and bring wholeness to fragmented lives.

Can we be one? I believe I hear the Spirit saying, "Yes, only believe; all things are possible."

Are you asking, "It sounds good, but what does it mean for me?" It means that God wants the church of Christ upon earth to be united. This unity cannot be complete until you are in the place God has prepared for you in the church, the body of Christ.

Ronald Osborn

Ronald E. Osborn (1917–1997) was a denominational and ecumenical leader, theological educator, and scholar who received the AB, MA, and MDiv from Phillips University, and the PhD from the University of Oregon. He taught at Northwest Christian University, Christian Theological Seminary, and Claremont School of Theology. Osborn was a leading spirit in the restructure of the Christian Church (Disciples of Christ), and was the first Moderator of its General Assembly (1968). A prolific author, Osborn made a signal contribution to preaching with *Folly of God: The Rise of Christian Preaching,* a history of preaching in the first three centuries C.E.[1]

Osborn, a European American, was a noted preacher. The sermon below is the first in a series on faith, hope, and love (three sermons) from the Regional Assembly of the Christian Church in Oregon in 1997. He uses the NRSV, except as otherwise noted.

This sermon is typical of many in the first wave of the restructured church. It begins with Scripture and broadens into more wide-ranging theological considerations of the theme, including facing squarely a hard theological question raised by the offering of Isaac. While the preacher refers to the Bible, the sermon does not probe the text in great exegetical detail. The sermon is warm and contains engaging illustrations. Osborn invokes an important theme to Disciples, the *rational* nature of faith.

"Faith"

Fly now with me in imagination to the Land between the Rivers, the Tigris and the Euphrates. We call it Iraq, but 4000 years ago it was named Chaldea. Set out with me from the prosperous city of Ur, pushing to the northwest across Syria and into southern Turkey, into the region then called Haran. Make your way with me through the crowded mall, quaintly known as the market square. As people squirm and shove through the crowd, we overhear a conversation.

"Have you heard the latest about Abram?"

"You mean that foreigner who came up here from Ur with old Terah and all his clan? They never seemed at home here. Won't even worship our moon-god… What about Abram?"

"Well, he's leaving Haran just like his old man leaving Ur. Guess he's not happy *here* either, for all his flocks and herds. Says *his* God will show him a better place."

"Yeah? I say, let him go. Good riddance! We have a nice community here in Haran. No need coddling outsiders with their foreign ways. See the bumper sticker on my camel? It's my motto: 'Haran: Love It or Leave It.'"

So at 75 years of age Abram packs his belongings, rounds up his sheep and goats, takes his wife Sarai and his nephew Lot, with Lot's herds, and heads south into the unknown. On that pilgrimage God makes a covenant with the couple, renaming them Abraham and Sarah.

The preacher who gave us the letter to the Hebrews sketched a telling characterization of the patriarch: "By faith Abraham obeyed when he was called to set out for a place that he was to receive as an inheritance; and he set out, not knowing where he was going" (Heb. 11:8).

Because of that faith, Abraham became known as the "friend of God" (Jas. 2:23). (How many friends would you trust as implicitly as Abraham trusted God?) And we are related to him. All who have the kind of faith he acted on, all who "trust and obey," Paul calls "children of Abraham" (Gal. 3:7, KJV).

OK, I can't ignore it any longer! Someone keeps tugging at my sleeve. I'd better see what this is about. The question is: What about Sarah?

Good question! I wish we knew more about her. The people who told the old stories lived in a culture where the men made the decisions and the women's part was normally incidental or subordinate. Marriage was not an equal partnership, as we Christians have come to believe it should be. Even the New Testament commends Sarah for fulfilling the traditional, subservient role, as in 1 Peter 3:6. Because of that traditional mindset, the story-tellers often fail to tell us things we'd like to know about our mothers in the faith. Though we commonly say Abraham-and-Sarah, Isaac-and-Rebekah, Jacob-and-Rachel, we wish we knew more about these women.

At the very least, we know that Sarah went along for the ride. It is safe to say of her what Mark Twain said of the wives of the pioneers: The wives, he observed, put up with everything the pioneers put up with; and besides that they had to put up with the pioneers. Remember that Sarah, too, made the trek from Ur up to Haran and south to Hebron, and the journey was just as long for her as it was for Abraham. We are told that she was a woman of rare beauty, so much so that Abraham feared for his life when some of the desert sheiks cast obvious glances at her–glances both covetous and scheming.

Like our pioneer women, Sarah was strong, honest with herself, and realistic–not always caught up in Abraham's childlike trust. The two of them were old people–older than anyone at your local retirement home; and, when a strange guest announced that she and Abraham would have a son, Sarah laughed. Nevertheless, without resort to a fertility clinic, a son was born, and those two oldsters called him Laughter (the meaning of "Isaac"). Along with *The Jerusalem Bible,* the *Revised English Bible* places Sarah on equal footing with the other great exemplars of faith, translating the confusing Greek of Hebrews 11:11: "by faith even Sarah herself was enabled to conceive, though she was past the age; because she judged that God who had promised would keep faith" (REB).

Clearly, all who live by faith, by trust in God, are children of Abraham and Sarah. Though some of the stories focus on him, he couldn't have done it alone! Both Abraham and Sarah are our ancestors in faith, and we who live by faith are *their* children.

Now, after these stories about their faith, it is time to ask, *What is faith?*

To begin with, faith is trust in God. In commending faith as one great reality that remains, along with hope and love, when all else is gone, Paul is not playing pop psychologist, nor is he a faddish guru peddling a nondescript spirituality of faith in faith. In Paul's thought, as in that of the preacher who wrote Hebrews, faith is the Christian's global positioning system, setting our course—not by directions from a satellite, but by God's will, as best we understand it. It trusts God—and acts accordingly.

There go Abraham and Sarah, "pressing on to the South," looking for the land God has promised. In the desert the herders begin to squabble over water, and Abraham lets his nephew Lot choose the way he wants to go, then takes a different way.

The hardest part of the whole story for me to understand is Abraham's notion that God was commanding him to offer Isaac, the child of promise, as a human sacrifice. Does Sarah know about this? What does she think? With the boy, the old man sets out to climb the slopes of Mt. Moriah. "Father, we don't have an animal for the sacrifice." "Never mind, son. *Jehovah-Jireh* (God, will provide)" (preacher's translation). What do you suppose he means?

The father goes so far as to truss up his little son, the child of promise, and lay him out on the altar. But as he raises his knife for the death stroke, he hears his own name called with urgency: "Abraham! Abraham! Do the child no harm!" Looking about for the source of the voice, he sees a ram caught in a thicket and, taking that as a sign from God, he unbinds his son, offers the ram on the altar—and names the place *Jehovah-Jireh*: "God Will Provide."

The peoples among whom Abraham lived commonly sacrificed one or more of their children to the strange gods they worshiped. And as Abraham had laughed at his little son at play, the awful question had begun to trouble his mind: *Would I honor Yahweh as they honor their god Hadad? Would I sacrifice Isaac to my God?* The conviction seized him that God was prompting him to do this unthinkable thing. Even the author of Hebrews saw the terrible incident as a test of Abraham's faith.

As a Christian, I find it hard to believe that the God revealed in Jesus would ever ask such a horrible thing of any one. The real point of the story—and we must not miss it in any show of piety about taking the Bible literally—the real point is the divine guidance Abraham received to *prevent* the slaughter of Isaac. We must notice too that, from that day on, the Hebrews–the descendants of Abraham, the people of the covenant–abhorred human sacrifice. The God they trusted had taught them another way.

When we lived for a time in Scotland during my boyhood, my father took us down to Musselborough one Sunday, where he was to preach at a little chapel of the fisher folk there on the Firth of Forth. The most impressive man in that congregation was David Ritchie–a tall, brawny, gray-bearded old Scot who every spring had gone out with the fishing fleet, as far as the Grand Banks off Newfoundland, out of touch with home through the long weeks of summer. No mail service. No telephone. No radio powerful enough to reach across the Atlantic. Every fall when the fleet returned, the women and children and men too old to sail anxiously crowded the shore, straining eyes to identify the boat of husband or father or son. On many such an anxious day hearts would turn cold in the realization that one of the boats had gone down at sea.

That Sunday in the little chapel at Musselborough, old David Ritchie stood up to witness to his faith. He spoke the name of his boat. It was *Jehovah-Jireh.* Many of the fishermen were not so godly as Brother Ritchie. They did not know the story of Abraham very well. Now and again a curious sailor or dockhand would look at the transom of his boat, sound out *Jehovah-Jireh,* and ask, "Where'd you get that name? Never heard that one before." Then David Ritchie would tell the story of Abraham and affirm his faith that the Lord will provide.

When we think of Abraham and Sarah setting out for the unknown and of all their spiritual children who walked by faith, pressing on serenely where they believed God was calling, we fix our minds especially on their greatest descendant, the pioneer and perfecter of our faith, who set his face steadfastly to go to Jerusalem–there to suffer rejection, arrest, scourging, and crucifixion–and to die...with a prayer of faith on his lips: "Father, into your hands I commit my spirit" (Lk. 23:46, REB). Faith is our whole-souled response to God's intention for us. It is trust in the Living God, who is supremely to be trusted.

And why do we trust? Because of what Scripture and church tell us about God; the faith that trusts is founded in belief. *Credo,* the Latin word for "I believe," gives us our English words *creed, credible, credit*–all of which suggest solid ground for trust.

Stretch your minds and souls, then, to the great dimensions of biblical faith–faith in God the Creator; faith in Jesus Christ, God's Son; and faith in the Holy Spirit of God, ever with us. Christian faith as taught by the church embraces the fullness of the New Testament witness concerning the One we confess as "Truly Human, Truly Divine." Our faith is not limited to a few scattered items that the Jesus Seminar concludes may be certified with historical assurance about the man Jesus of Nazareth. Rather, it pays close heed to all that the New Testament claims about the Son of God, the *Logos,* the divine Word who became flesh and lived among us, full of grace and truth.

In describing ourselves as non-creedal, even non-theological, because we require only the *Good Confession*–"I believe that Jesus is the Christ, the Son of the living God"–we modern Disciples do a grave injustice to our heritage and to the faith of our founders. When they popularized the slogan "No creed but Christ, no book but the Bible," they made it clear that the term "Christ" is no vacuous, ethereal expression without meaning, but a term given richness of content by the witness of Scripture–prophecy and Psalms and Wisdom and Gospels and Epistles and Revelation. The testimony of all these inspired witnesses is sufficient for our common understanding, faith, and worship, without need for extended theological negotiation or philosophical definition as a basis for the church's life. But they were thoughtful men and women who prized the gift of reason, and they expected faith to be illumined and guided by it. When you come down to it, that is the classic definition of theology: "faith seeking understanding." (Consult St. Augustine and St. Anselm.)

Any true understanding requires the fullness of biblical faith. I have just been working through *The Christian Hymn Book* compiled by Alexander Campbell, Walter Scott, Barton W. Stone, and J.T. Johnson–"Elders of the Christian Church"–and published (second edition) in 1853 at Bethany, Virginia, as *Psalms, Hymns, and Spiritual Songs, Original and Selected.* What has impressed me most about these hymns is their high Christology–an exalted doctrine of Christ derived not from the Council of Nicea or Thomas Aquinas or any of the Reformation theologians, but from the imagery of the New Testament itself.

Remind yourself of the corporate nature of biblical faith. When we think of the content of Christian belief, we confess it with the whole church– through the centuries and around the world. We anchor our souls, not in the peculiar speculations of this thinker or that, no matter how brilliant, but in the consensus of the faithful as set forth in hymn and praise song and Scripture and sacrament and creed.

The first hymnal I remember was called *Hymns of the Faith.* (It had a green cover.) From it we sang "More about Jesus Would I Know," and "Faith of Our Fathers"–which, on Mother's Day, the preacher always made a point of changing to "Faith of our Mothers"–and "'Tis Midnight, and on Olive's Brow," and "My Jesus, I Love Thee." My dear little Grandmother Osborn worked hard in the church, organizing a local auxiliary of Christian Woman's Board of Missions, leading the Children's Temperance League, sponsoring Christian Endeavor, slaving with the Ladies Aid Society, never missing midweek prayer meeting or Sunday services, singing in the choir, sending her son into Christian ministry. When deafness struck her, she could hear not a word of the worship, not a note of the music, not a phrase of the sermon. A woman of intense nervous energy, suffering from arthritis, she found sitting through church a painful ordeal. She grieved to my father about how much she missed the sounds of what had always been the center of her life. He said, "Mom, you know all the church songs by heart. Each morning pick out one as your hymn for the day, and sing it as you go about your work, remembering all the dear people who have sung it with you through the years." So, when we visited her house, we would hear her aged voice singing all day long "Trust and Obey" or "What a Friend We Have in Jesus" or "The Old Rugged Cross." And she was upheld by the faith of the whole church.

Take note of the rational nature of faith. A conviction as to the reasonableness of the Christian religion is an important ingredient in Disciples thought. Our religious movement came on the scene after the Enlightenment, and we strive to love God with all our mind as well as all our heart. On the frontier, our preachers engaged the minds of their hearers so intently that emotional evangelists from the camp meetings accused us of having head-religion instead of heart-religion. We accepted the charge as a compliment.

I take personal pride in wearing the button of the Disciples Society for Faith and Reason, an honor awarded us who have spent our lives in Christian Higher Education. I like the way Fred Craddock puts the issue of thought and emotion: "[F]aith is not generated by an experience of being overwhelmed but by gaining clarity about the true meaning of scripture."[2] Let me add that, when we understand, we may well be overwhelmed.

Think of the contribution of our people to education in this state— Pleasant Hill Academy, Oregon Christian College at Monmouth. (You can still read that name on the cornerstone of the old red brick building on the campus of the state school.) Recall Prince Lucien Campbell, first president of the University of Oregon; scholars like Victor P. Morris and Grace Morris and Ray Hewitt, who served both the academy and the church with distinction; Ross J. Griffeth and all who through the years have led Northwest Christian College toward the maturity it is achieving today led by President James Womack, Dean Song-Nai Rhee, and faculty. Keep in mind the personal nature of biblical faith. We confess a *person,* Jesus the Christ, whom the church proclaims and we love and follow. Personal commitment, not confessing this or that,…but *Him,* is the primary ingredient of biblical faith: "My Faith Looks Up to *Thee.*"

We conclude by reflecting on faith as faithfulness. From two Latin adjectives, which describe those traits, we have formed our words, *piety* and *fidelity. Piety* really means faithfulness, devotion, allegiance. *Fidelity* occurs in the motto of the United States Marines, *Semper Fi.*

Remember when President Reagan visited the hospital to cheer our service people wounded in action. As he sought to encourage one Marine who was in bad shape, the young man gave the president thumbs up and whispered *"Semper Fi"*–"ever faithful."

Recall the haunting refrain that ran through Judy Dyer's song, the theme of last year's Sesquicentennial Convention at Pendleton, celebrating 150 years of our Disciples life and witness in Oregon: "Oh, may all who come behind us find us faithful. May the fire of our devotion light their way." Our pioneers sang that in our historical pageant, and, in their honor, we sang it as our prayer for ourselves. Look out with me now across the hills of time. Can you see that man and woman tramping slowly to the south? Listen closely! Abraham and Sarah are singing that song! And that strapping lad striding along after them–Isaac is singing it too!

When all is said and done, what's left? There are three things that last forever: faith, hope, and love,...and the first of these is faith. That's what really matters.

Ah, yes! May all who come behind us find us faithful!

Michael Kinnamon

Michael Kinnamon–well-known Disciples teacher, scholar, and leader in the ecumenical movement–holds an AB from Brown University and a PhD from the University of Chicago Divinity School. He served on the staff of the World Council of Churches and as General Secretary of the National Council of Churches in the USA. He was on the faculty of Christian Theological Seminary, served as Dean and Professor of Theology at Lexington Theological Seminary, and is a frequent speaker at Disciples conferences and assemblies. In addition, he is a popular speaker in interfaith and ecumenical settings. Rev. Kinnamon is European American. His books include *The Vision of the Ecumenical Movement and How It Has Been Impoverished by Its Friends,*[1] *Disciples: Reclaiming Our Identity, Reforming Our Practice*, with Jan Linn,[2] *Can a Renewal Movement Be Renewed? Questions for the Future of Ecumenism,*[3] and *The Witness of Religion in an Age of Fear.*[4] Typical of Dr. Kinnamon's ethical and theological foci, this sermon was preached at a community-wide, ecumenical service for the Week of Prayer for Christian Unity, in January 2001 in St. Louis. John 14:6 was the focal text for that year's observance. He uses the NRSV. The specific Disciples themes of the role of Jesus Christ and the place of other faiths are investigated with insights from biblical interpretation and events from our denominational history.

"Bold Humility"

John 9:1–41

Let's start with a bold statement: The single biggest theological challenge facing the church in our era is not human sexuality, but how to understand the place of other faiths (Jews, Muslims, Buddhists, Hindus, Bahais) in God's plan of salvation. It goes without saying that we, Christians, are to treat every neighbor, of whatever faith, with compassion as a child of God. But how are we to understand the relationship they have to the God we have known in Jesus Christ?

In the late 1980s, a group within my denomination, the Christian Church (Disciples of Christ), brought a resolution to our General Assembly asking the church to declare that unless people confess Christ as their savior, commit their lives to him, they cannot be saved (forgiven, reconciled to God). After all, said the authors of the resolution (and on this they were correct), this is what the church has generally taught for most of its history. And for support, the resolution cited two scriptural passages: Acts 4:12 ("There is salvation in no one else, for there is no other name under heaven given among mortals by which we must be saved.") and our key text for this year's Week of Prayer for Christian Unity, John 14:6 ("I am the way, and the truth, and the life. No one comes to the Father except through me.").

The issues raised by John 14 are always important, but especially so now that we live in ever closer proximity to Jewish and Muslim and Buddhist neighbors. What witness are we to make to them? Do we affirm them as they are? Do we call them to Christ for the sake of their salvation? Do we live and let live? If we are convinced, as I suspect many of us are, that God is present in other religious communities, then what sense are we to make of these more exclusive parts of Scripture? Let's look at the text.

John's Gospel gives us a picture of a church facing persecution. The community to which this Gospel is addressed had apparently been part of the synagogue; but, at some point, its members were thrown out because of their conviction that Jesus is the Messiah, the Incarnation of the living God. John's Gospel, of course, doesn't report this as history, but rather incorporates this later conflict as part of its narrative about Jesus.

In chapter 9, for example, Jesus heals a person born blind. The Pharisees investigate the report of this healing by interrogating the person's parents. Do you remember the story? If so, you may remember that the parents are evasive because, according to the text, they are afraid of the Jews "for the Jews had already agreed that anyone who confessed Jesus to be the Messiah would be put out of the synagogue."

Such exclusion, however, didn't happen at the time of Jesus. We know from the rest of the New Testament that the early Christians had access to the synagogue; several passages talk about their going there daily to pray. No, the intense hostility between church and synagogue only appears toward the end of the first century, about the time that John's Gospel was being put in its present form. It was around the end of the first century, for example, that the Jewish community, itself under persecution, added the following words to its daily prayer: "May the Nazarenes (the followers of Jesus of Nazareth) and the heretics perish quickly; and may they be erased from the Book of Life"!

Given this, it is hardly surprising that John's Gospel contains harsh references to the Jews—some of which, we need to say it honestly, have been used to justify anti-Semitism down to the present. And it's also not surprising that John has explicit words of assurance for this beleaguered group of disciples.

Chapter 14, on which we are focusing, is the beginning of what is often called the "farewell discourse": Jesus' taking leave of his followers. This leave-taking gets lengthy attention in John, unlike the other three Gospels, because, I suspect, this community felt so abandoned. The text is filled with words of consolation that we don't find in Matthew, Mark, or Luke: "Do not let your hearts be troubled... I go to prepare a place for you... I will come again [to] take you to myself, so that where I am, there you may be also" (14:1a, 2b, 3b). Do you hear the message? You are not alone! You are not forgotten! You are loved! Despite present persecution, you will be saved!

Now comes a question from our skeptical ancestor, Thomas. (If Thomas were an American, he would be from Missouri: "Show me" the marks.) In this case, he complains: "We [don't even] know where you are going, [so] how can we know the way?" To which Jesus replies (you can say it with me), "I am the way, and the truth, and the life" (Jn. 14:5–6). To put it another way, the one I call Father, the one God of heaven and earth, is revealed in me. Thus, if you would have life with God, trust in me.

I was for several years on the staff of the World Council of Churches; and, I know from my experience with the World Council that these verses in John 14 are heard as very good news by Christians who are today facing their own times of persecution. I heard a sermon on this text in Bangladesh, where Christians make up a tiny fraction of the population. I heard a sermon on this text in the Evangelical Lutheran Christmas Church in Bethlehem. And I have heard this passage preached on in African American congregations in this country.

As you may know, the theme for each year's celebration of the Week of Prayer is selected by some local working group, and it's not at all surprising that the theme for this year, based on John 14:6, was chosen by a group of Protestants, Catholics, and Orthodox in Romania–where Christians, in the years after the Second World War, lost almost all their land, their schools, their hospitals, and where they were not allowed to build new churches. The Catholic Church in Romania suffered particularly harsh treatment at the hands of the Communist government. That church was totally banned, many of its clergy imprisoned or killed, and its property confiscated–which is why a papal visit to Romania in May of 1999 was so pastorally important. From Pope John Paul II–and from John's Gospel–the church in Romania heard the wonderful news: You are not alone! You are not forgotten! You are loved! Despite persecution, you will be saved!

This next part needs to be said carefully. There have been many times when the LGBTQAI community in the church needed to hear–in many places, still needs to hear–this good news: You are not alone. You are not forgotten. There have been many times when the black community needed to hear, still needs to hear, this comforting, uplifting word. But speaking now about "mainline" Christians as a whole, we are not a persecuted church; and, when we use this language, it can sound very different. A few years ago, *The Disciple* magazine, our national journal, included a letter to the editor with these words: "The Mahatma Gandhis and Elie Wiesels of the world may merit praise, but until they confess Christ as God's Son, and perform their good deeds in his name, they have no promise of eternal life with God, because, as Jesus said, 'I am the way, and the truth, and the life.

No one comes to the Father except through me.'" This is not the blessed assurance that God is with us. This is a triumphal assuredness that God is with *us* only. And there is a very big difference.

This leads me to the most important part of this sermon. My former colleague at Christian Theological Seminary, Clark Williamson, has helped me see that there are two prominent themes running throughout Scripture that must be held in tension. What we might call the "reassurance theme" reminds us that God loves us in a special way. From Exodus: "I will redeem you with an outstretched arm and…mighty acts of judgment. I will take you as my people, and I will be your God"(6:6b–7a). But alongside this is what might be called the "prophetic theme," which reminds us that God loves our neighbors in a special way–and that, too, is good news. From Amos: "Yes, I brought you up from the land of Egypt. But didn't I also bring the Philistines from Caphtor and the Arameans from Kir?" (9:7b, preacher's paraphrase). "Are you not like the Ethiopians to me?" (9:7a).

The prophetic theme without the reassurance theme says to the community that God loves *others,* but not us. The reassurance theme without the prophetic theme says that God loves *us,* but not others. Neither of these, by itself, is good news; but, taken together, they enable us to live with bold humility: bold in our proclamation that Jesus is the way, the truth, and the life, that in him the Creator is truly revealed–but humble in our confession that we are God's, not that God is ours. And that it is up to God's wise mercy to decide who is saved. Our task, our privilege, is to witness to what we know: that in Jesus Christ we see revealed the nature and purpose of God, which is not to divide people but to reconcile those who are estranged, to heal that which is broken.

I will end by going back to that resolution submitted to the Disciples General Assembly that I mentioned earlier in the sermon. The Disciples will never approve such a resolution, in large part because it sounds like a creed; and, as you may know, Disciples are allergic to creeds! But our General Assembly didn't want simply to dismiss it–they could imagine headlines like "Disciples vote no on Jesus"–so they asked a commission I was on to study the resolution and bring back a report. Doesn't that sound like a typical Protestant thing to do?!

As one of the authors of that report, I got hate mail about it for years; but I still like what we said. For one thing, we urged the church to keep in mind that Acts 4:12 and John 14:6 are not the only portions of the Bible that speak to such matters. Think, for example, of the parable of the good Samaritan, in which Jesus, in response to the question, "What must I do to inherit eternal life?" tells the story of this complete outsider who helps the neighbor by the side of the road. Or, think of the separation of the sheep and the goats in Matthew 25, where the criterion of judgment is not, "Did you confess my name?" but, "What did you do for the least of these?"

According to Matthew, Jesus even declares, in the Sermon on the Mount: "Not everyone who says to me, 'Lord, Lord,' will enter the kingdom of heaven, but only the one who does the will of my Father in heaven" (7:21).

But beyond that, the essential logic of the New Testament, we argued in the report, is not that only Christians are saved, but that *even* we are included in the gracious, redemptive love of God. I don't know how God relates to Muslims or Hindus; but, I have reason to pray that God will be merciful to them, just as the God who was in Christ has been merciful even to me. Will this approach heal the rift within Christianity over the place of other faiths in God's plan of salvation? Probably not. But it may go a long way toward healing the rift between Christians and other children of our gracious Creator.

Bold humility: Bold in our witness that Jesus is the way, the truth, and the life; humble in our love because the divine grace we see in Christ is far greater, far wider, than we can ever imagine.

This, I confess, is the gospel! Thanks be to God!

Lisa Davison

The Christian Church legacy of feminist scholarship and scholars includes our next sermon contributor, Lisa W. Davison (1966–). Rev. Davison is a member of the Forrest-Moss Institute (an association of Disciples women scholars formed in the early 1990s), the Society of Biblical Literature, and the Association of Disciples for Theological Discussion. She is the Johnnie Eargle Cadieux Professor of Hebrew Bible at Phillips Theological Seminary. A native of Radford, Virginia, Davison has earned degrees from Lynchburg College (BA), Brite Divinity School (MDiv), and Vanderbilt University (MA and PhD in Hebrew Bible). She has previously held professorships at Lexington Theological Seminary and Lynchburg College. She also has served congregations in Texas and Kentucky. Dr. Davison is European American.

The following sermon was delivered on July 25, 2005, at the Disciples General Assembly in Portland, Oregon. She uses the NRSV. The theme of the meeting was "Jesus Calls Us." At this assembly, Sharon Watkins was elected General Minister and President, the first woman to serve in this capacity. How would the church be formed with this historic presence at the helm? Davison brings her expertise in Hebrew Bible–the Prophets especially–to this question, asking: To what ministry is the *denomination,* not just a new General Minister and President, called in particular? Davison answers with themes of social justice in our time and a call to an active ministry of all believers.

"To What Ministry Are We Called?"

Isaiah 61:1–9

It was not at all like they had imagined it would be. For decades, the exiles in Babylon had dreamed about finally being allowed to return home to Jerusalem. Prophetic voices had promised them a glorious return, painting pictures of dry bones coming to life and a great highway leading them home. But when Cyrus of Persia issued the edict that freed them from exile, what they found in the city was anything but glorious. The walls of the city had been destroyed in the attack by the Babylonian armies. Their homes had been inhabited by others. They had no land, and their jobs were gone. Worst of all, their place of worship, the beloved Temple built by Solomon, lay in ruins. Instead of a wonderful homecoming celebration, they were faced with desolation. They were strangers in their own land. Disappointed and discouraged, some returnees must have envied their friends and family who had remained in Babylon, where at least they had a life and a livelihood. With the remains of the once great city of Jerusalem at their feet, all they could think about was the work that needed to be done. The dominant concern was to get the Temple and the city walls rebuilt as soon as possible, to have at least some sense of security. But where would they get the resources for the construction? Not only was their city in shambles, but so was the community. There were divisions among them, arguments about how to start and who would be in charge. It seemed utterly hopeless.

Out of the laments of mourning and despair, a voice declared: *ruach 'adonai 'elohim 'alay*: "The spirit of the Lord GOD is upon me!" (Isa. 61:1a). A prophet stepped out from among the people and proclaimed words of encouragement. Without denying their pain and disillusionment, this messenger of God was called to preach release, freedom, healing, and hope. These promises of God, spoken by the prophet, were indeed good news. After having lost their land and their dignity, the idea of no longer laboring to benefit others must have been a powerful dream. But the prophet not only proclaimed restoration of property but also restoration of responsibility. Like strong trees, this new community would stand as a testament to the God whom they worshiped and served so that one day, soon, all other nations would look to them and to their future generations and recognize that they were a people blessed by God, that through them others would be blessed. This was just the motivation the people needed to begin the process of rebuilding their city and their lives. But the impact of these words would not end there, for this mission was not for the prophet alone. The spirit of God also had anointed the whole community to fulfill this call to make the messages of release, healing, freedom, and hope a reality. As with all authentic prophecy, these words from Isaiah 61 continue to call future generations to ministry even unto today.

"Tell us about your call to ministry?" This is the most frequently asked question of seminary students. I remember all too well the day the question was asked of me during an ordination interview. Oh, how I had wanted to tell some great story of a burning bush or of hearing a voice saying: "Who will go for us?" Unfortunately, that would have been a lie; yet somehow my experience of just feeling "drawn to ministry" did not seem too impressive. The idea of "call" is an important concept in the church. We read stories in the Bible about people who experienced a divine invitation. God's call, though, is experienced not just by those preparing for ordination or by those being asked to lead slaves out of Egypt. God calls all of us to participate in ministry in many ways. Tonight, the youth have shared some of their experiences of hearing God's call in their lives, and I'm sure each of you has experiences you can share. So rather than asking, "Are you called to ministry?" the more important question that needs to be asked is: "To what ministry are you called?"

I imagine this question was on the minds of those from Jesus' hometown, when he first showed up claiming to be called by God. Sitting in the synagogue before what was essentially his own "ordination committee," Jesus turned to the words of an ancient prophet, found in Isaiah 61, to explain the ministry God had called him to do. As those who proclaim Jesus to be the Christ of our lives and who seek to follow his example, this text should be the place where we go to answer the question: "To what ministry are we, the Christian Church (Disciples of Christ), called by God?

Much like the ancient audience for whom the words of Isaiah 61 were originally spoken, we, the Christian Church (DOC), are in a familiar, but new, place. We have experienced exile, loss, broken hearts, and uncertainty about the future. For quite some time now, it has seemed like we have worn the ashes of mourning and despair. As a denomination, we have lost numbers, and money seems to be an ever-dwindling resource. Like those who faced rebuilding Jerusalem, many of us feel that our beloved church has suffered the brunt of attack, and we wonder if it's even possible to rebuild it so that this denomination will be around for more than another generation. One possible response to this situation would be for us to seek protection by building walls that keep us safe, with sure answers and the confidence that we alone have the truth. Another possibility would be for us to be like the exiles who remained in Babylon because it was comfortable, and try to fade into the religious backdrop, losing our identity to be just like everyone else.

Or, we can respond by heeding the prophet's call in Isaiah 61—whose message was not a call to grasp at security or to embrace uniformity. These were words of challenge, risk, and service. Is not the message still relevant for us today? At the 2003 General Assembly, meeting in Charlotte, North Carolina, a modern-day prophet—the Rev. Dr. Peter Gomes—spoke a similar message to the Christian Church (DOC). As an outsider, Gomes described what he saw as the uniqueness of the Christian Church (DOC). He talked about how this denomination had always been a leader, showing the Church a new way. But he also warned that if we Disciples keep trying to blend into the landscape, then we would deserve whatever troubles came our way. And we have had our troubles.

Now is the time to reclaim our uniqueness and to fulfill our call to ministry, to bring into reality the ideas described in Isaiah 61. The Gospel writers tell us how Jesus fulfilled this call to ministry, but what would it look like if we, the Christian Church (Disciples of Christ), were to do so today? Who are the oppressed who need to hear good news? Where are the broken hearts that need our binding? Who are the captives that need to be liberated? Where are the ones who need to be released from the things that keep them imprisoned? Who needs to hear a word about the Lord's favor? Is this not the ministry to which we are called? What would this call to ministry require of us in this time and in this place of exile?

The Spirit of the Lord is upon us to preach good news to those who are oppressed! For those oppressed by unjust economic systems that penalize working single-moms because the cost of daycare is too high for them to afford on their salary, we can work to make a living wage a reality, not just a resolution we approve. On behalf of those oppressed by political systems that protect the rights of the powerful few while exploiting the powerless, we can demand that all votes are counted in elections. For those oppressed by the high cost of health care that forces them to choose between food and medicines, their children's education and a life-saving operation, we must risk increased taxes to ensure that all of God's people have health insurance.

The spirit of the Lord GOD is upon us to bind up the broken hearts in our world! For, hearts broken by dishonesty in relationships where covenantal trust has been shattered, we can offer the balm of compassion. To the hearts broken by the diagnoses of loved ones with terrible diseases that seem to defy treatment, much less healing, we can provide the dignity of hospice care and ensure that all avenues of medical research are pursued. On behalf of the hearts broken by abuse at the hands of those who were supposed to protect them from harm, we can provide safe places for them to go and find security

The spirit of the Lord GOD is upon us to declare liberty for the captives! For those enslaved by systems that discriminate based on differences in physical abilities, religion, sex, and race, we can support policies that ensure fair hiring practices and protect against discrimination of any kind. On behalf of those enslaved by addictions to power, money, drugs, and anything else that dulls the pain of feeling unloved, we can work for better educational opportunities, compassionate treatment centers, and provide them with a sense of self-worth. For those enslaved by the pandemic of AIDs, unable to get the treatment that will save their lives, we can demand that our government not only give adequate financial relief but also support the providing of condoms and the education on how to prevent the spread of this horrible disease.

The spirit of the Lord GOD is upon us to proclaim release to the imprisoned! To those imprisoned by the fear to be who God created them to be, we can work for laws that enlarge the definition of hate crimes and for fairness ordinances throughout the country. For those imprisoned by others who say that they are not created in the image of God, but are inherently flawed, an abomination because of whom they love, we can acknowledge such language as spiritual violence and no longer tolerate such hateful behavior in the name of "Christian love."

To respond to this call to ministry, we will have to take off our mourning clothes, tear down our walls of security, and take the risk of being unique.

We, as individuals and as a church, will stand strong and tall, like trees planted by God, giving witness to the God whom we worship and serve. Our future will not be one of foreign occupation or despair but of hope and promise. Then, all peoples of the world will look at the Christian Church (DOC) today and in the future, and they will recognize us to be a church blessed by God.

Indeed, already many have responded to this call. On June 12 of this year, First Christian Church in Radford, Virginia, my home congregation, was the victim of arson which did over a quarter of a million dollars' worth of damage. Within 24 hours, the church received a check from Week of Compassion. The trustees in charge of dispersing the funds left from the closing of Hanover Christian Church in Richmond, Virginia, sent a $1,200 check. Fort Lewis Christian Church in Salem, Virginia, donated $1,000 for the restoration of the nursery school rooms that were destroyed in the fire. The spirit of the Lord is at work binding up broken hearts in Virginia.

As of this assembly, at least 68 Disciples of Christ congregations have taken a stand for justice by identifying themselves as Open & Affirming. They have risked condemnation by other churches to provide a place where all of God's children are truly welcome. These congregations have faced protests by Fred Phelps and others like him, so that everyone will know that theirs is a church that celebrates the beautiful diversity of God's creation. The spirit of the Lord is at work in these churches proclaiming liberty and release to the captives.

Instead of going to the water park or the zoo, 260 youth and adults participated in mission opportunities around Portland today. Overcoming what is for some a very real fear of needles and passing out, we collected 120 pints of blood during this assembly. That is 360 lives saved. The spirit of the Lord is at work here in Portland preaching good news to the oppressed.

This is only a beginning. Church, there is so much more to be done in responding to this call to ministry.

"Ruach 'adonai 'elohim 'aleynu"..."The spirit of the Lord GOD is upon *us* all!" May the words of the prophet Isaiah be fulfilled in our living!

Delores C. Carpenter

African American Disciples pulpits, like Eurocentric ones, were primarily male in the first decades included in this volume. However, some women have always been in the pulpit, including Delores C. Carpenter (1944–) who received a call to ministry at age 14 and first preached at age 16.[1]

Delores Carpenter received a BA from Morgan State University, a MDiv from Howard University School of Divinity, and an ED from Rutgers University. She served simultaneously as Professor of Religious Education at Howard University School of Divinity and as Senior Minister of Michigan Park Christian Church (Disciples of Christ) in Washington, D.C. Among her many publications is *A Time for Honor: A Portrait of African American Clergywomen.*[2]

On the Sunday mornings of General Assemblies, Disciples preachers typically fill local pulpits. Dr. Carpenter initially preached "God's Female Activists" in this role as part of the 2007 General Assembly in Fort Worth, Texas. She uses the NRSV. This preacher uses three biblical women as paradigms of God's working through women to bring liberation. Such activism involves risk and danger, but, just as God empowered biblical women, so God empowers women for personal and social transformation today.

"God's Female Activists"

I have draped my windows with praise, covered my walls with faith, carpeted my floor with gratitude, and filled every corner of my room with prayer. I have sat upon the cushion of confidence, leaned in the recliner of hope, and stretched out on the bed of trust. And today, while others have dropped out or fallen out, we have walked out into the kingdom of God.

Therefore, I will not hesitate at the hint of adversity, negotiate at the table of the enemy, meander in the maze of mediocrity, or ponder at the pool of popularity. I am a part of the fellowship of the unashamed, and a disciple of Jesus Christ. Jesus is the Way, the Truth, and the Life. Without the Way, there would be no going. Without the truth, there would be no knowing. And without the Life, there would be no growing.

Deborah. Abigail. A woman we know as the woman who had a flow of blood. What do these three women have in common? One an older, widow woman; one a married woman; and one an unnamed woman on her own in the text. Each is sent by God to use her gifts for the salvation of the nation, her family-tribe, and herself. Each receives an important affirmation, which leads to a rich reward—the reward of faith. Faith always calls upon us to act—to be God's activists.

Let us turn to Judges 4:8. "Barak said to her, 'If you will go with me,
I will go; but if you will not go with me, I will not go.' And she said, 'I
will surely go with you; nevertheless, the road on which you are going
will not lead to your glory, for the LORD will sell Sisera into the hand of a
woman'"(4:8–9).

We find that devoted Deborah was a woman of public dignity and
supreme authority. She was not always a judge and prophet. She had been
the keeper of the tabernacle lamps, but God elevated her to become the
superintendent of a new vision that was to light up all Israel. She trusted
God and inspired others to trust in God. Unafraid of Sisera and his 900
chariots, when fear and complacency gripped Israel, she alone became a
military advisor. She reminded Barak that God would rescue Israel. She
sensed a common danger and kindled an enthusiasm for an immediate
action. She, unlike others of her day, was not frozen in what MLK called,
"the paralysis of analysis." She got up and did something about it.

Where did she get such optimism and faith? Well, we know that she
was a singer; she had heard and sung Miriam's song "Pharaoh's army got
drowned in the Red Sea." She knew that if God could deliver her people
from so mighty a ruler as Pharaoh, surely God could deliver them now.
Deborah said to Barak, "I will surely go into battle with you, for the battle
is not yours; it's the Lord's" (preacher's paraphrase). She told the army
what day to go to battle. She was the wakeup call for the camp. She was the
weather forecaster. She shouted that morning, "Wake up, get up and out of
here! This is the day the Lord has given you the victory" (4:14, preacher's
paraphrase). And a storm of hail and sleet burst over the plain, beating
cold rain into the faces of the enemy. At the same time, flood water rushed
down the Kishon River. The enemy chariots got stuck in the mud. Sisera
dismounted and ran for cover. A woman, named Jael, welcomed him into
her tent. She proceeded to drive a stake through his head; thus, Deborah's
prophecy was fulfilled.

Deborah did not take credit for the victory. She wrote a new song,
called Deborah's song. It was much like Miriam's song, only she added,
"To God be the glory, great things he has done."[3]

Let us shift now to the second passage, 1 Samuel 25:32. "David said
to Abigail, 'Blessed be the LORD, the God of Israel, who sent you to meet
me today! Blessed be your good sense, and blessed be you, who have kept
me today from bloodguilt and from avenging myself by my own hand!'"
(25:32–33).

We find determined Abigail, a woman of good understanding. She
admonished David and contributed to his becoming the greatest king
of Israel. Abigail was a beautiful woman, but she was married to a rude,
drunken husband. They were not a good match, but Abigail was patient
in a bad situation. Being married to an alcoholic resulted in her becoming

the first diplomat in the Bible. Nabal, her husband, was a wealthy man. Perhaps she had married him for his money, but her story exposes the truth that a rich husband is not always a good husband. But Abigail endured her situation. And God blessed her mightily in the end. Won't God do it?

David had been living in the hills, a renegade from King Saul. He had put together a fierce army of 300 men, a motley crew. Having lived far from conversation for so long, he had lost most of the social graces which he had learned in Saul's court. David was running wild in the mountains, killing everything in sight. We must understand that although Samuel had anointed him king, it took him many years to become King David.

Now Nabal was a big businessman down in Mt. Carmel. He had sheep grazing down the backside of the hill where David's army was camped. When shearing time came, David was running low on food, so he sent a delegation to request that Nabal send them some of the leftovers after the big feast of shearing. But Nabal, in a drunken state, denied David's request. Nabal asked, "Who is David? These hills are filled with upstarts and renegades from the king's palace" (1 Sam. 25:10, preacher's paraphrase).

Such a response threw David into an angry fit. David was especially angry since, all year, he had protected Nabal's sheep from invasion and slaughter by foreigners. He had given protection to Nabal, and now Nabal had the audacity to refuse his request and to disregard him, the epitome of ingratitude. David called for the annihilation of Nabal's family and village. David declared that he would lead the effort to wipe out the family, so that not one man would be left alive by the morning.

In the meantime, Abigail, upon hearing through the servants what Nabal had said, moves into action. Watch her when one of the servants goes to her and tells her of the conversation between her husband and David's emissaries. Abigail does not wait to ask her husband's permission. She initiates crisis intervention—asking for two hundred loaves of bread, five sheep, and sufficient grain, wine, raisins, and figs to feed an army. She makes up her mind that she will try to intercept David, already having figured out that his wrath is soon to follow. Imagine now—she is coming one way, and David another. Fortunately, they meet up. When they do—watch a skilled diplomat at work. She gets off the animal she is riding and gets on her knees. She commences to say things that David has not heard in a long time—things of his great destiny.

> I know who you are David, you are a prince in Israel. The hand of the Lord is on your life. Please do not slaughter my husband's family. He was drunk and did not know what he was saying. You are a better man than to kill all the innocent people in our camp. Stop and think about what you are about to do. Guilt-blood will be forever on your hands. Now you don't want that, do you? (excerpts from 1 Samuel 25, preacher's paraphrase)

And by the time Abigail finished complimenting David and apologizing for her husband, David goes to complimenting her. "Blessed are your good sense and you. Thank you for talking some sense into me. Go to your house in peace. I grant your petition" (1 Sam. 25:33a, 35b, preacher's paraphrase).

Back at home, a few months later, Nabal dies. We don't know exactly how, but I figure that when he woke up the next day and was informed of how he dealt with David's request, he had a stroke from fear of the danger to which he had exposed his family and servants. At any rate, David never forgot Abigail, and as soon as he learns of her husband's death, he sends for her. He couldn't forget how she was sent by God to him. And when she comes, "sistas," she does not come empty-handed. She places all Nabal's wealth at his disposal. David is never the same again. Through Abigail, he went from a poor, rough, cursing renegade toward becoming the king of Israel. Abigail gave him renewed hope and a new self-understanding.

Oh, it's a wonderful thing to be sent by God on a mission of salvation and transformation! After revival, I want to be an activist.

Now we turn attention to our final example, in Mark 5:34. "He said to her, 'Daughter, your faith has made you well; go in peace, and be healed of your disease.'"

The woman with the issue of blood comes up behind Jesus and touches the hem of his garment, for she said, "If I can but touch the hem of his garment, I know I'll be made whole." (Mk. 5:28, preacher's paraphrase). The crowd was pressing in, but Jesus stops what he is doing and says, "Somebody touched me. Power has gone out of me." No longer content to stay home and hemorrhage, this woman got up, and went to find Jesus—sent by her own faith in God's goodness and God's ability to heal her body. She has so emptied herself and allowed faith to fill her that she was able to pull down the power of God. She was able to reach inside the essence of Jesus and snatch her blessing, without the help of any mortal. She did it all on her own (with God's help).

But there was a problem. The woman thought she could keep her healing a secret, but not so. There are no closet Christians. Jesus demands the public recognition of this woman. She not only identifies herself, but also tells her story—the whole story. Jesus asks her to tell the truth, the whole truth. Jesus demands the same of us—if we don't tell the whole story, God can't get all the glory. Jesus wants us to tell all—trials great and trials small! Some privacy and confidentiality are necessary, but too much causes us to hide the goodness of God. This woman's story can be added to others of faith, and so can yours and mine, if we are open to reveal our private healings.

Also, notice Jesus was not disturbed that the woman got in the power line and… drained him. I wonder why? I'm glad you asked. It is because Jesus knew the source of his power. And that source is inexhaustible. That's why I believe in the creation of new power. People-to-people power is the best kind of power. We don't have to worry about running out! Jesus was on his way to healing Jairus' daughter, and they were upset that Jesus was taking time with this woman while the child was dying—and, in fact, *did* die before he arrived. But Jesus didn't cancel his trip because it was delayed. He simply raised the girl from the dead. How could he do this? Because he knew how to replenish his power. Jesus was such an expert on power that he said, "All power is given unto me in heaven and in earth." (Matthew 28:18, KJV). And Jesus still has all the power we will ever need to get the job done. It makes this woman's witness even more precious. Never before in the Scripture had the title "Daughter of Abraham" been used. She receives this great affirmation, "Beloved Daughter." It is another version of God's pleasure, as shown to Jesus at the time of his baptism. Instead of, "Thou art my beloved Son, in whom I am well pleased" (Mk. 1:11, KJV), the text is shouting, "Thou art my beloved daughter, in whom I am well pleased." God is always pleased when we exercise faith. Do you know that you have more power than you realize? It was her faith that made her whole. Let's ask God to help us to walk every day—not by sight, but by faith! Sometimes faith is sneaking up behind Jesus and touching the hem of his garment.

Three women—all three activists, all risk takers. There were no guarantees that things would work out in each case. Each was willing to exercise a drastic measure. Each had to struggle with the vision of what God wanted them to do. Once the vision was in view, they acted decisively and quickly. They were faithful to the task. Each rose in the midst of a crisis—national for Deborah, family for Abigail, and personal for the woman with the issue of blood. Each realized that, in every danger, there is an opportunity. They all had power or access to power. Deborah lent her power to Barak and Abigail hers to David. The unnamed woman tapped into the power of Jesus. This teaches us that our spiritual gifts are not for us, but for the benefit of others.

To be called and sent by God is itself a dangerous thing. It means we are willing to participate in the solution of problems. It means that we stand for truth in a world of deception. It means we become the conscience and faith of a nation. Spiritual gifts used in conjunction with spiritual fruit are God's way of using us to bring the kingdom of God to earth, as it is in heaven. Whatever faith you have come prepared to consecrate before the Lord today, remember these three women.

May they inspire you to be active, agitating, and reconciling; reaching out; creating and giving away the new power of faith. As you go, remember the sick, the hungry, the poor, the lowly, the castaways, and the throwaways, abandoned babies and the elderly frail, the homeless and the lonely, and twelve-year-olds dropping out of school.

As you go, remember the three affirmations of these biblical women. First, if you go, I will go with you. Second, blessed is the Lord who sent you, and blessed are you! Third, your faith has made you whole: "Go in peace, heal and be healed!"

And as you go, learn to call His name–"Jesus." It's a mighty name–an anthem in one word. An oratory in two syllables. "Jesus," I love to call His name. I heard a brother say, "It's a life-giving, sin-destroying name. His first lullaby He heard on the moon-drenched hills of Bethlehem."

Learn to call His name. One day, He looked down at water and looked up to God. He looked down again and when He blushed, plain water turned to fine, red wine.

Learn to call His name. His humanity did not subtract from His divinity. He conquered death and the grave.

Learn to call His name. When my soul is under siege, "Jesus my Lord"–I love to call His name. His name is all my boast. He will not put my soul to shame, or let my hope be lost. I just love to call His name.

Today, we can be activists because of who Jesus is.

He's the Paraclete of God. His Holy Spirit is our advocate and our defense. He comes alongside us in the time of trouble.

Jesus is the Paraphrase of God. When God seemed unknowable, unseeable, and mysterious, the Word was made flesh and dwelt among us and we beheld His glory, the glory of the matchless Son of God.

Jesus is the Parachute of God. He will not keep you from falling, but He'll let you down easy. I've been up and I've been down. I learned that down is not final. Down is not fatal.

Not only is Jesus our Paraclete, Paraphrase, and Parachute. He's the Parasol of God. We see the lightning flashing and hear the thunder roar. He covers us during life's storms.

He's the Paramedic of God, a doctor when we're ill. When we can't get up to go to the doctor, the Paramedic will show up. If you're sick and can't get well, just call Him up.

He's the Paragon of God. All names fade when we lift his name, which is above all other names. At that name, every knee shall bow and every tongue confess. He's in a class all by Himself. And if you want virtue, compassion, and justice–He's our Paragon.

Not only is He our Parasol, our Paramedic, and our Paragon, but finally Jesus is the Paradise of God. Wherever He is, is heaven to me. He'll be there when we face our exit into eternity. He said to the thief on the cross: "Truly I tell you, today you will be with me in Paradise" (Luke 23:45). In the end, where He is, there we shall be also. When He appears, we shall be like Him, for we shall see Him as He is.

I remember a little ring game we played as little girls: "Little Sally Walker, sitting in her saucer, wiping her weeping eyes. Rise Sally Rise!

Wipe your weeping eyes. Put your hands on your hips and let your back bones shift. And shake it to the east and shake it to the west. Shake to the one that you love best."

I heard that some "sistas" in the hood still play the game, but have changed the words to "Little Sally Walker, out of the saucer, walking down the street. Go on girl, do your thing!" Before we can move out in power, we've got to get Sally out of the saucer, no longer sad, confused, abused, or misused. Women of color must rise upon their feet and move out in God's power.

Cynthia Hale

Cynthia L. Hale was born in 1952 in Roanoke, Virginia. Since 1986 she has served as the founding Pastor and Senior Pastor of the Ray of Hope Christian Church in Decatur, Georgia. Rev. Dr. Hale received her BA in Music from Hollins University, her MDiv from Duke Divinity School, and her DMin from United Theological Seminary in Dayton, Ohio. She holds several honorary doctorates from colleges and seminaries, and is a frequent preacher and teacher in various settings beyond Ray of Hope. She is the author of *I'm a Piece of Work: Sisters Shaped by God*.[1] Dr. Hale is African American.

While Ray of Hope as a Disciples Church has been celebrating the Lord's Supper since its beginning 30 years ago, most people who join the church have no denominational affiliation. As such, the church has had to teach and re-teach the significance of the Lord's Supper. Nevertheless, it had gotten old and familiar, with some not excited about its observance—and even leaving worship prior to communion. As a way of refreshing its meaning, the pastoral staff and elders decided to have it only on the first Sunday of the month, with a much more elaborate, celebratory liturgy. As central to the experience of worship, the points of this sermon talk about the significance of our time at the table, and the impact of communion on corporate and daily living. The sermon uses the NIV, except as otherwise noted.

"Do This in Remembrance of Me!"

1 Corinthians 11:23–26

Well, it's the first Sunday of the month, communion Sunday, the Sunday when most people make it their business to come to church. It's traditional, but there is also something—in the minds of many—mystical and magical about communion. I suppose this is particularly true when you grew up in a church where the deaconesses held up a crisp white sheet in front of the table, hiding the pastor who was behind the veil. Back in the day, I always wondered what that dude was doing behind that sheet; didn't you?

There is something magical and mystical about the Lord's Supper. The Catholics teach the doctrine of transubstantiation. They believe that the bread and wine become the body and the blood of Jesus.

As Protestants, we don't believe that the body and blood become the actual presence of the Christ. We do, however, have our own interesting thoughts about the Lord's Supper. Some of us think that we can live any way we want all week—but, if you can just get to church and take communion on the first Sunday, your sins, which are many, will all be washed away. I don't think so! Those who are sick or brokenhearted may feel like there is something in the bread and wine that will bring healing. While I am convinced that the observance of the Lord's Supper will make you whole, I assure you that it is not in any sense a magical potion that makes everything all right. What makes communion so powerful is who and what it represents.

There are many denominations that have, as their custom, communion on the first Sunday, but some of you know that as Disciples, it is our longstanding practice to have the Lord's Supper every Sunday. We call ourselves people of the cup. Our denominational emblem is a chalice with St. Andrew's cross on it.

Having communion every Sunday gives you a choice of Sundays to choose from if you only want to come once a month. Having communion every Sunday has its benefits, but it also has its dangers. That is one of the reasons we thought we would try having it once a month. When you do something too often, there is a danger of becoming too familiar with it. There is the danger of the meal becoming common—a routine ritual, a pious practice, or an unholy habit that has lost its power and significance.

This is what the apostle Paul is addressing in the 11th chapter of his first letter to the church at Corinth. The entire chapter focuses on what is appropriate in worship. Paul is dealing with worship in the church in Corinth—specifically, irreverence in worship, and, in this instance, at the table of the Lord.

It seems that the observance of the Lord's Supper had become the arena where the divisions and schisms in the church were manifesting themselves, and certain attendees' selfish attitudes were becoming apparent. Paul makes clear that what is going on is serious and destructive to the life of the church and its members.

In verse 17, he says, "In the following directives I have no praise for you, for your meetings do more harm than good." This is serious! Back in verse 2, he had commendations for them, but none here. He continues, "In the first place, I hear that when some of you come together as a church, there are divisions among you, and to some extent I believe it" (11:18).

At Corinth, as is true of the church from its inception, the members observed as a part of their worship time an *agapé* feast. *Agapé,* as you know, is the Greek word for love. The love feast was a time when the saints came together to share a time of sweet fellowship with one another. At the conclusion of the meal, they celebrated the Lord's Supper. This was a good practice until some abuses of the meal and the fellowship started taking place.

Apparently, everyone brought dishes from home to share with one another, in typical potluck fashion. The wealthier members of the fellowship, those who did not have to work, or could leave whenever, came early, brought their dishes, and rather than wait on the others began the meal without them.

Those who could not get off work early, because they were servants or slaves, did not own their own businesses and thus could not determine their own schedules, arrived later to find the food gone and the folks who had consumed it also had had too much wine and were drunk. Yes, this was in church and, no, they were not drunk with the Spirit, as on the day of Pentecost. That's one reason why we serve grape juice and not wine. Some of *you* all…might try to take two or three of those little cups.

The working class, the poorer members, were feeling hurt and left out. They, too, brought dishes, but not what the others had brought. Many of them depended on the love feast for their most substantial and healthiest meal of the week. They were feeling embarrassed and ashamed that they were in the social condition they were in and did not have what the others had, and, for that reason, were being excluded in the church.

It was a mess. The fellowship was shot. The whole point of the meal was to share love with one with another, but there is no love flowing when persons are excluded or feeling left out.

Given the condition of our society, as African Americans we know what it feels like to be excluded or left out. All of us know what it's like not to be invited to a party, to join a certain club, or to hang with a certain group. Somehow, it's a little easier to understand this in the world; but, when you come into the church, you expect things to be different.

In the church, you don't expect persons to walk by you without acknowledging you. In the church, you don't expect to be excluded from certain ministries because you don't have money. In the church, you don't expect to have people overlook you in the selection of those who they want to socialize with because you aren't wearing designer clothes, don't have the right look, aren't considered upwardly mobile—or already there. In the church, you don't expect to have to prove yourself like you do every day of your life: on your job, at school—especially when you are a woman in a sexist society, a Black man in a racist society, a white man who is a nonconformist, a youth who is trying to be different, any person who is physically or mentally challenged or is living on an income that is substandard.

We don't expect it in the church because as Paul says in Galatians 3:28, "There is neither Jew nor Gentile, slave nor free, male or female; for you are all one in Christ Jesus." In Christ, we are one. Our differences shouldn't matter. We are all members of the body of Christ. In the church, we believe in unity with diversity. Each of us is unique and different, like the parts of the human body, and that's what makes the church so special and our community so affirming and appealing. Everyone has a place. That's what being the church is all about. Anybody and everybody can come up in here and know that they are unconditionally loved and accepted. You can be tattooed or pierced to the nines—with a blue, purple, or yellow punk hairdo. Folks might think you are a little weird, but they thought Jesus and John the Baptist were back in the day. We are to accept one another as Christ has accepted us.

Paul was ticked. These folks were turning the celebration of the Lord's Supper into a private and personal dinner party, and he let them know it. This is how we know he was angry. In verse 19, he says to them, "No doubt there have to be differences among you to show which of you has God's approval."

Another version says, "For [doubtless] there have to be factions among you, so that those who are of approved character may be clearly recognized among you" (Amplified Version). It is clear that Paul is using a bit of sarcasm here, when he tells those who are guilty that some good has come out of their indiscretions. Now those who are genuine, those who are truly faithful Christian will be evident and recognizable.

Just as light exposes darkness, deeds of darkness make the light or right more apparent. Furthermore, he asks them in verse 22, "Don't you have homes to eat and drink in? Or do you despise the church of God and humiliate those who have nothing?"

What Paul makes clear to them is: "You think this is just about you. If that were the case, you could eat and drink at home. You have disgraced the church, hurt the fellowship, and humiliated the poor. That's not love!"

That's not what the church or the Lord's Supper is all about. As a way of addressing the abuses, Paul gives the people of Corinth, you, and me instructions about what the Lord's Supper is. Verse 23 says, "For I received from the Lord what I...passed on to you."

You should know that this account of the Last Supper was written before any of the Gospel accounts. It is the first account of how Jesus instituted the Lord's Supper and why. Paul said he received the account from the Lord. He obviously received it in his vision of the risen Lord; because he wasn't there at that Passover meal that Jesus had with his disciples. Perhaps he received it from the oral accounts that were passed down from those who were. Whatever the case, for Paul it was from the Lord that he received this tradition, and that gave it validity and power. And he had passed it on to us to observe.

Notice, there is no record here of how often we should observe it. So if churches do it once a year, once a quarter, once a month, once a week, every day of the week...it doesn't matter. Some folks get in a huff about how often to have the Lord's Supper; churches have split, and new denominations have been developed over disagreements about the regularity of it. All Jesus said is to do it.

The first thing that Paul wants them/us to understand about the Lord's Supper is that it is relational.

When Jesus instituted the Last Supper, he was with his disciples in an upper room. Just as Jesus and his disciples met around that table on the night he was betrayed as a unit, every time we meet at the table of the Lord, we meet as family–brothers and sisters in Christ. At the table, we affirm our unity and our equality. At the table, there are no big "I's" and little "you's." The ground is level at the foot of the cross.

When we come to the table, we are to focus on the death of Christ and the fact that because of his death all the things that might be used to separate us have been done away with. Those of us who were excluded and those who excluded us are reconciled at the cross through Christ. In Christ, we are one. And we need to act like it. Paul says in 1 Corinthians 10:16–17, "Is not the cup of thanksgiving for which we give thanks a participation in the blood of Christ? And is not the bread…we break a participation in the body of Christ? Because there is one loaf, we…all [partake of] the one loaf." Perhaps the image of our being one body, participating in a meal as one, would be clearer if we all ate of the one loaf of bread, rather than the individual pieces; or drank from one cup rather than individual cups. But you will notice that we hold the elements and all eat together. At least, those of us who are here, eat together.

Some people don't understand the whole concept of a family meal. Given the hustle and bustle of our lives, families don't sit down at the table together any longer, like we used to, but we should. Some of us don't understand the significance of the Lord's Supper as a family meal. If we did, you wouldn't stay at home and stream, when you are physically able to come to the table. You wouldn't skip out before the meal is served–in a hurry to get to breakfast, brunch, lunch, or wherever it is you are going. You clearly don't understand that you are skipping out on the family meal, the most intimate time of sharing in our worship experience as a congregation. I know that some of you see the meal as an intimate time between you and the Lord, but it's also about our relationship to one another. I know that you think it's all over after the sermon. The sermon is important. The Word is key, but so is our time together at the table. There ought to be at least one time when we intentionally come together as one.

Our participation in the Lord's Supper is crucial for us as baptized believers, not for curious children who want to have their way or have whatever they see, not for folks who want no part in the body of Christ, but for those who come seeking the Lord and those already surrendered to him. Not only is the Lord's Supper relational, it is an act of receiving. Paul said, "For I received from the Lord what I…passed on to you."

When we come to the table of the Lord, we receive the elements, even as the disciples received them from Jesus. Notice that he used ordinary elements—common things like bread and wine. Those things were present in every household and a part of their meals. These elements were a part of the Passover meal that Jesus shared with his disciples.

It is just like God to take ordinary things, touch them with his glory—transforming them into something extraordinary. He took a little boy's lunch of two little fish and five barley loaves and fed a multitude. Little becomes much when we place it in the master's hand. I can't help but reflect on what he did with my life and yours when we gave them to him.

Think what God does with ordinary things: he infuses them with new meaning and new life. The bread represents his body, the cup his blood. Communion is a meal that we have the responsibility of receiving.

When we receive the bread, we are witnessing that we have received the Bread of Life into our very being, and he has given us new life. We have new life because we have received and trusted the Savior who shed his precious blood on the cross for us.

Those who have not received him are yet to receive that life. You are existing, but not really living. You know that; you know that you are just going through the motions, wondering if and when things will get better, but they won't without him. Without Christ, there is a hunger and thirst that cannot be satisfied, even though we have tried just about anything and everything to do it. Time after time you have been offered the Bread of Life and you have not received it—and you wonder why you are still not satisfied. Only Jesus can satisfy the hunger that you feel.

He said of himself in John 6:35, "I am the bread of life. [He/she who] comes to me will never go hungry, and [he/she who] believes in me will never be thirsty." You know that you need him; why not receive him and turn this meal and your life into more?

For those of us who have received him, receiving the bread and cup when we come to the Lord's table is a graphic way of showing that we have taken Christ into our innermost being and that he is alive—not just in the world, but in our lives.

For us, the Lord's Supper is not just relational, or a meal that we receive; it is an act of remembering:

> On the night [that Jesus] was betrayed, he took bread, and when he had given thanks, he broke it and said, "This is my body, which is for you; do this in remembrance of me." In the same way, after supper he took the cup, saying, "This cup is the new covenant in my blood; do this, whenever you drink it, in remembrance of me." (1Cor. 11: 23b–25)

The Lord's Supper is a time to remember Christ and all he has done for us. The meal, the initial setting of the meal, the occasion of the meal, the elements of the meal—are all significant.

Paul says the meal took place on the night Jesus was betrayed. The Gospel of Luke says that it was during the Passover meal. The Passover for the Jews, according to Exodus 12, is the commemoration of the Lord's deliverance of his people from bondage in Egypt. The night they were delivered, they were told to sacrifice a lamb without spot or blemish and put the blood of the lamb on their doorposts. When the death angel that was sent to kill the firstborn of every Egyptian family saw the blood, it would pass over that home. The blood of the lamb saved the firstborn; it was the blood of the lamb that provided for their deliverance from Egypt. It was the blood that set them free.

As Jesus shared the Passover meal with his disciples, he used the occasion to help them see who he really was: "the lamb of God who takes away the sins of the world" (Jn. 1:28). He used the bread to let them know that his body would be broken for them. "This 'is' my body," he said, "which 'is' for you." The word for "is" in the Jewish religious understanding means "on your behalf." He was broken so that we might be made whole. He took the cup, saying, "This is the new covenant in my blood." He was talking about humanity's covenant relationship with God. There was a need for a new covenant because the old one wasn't working.[2] The blood of bulls and goats had no power to take away the sins that prevented us from being in relationship with God. We can have complete confidence in the new covenant because it was ratified by none other than the Living God.

When we remember what Christ did for us, we are reminded of the fact that we were sinners and had no power to change. The old covenant depended on our being able to keep God's laws, and we couldn't do it. You know that, as hard as you try, you just can't seem to get it and keep it right in your own strength alone. Sin is like that. It separated us from God, and it wants to keep us separated.

But God loves us and wants us back. So he sent Jesus to earth to establish a new covenant, a new relationship between us. The new relationship was established with his blood. A death had to occur to pay for our sins, and so he died in our place. The Gospel of Matthew says in 26:28, "This is [the] blood of the new covenant, which is poured for many for the forgiveness of sins." The songwriter said it this way, "What can wash away my sins, nothing but the blood of Jesus, What can make me whole again, nothing but the blood of Jesus?"[3]

It was the blood of Jesus poured out on our behalf that set us free from sin and gave us peace within. It was the blood that gives us power to live free from sin. Every time we meet at the table of the Lord we are reminded that Jesus

was wounded for our transgressions,

He was bruised for our iniquities;

The chastisement of [His] peace was upon Him,

And by His stripes we are healed. (Isa. 53: 5, NKJV)

For righteousness and by his wounds we are healed. Whether you have received it or not, he died for you. When you receive him, his forgiveness will be made real in your life.

What all of us need to be aware of is that the word translated "remembrance" means much more than "recalling something or someone from the past." To participate in the Lord's Supper is not simply to recall a past event; it is to experience Christ's presence in the breaking of the bread and the drinking of the cup. It is to commune with him and be made confident in God's love for us. To remember Christ is to receive strength for each new day, power to do the impossible, peace to handle the confusion, faith to face the madness, love to love the unlovable, and hope to manage the feelings of helplessness.

To remember Christ is to appropriate his saving benefits in our lives daily. Now that we are saved, we need to act like it. Now that you have been delivered, live free; why keep getting entangled again, coming to the table in bondage or in sin?

Paul makes clear that we have a responsibility to come to the table prepared, not in an unworthy manner. He said that we do not come to this table as one who is worthy; none of us is worthy. It is through Christ's death on our behalf that we are made worthy. He is our righteousness; we stand complete in him. But to come to this table in an unworthy manner is to come with unconfessed sin in your life, therefore bringing judgment upon yourself. God's judgment is tough. When the Lord judges us, we are being disciplined, so that we will not be condemned by the world. God disciplines those whom he loves in order to mature us and keep us from being condemned by the world. We have a witness to be concerned about. People are watching us to see if we really are who we say we are. But if we judge ourselves, we will not come under judgment.

We are to judge ourselves, examine ourselves, come clean with ourselves and with God–confessing our sins and repenting of them before eating and drinking of the cup.

Paul wanted the folks in Corinth to get it right. They were not recognizing the body of the Lord in their actions, and neither do we. But if we confess our sins, God is faithful and just to forgive us and cleanse us from all unrighteousness. We are reminded of that at the table of the Lord.

The Lord's Supper is relational; it is an act of receiving. It is remembering all that Christ has done for us, and it calls for a renewal of our commitment to him. Christ said in verse 26, "For whenever you eat this bread and drink this cup, you proclaim the Lord's death until he comes" (1 Cor. 11:26). Every time we eat at the table of the Lord, we proclaim–we are giving notice to the world with our lips and with our lives—that we are living for him.

That's what we are to do until he comes: proclaim his death, tell folks that he died, tell them why he died, and give evidence of what a difference his death can make in their lives. We are to show them in our way of life that the blood still works.

To proclaim is to also give him thanks and praise. Another word for the Lord's Supper is *Eucharist,* which means the giving of thanks. I learned this when I was a little girl. My grandmother Hale was a big woman who suffered from arthritis and other ailments that kept her from going to church on a regular basis, but when she was able she pressed her way. She loved to go on the first Sunday because she could have communion. I will never forget the times that my daddy and I had to help her up from her seat, down the aisle to the altar. She was A.M.E. and they went to the altar for communion. Every time my grandmother knelt at that altar, as soon as the pastor put the communion wafer in her hand, she would shout, "Thank you, Jesus!"

I had always been taught that communion was a solemn time, a time to be quiet, and I was embarrassed at my grandmother's behavior. But now, I know what she knew then. When I think of the goodness of Jesus and all he's done for me, my soul cries out, "Hallelujah!" I thank God for saving me.

Allen Harris

Allen V. Harris is the Regional Minister for the Christian Church (Disciples of Christ), Capital Area. He served as Senior Pastor of Franklin Circle Christian Church in Cleveland, Ohio, for fourteen years, where he helped transform that congregation's ministry within its richly diverse urban neighborhood just west of downtown. He served as Associate Pastor/Transitional Senior Pastor of the Park Avenue Christian Church of New York City for a decade—the congregation in which he was ordained into ministry in 1991. He is a graduate of Phillips University with a BS in Religious Education; and of Brite Divinity School, Texas Christian University, with a MDiv concentrating in Christian Education. Rev. Harris is European American.

This sermon was preached on Palm/Passion Sunday 2014 at Franklin Circle Christian Church, using the NRSV. It was offered at the conclusion of a Lenten Mid-Week Bible Study exploring the theme of atonement. The sermon invites an understanding of atonement that differs from the familiar cultural understanding of atonement constituted by Jesus' violent death as a condition for God's justice to be satiated and for redemption of sinful human nature. In doing so, Harris encouraged an environment in which spiritual exploration and thoughtful reflection about faith, life, and (most especially) Scripture was actively nurtured. The sermon offers a clear and perhaps demanding alternative to an embedded cultural theology.

"Palms, Principalities and Powers, and Passion"

Matthew 21:1–11

Palm Sunday. Exactly one week before Easter. The waving palms, the cheering crowds, the slow but steady march into a week that will be filled with passion and eternal significance. Palm Sunday and Passion Week. Filled with struggle over the meaning of agony and pain. For some traditions, the pain of Jesus is actually taken on in the life of his followers, either through some ritual action of penance and obedience by the masses, or by an individual who re-enacts the way of the cross—sometimes even to the point of scourging and wearily dragging the cross through the streets of this or that town.

For centuries, even millennia, this week has come to symbolize the ultimate price the Son of God paid for our sins: death, even death on a cross. For the vast majority of Christians, and many onlookers, this week answers the question, "Why did God send Jesus into the world?" with a resounding reply: "To die. And to die as the ultimate payment for the forgiveness of our sins." Many Christians believe this; perhaps, by any standard, *most...* but not all. Not me. Not me.

I stand here before you today to proclaim that I do not believe that God sent Jesus, God's very self, into the world with the express intention that Jesus was to die, and die a painful, agonizing, humiliating death on a wooden cross. I do not for one second believe that the Creator of the universe, whom we know in Holy Scripture only through hints and glimpses and the complex, twisting storylines of the people who worshiped and followed that God, sent Jesus just to die. But before you cry out, "Blasphemer!!!" hear me out.

I don't believe God sent Jesus into this world to die because, if that were true, it would spawn a wretched and epic saga of violence and brute warfare on the part of God's followers. Which, of course, it has. Disciples scholar and preacher, Rita Nakashima Brock, is one who reminds us that for the first several centuries Christians focused, not on the death of Jesus, but on the resurrection of Jesus. We know this because the artwork Christians created in those centuries closest to the birth, life, ministry, death, and resurrection were almost exclusively representations of a transfigured Christ or a resurrected Christ. In catacomb, tomb, house church, and then later sanctuary, basilica, and cathedral, the images our forebears of the faith crafted to remind them of Jesus the Christ were without blood and were rarely of him dead on the cross.[1]

Nakashima Brock reminds us that it wasn't until after the faith of Christianity was consumed by the power of the empire that the gory death of Jesus became frequent fodder for artists and writers. Brock writes:

> On "good" Friday, in 1095, the First Crusade's pilgrims–headed to Jerusalem to take the city back for Christ–paused in the Rhineland to slaughter 10,000 Jews as "Christ killers." This focus on genocide against all "infidels" was supported by a new idea claiming that Jesus' crucifixion saved sinful humanity from the penalty of sin and that dying for Christ in holy war was the best, most effective form of escape from hell. In launching the crusades as Christian holy war, Pope Urban II proclaimed, "God wills it!" He promised all who died that their sins would be totally forgiven and they would go straight to paradise, effectively making killing penance, while the early church had regarded killing as a mortal sin requiring penance for a full return to the church as the paradise in this life.[2]

It was only three years later, in 1098, that the cleric Anselm of Canterbury would write his tome articulating the theology that claimed that the only purpose of the Incarnation was for Jesus to die, a theology now called "substitutionary atonement." Humanity's sinfulness, so this theology says, had dishonored God and carried a magnitude of debt from sin that was impossible to pay. God sent Jesus to be tortured and murdered as the only way to deliver salvation, according to Anselm. The fear of eternal damnation and hell kept Christians in line, and remorse for what we had done to Jesus kept us in shame. Both the fear of hell and the shame of killing Jesus has provoked in those who call themselves "Christians" some horrific actions toward others, their loved ones, and even themselves.

That theological innovation has now morphed into multiple complex and convoluted theologies, as we have explored the past few weeks in Mid-Week Bible Study, and worked its way into almost every hymn of our upbringing. But as I have examined these perspectives more intensely, and read the Scriptures that supposedly support them, and prayed mightily for the Holy Spirit to guide me, I have heard a clearer and what I consider more faithful understanding of why God sent Jesus to us, as well as what response my faith in that Jesus could and should be.

I do not believe that God sent Jesus into the world to die. Not for a minute. Rather, and confidently, I believe that God sent Jesus—or, more accurately, God became incarnate among us—to live. God sent Jesus to live! God became incarnate in the very creation God had formed in order to grow and mature, learn and listen, teach and heal, preach and cry, dance and drink wine, laugh and love. This is what the early Christians believed, and for centuries after Jesus walked amongst them! For the earliest Christians, violence was abhorrent, and going to war was against everything that Christ taught! Jesus came that we might have life, and have it more abundantly! (Jn. 10:10).

So, you ask, did Jesus "have to" die? I think that is the wrong question completely, if you begin with the premise that the only thing that Jesus "had to do" was to live, and live an abundant, God-centered, faithful life—which he did! End of proposition!

Did Jesus die? Now that's a very different question. Yes! Yes, Jesus died a horrible death after the betrayal of his disciples, the comedic antics of religious and political leaders, the abuse of those in power, and finally being nailed to the imperial device of torture, shame, punishment, and execution: the cross. Yes, Jesus died and he died long before his time.

So then, you might ask, how could the God of the universe not know that Jesus was going to die? How could the one who was Messiah himself not know that he would be tortured and hung upon a tree? Of course, they may have expected, assumed, anticipated, even known! But that is an entirely different proposition from saying "God sent Jesus *to die!*"

So the second part of my theological stand is this: God became incarnate amongst us as Jesus the Christ in order to live! But knowing well how life amongst us humans is, it would be expected that one who lived a faithful life would come up against misunderstanding, opposition, hostility, even violence. And furthermore, one who lived a life in tandem with God so closely, so purely, so honestly as the Messiah would, therefore inevitably would encounter all the more the antagonism of those in power who had the most to lose because of their investment in the ways not of God! God sent Jesus to live life abundantly, and this enraged those in power!

And this is where Palm Sunday comes into play! It is no accident that Jesus chose Jerusalem as the location into which he would enter to confront the powers that be with the God-life that he was living! Walter Brueggemann, in his brilliant book *Mandate to Difference: An Invitation to the Contemporary Church,* reminds us that Jerusalem had become the symbol of all that was wrong with the world in that day. Since David's conquering of the old Canaanite city of Jebus (2 Sam. 5:6–10), it became a symbol larger than itself. But it was under his son, Solomon, that the city became a place of royal power and compromising ethics. Quickly it moved from being sacred center of the humble nation of the Hebrews to a symbol of royal power, wealth, and grandeur–built on the backs of the peasants of the countryside from whom Solomon extracted enormous taxes to pay for his opulence (1 Kings 10:11, 25). It quickly became a fortified city with a standing army, forced labor, and highly dubious political-economic arrangements, including sexual politics![3]

We know this to be true because of the heavily negative associations with Jerusalem by the prophets of ancient Israel. Micah declares, "Hear this, you rulers... / who abhor justice / and pervert all equity, / who build Zion with blood / and Jerusalem with wrong!" (3:9–10). Isaiah is scathing when he intones, "How the faithful city / has become a whore! / She that was full of justice, / righteousness lodged in her– / but now murderers... thieves!" (1:21, 23d). Jeremiah hauntingly proclaims regarding Jerusalem, "This is the city that must be punished; / there is nothing but oppression within her" (6:6b).

And it is no accident that Jesus would enter Jerusalem on this very day! Marcus Borg and John Dominic Crossan, in their pivotal book, *The Last Week: What the Gospels Really Teach about Jesus's Final Days in Jerusalem,*[4] remind us unequivocally that on that fateful day there were not one, but two processions into Jerusalem. From the west rode Pontius Pilate, Roman governor of the area, in a regal procession with all the accouterments of control, power, and domination in full view: soldiers decked out in armor, cavalry horses stirring up dust, armaments glistening in the sun, and Pilate held high and aloft. All this pomp and circumstance echoed on the eve of the Passover, when thousands of faithful pilgrims were entering the city for their observance of their faith. Thousands of the faithful recoiled in horror, being reminded in no uncertain terms that though the Passover recalled a day when the Hebrew children got the best of one potentate, they should have no schemes to try to do the same for this one–that day, or any day!

On the other side of town, to the east, rode Jesus, humble and on donkey–and even a female donkey with her colt by her side–to perhaps a few hundred of those who had heard his words, seen his miracles, felt his holy presence. They cheered with what they literally had at hand: the branches of palm trees that were within reach, and even the top cloaks of the outfits they were wearing. On one side of town a monarch who ruled by fear and shame; on the other a sovereign who ruled through love and sacrifice.

Yes, Jesus did come to live and to live life abundantly. But this was no silly Messiah, this was no inattentive God. They knew that a life lived in accordance with Scripture, a life lived in tune with the holy, a life lived completely devoted not to the rulers of this world but the one who created life itself would rile the powers and anger the principalities. How many of us who say that we follow Christ have never even gotten one other person agitated or even miffed? But it is what might be expected from a life lived in line with the justice, righteousness, holiness of God. To me, this is salvation: to live life as Christ lived life, to walk in the way of Christ, to live life so holy as to risk infuriating principalities and powers. His life of atonement–at-one-ment with God–calls me to this and no less.

So let me tell you what I believe this theology of atonement calls me to during this week of Passion. First and foremost, it calls me to live out John 3:16: "For God so loved the world that [God] gave [God's] only Son, so that everyone who believes in [Jesus] may not perish but may have eternal life"–not interpreting "gave" as "gave up to die," but "gave God's only Son" as "gave to live life abundantly"![5]

Next, every day this week, I am going to remember the Passion of Jesus Christ by remembering something during his life that he was passionate about!

Today, Palm Sunday, as we remember Jesus' triumphant entry into Jerusalem, I am going to remember Jesus' humble entry into this world in his birth to Mary and Joseph, in a stable, lying in a manger.

On Monday, as we remember Jesus' driving out the moneychangers from the temple, I am going to remember Jesus' reading Scripture in the synagogue, reminding them, and us, of his mandate to bring good news to the poor, release to the captives, recovery of sight to the blind, to let the oppressed go free, and to proclaim the year of God's favor.

On Wednesday, when Jesus was tested again and again, being tempted to indict himself, I am going to remember Jesus' many confrontations with the religious leaders of his day–Sadducees, Pharisees, and Scribes–calling into question their collusion with imperial domination.

On Thursday, when Jesus gathered with his disciples and broke bread, shared the cup, and blessed them, I am going to remember all the times in Jesus' life when he fed people, literally and spiritually, taking what seemed like scarcity and making abundance a reality.

On Friday, when we recall the trial, scourging, and crucifixion of Jesus, I am going to remember Jesus' taking children into his lap, calling short tax collectors down from trees, eating with prostitutes, and treating demoniacs as children of God, and all those actions that stand up against the way things are and the way people think things ought to be.

On Saturday, when our rituals call us to a day of silence and reflection while Jesus' lifeless body lay in a borrowed tomb, I will choose to remember all those moments of silence and reflection in Jesus' life: when he crossed the sea, crossed the hillside, went to a garden to pray…but, most especially, I will remember those few seconds as Jesus knelt and drew in the sand with a stick, before looking at the woman almost stoned to death, saying, "Woman, where are your accusers?"

And on Sunday, Easter Day… Well, on that day I think we will all join and remember one thing: *Life.*

Janet Casey-Allen

Janet Casey-Allen (1954–) was born of Chinese descent in Malaysia, where she passed A-levels (i.e., graduated from high school). She holds a BA from DePauw University, and a MDiv and DMin from Christian Theological Seminary. Thought to be the first woman of Chinese ancestry to be ordained in the Christian Church, Rev. Casey Allen has served ministries in congregations, and was Chaplain at Indiana Girls' School and at Indiana Women's Prison for 24 years. She is a founder and a previous Moderator of the North American Pacific/Asian Disciples.

Dr. Casey-Allen first preached this sermon in the Indiana Women's Prison in 2008. She preached it later in another prison and in two Disciples congregations—one largely Eurocentric and one largely Zo (comprised of refugees from Myanmar). The biblical text is a narrative. The preacher uses the NIV. The movement of the sermon follows the movement of the text as the preacher goes back and forth, scene by scene, between the world of the text and the world today. Although the preacher does not directly invoke the category of shaman, the sermon portrays Jesus in ways like that figure, familiar to many Asian cultures. The preacher ends the sermon by inviting the congregation to engage in body movement that evokes some shamanistic rituals. The preacher thus hopes the congregation will have an embodied experience of the healing of which the sermon speaks.

"Healer of My Soul"

Mark 2:1–12

So let's go on back to those days, and pretend you wanted to see a healer. The story is about this man who is paralyzed. How long he has been paralyzed, I do not know. But what I do know is that he couldn't walk, and he was afraid. It was hard to be a paralyzed person in those days. Why? Because they had no "Depends," and they had no physical therapist who would work their muscles. He just lay there. I don't know what kind of care he got, but he was in a sorry state.

We don't know if he fell off a roof, or if he was a roofer and hurt himself. We don't know, but what we do know is that he was flat on his back. How many of you have been flat on your back? And you can't move after surgery during that time—being flat on your back, feeling hopeless, and feeling helpless. He was utterly helpless, and he didn't have Medicaid.

I am sure that he could have heard that there was this wonderful healer who was in town. His friends also heard that this healer was in town. So they came on over to him and said, "Come on, let's take a chance, what have

252

you got to lose?" They didn't call 911, and there was no ambulance to take him. They plunked him on a pallet, and carried him. This denotes that they weren't rich folks. They didn't have a nice car or carriage they could put him on. We don't know how far they walked, but they carried this person, one at each corner, until they came to this house where Jesus was staying.

Do you think any of those people had any sympathy when the man's friends said, "Yo, can we get on through? We've got a sick man over here, we need to get on through."? No, they just ignored him. They were so captivated listening to the word of God that they just ignored the poor fellow back there. He couldn't walk. His friends kept on saying, "Hey, let us through." But they were not going to give up their spot.

It's like going to see some pop star; I don't know whether I would give up my spot either. But anyway, they were all packed in, looking in. Those houses weren't very big, but they surrounded the whole home, trying to hear a little word. There was no microphone, and we don't know how well Jesus projected. But what we do know was that no one was going to get through to Jesus. The crowd didn't care about a paralyzed person.

Why didn't they care about him? Because they were so anxious listening to the preacher, listening to his message of hope. They were so enthralled, being in the presence of the holy, that they forgot the poor guy behind them.

But did it deter those four friends? No, they were determined that their friend was going to see this healer. They hoped that all they had to do was to get him to where the healer was.

But how could they get there? All these church people were not letting them through. The congregation was packed, so they couldn't get through. Then, they looked up on the roof. You know the story of the little pigs, and how the wolf wanted to eat the little pigs? Well, even the wolf got smart. The wolf climbed up on the roof, and said, "I'm going to jump down the chimney since I can't blow the house down."

The wolf comes down from the roof. Santa comes down from the roof. Santa had a chimney; the wolf had a chimney—even though he ended up in the cooking pot! So what could the men do? They had to lift him up on the roof.

So they told the guy, "We don't want to drop you, so we will tie you up." He was bound up. (This is in my imagination). So they bound him up. Now think about this guy, the trust that he had in his friends. He had to trust them enough so that they could lift him up. If they had dropped him, he could have broken an arm; then, not only could he not have walked, he couldn't have fed himself either. But he trusted his friends enough, as they had carried him this long distance, and they promised him, "We will take you to someone who will help you." He had enough trust in them. His friends had to have enough trust in themselves and faith in God that they could help their friend up over the roof, too.

Legends say that was Peter's house. Peter, the great big fisherman who would stand up tall and look at these folks like this. It was Peter's house they were going into. But it was not that there was any fear that it was Peter's house that they were breaking into, but they knew that Peter walked with the healer. Perhaps in the house, they said, "We will put the house back together, because we know that Peter would understand," even though they had no authorization to take the roof apart.

How would you lower a man down if he were on a mat? The hole in the roof had to be big enough to lower him straight down. Well, I would assume at that point they were going to be more careful. So they made a big, huge hole on the roof so they could lower him.

When you want to help someone, think of the risk you'd have to take. When helping someone, you could get sued. That's why we have the Good Samaritan law, because as you are trying to help someone and something else happens by accident, though with all good intention, you won't be held responsible. But it takes incredible risk and faith and belief in God, that God was there to help them. And they took that risk.

So these four friends could have dropped him, but they believed their strength came from God, who gave them the capacity to take risk. Now that is an important thing when you want to help someone. There is risk of rejection.

How many people may know some member of the family who's on drugs or alcohol and need to get them to treatment? It takes incredible risk for any family member to say, "No, you're not getting a dime out of me. I don't care if you have not eaten for five days, but you are going to check in at that place where you can get help." Well, the person says, "I hate you! I just hate you; I just don't want to see you again; you're mean; you're horrible; you don't care about me."

But it takes risk and it takes strength—sometimes, it takes physical strength, not just moral strength, when you want to help someone. It can take both. That's why you see people going out to help someone with Habitat for Humanity—pounding nails, lifting the beams, and doing that kind of hard work. People would go on down to New Orleans and help after all that destruction. Sometimes, it also takes physical strength and physical labor.

Well, after they got on top, and tore the hole out, they lowered him. The man who was paralyzed had trust. His trust had to be like that of a child. When you love a child, and you raise the kid up...oh, they just love it. When you lower the child down and then raise the child up and lower the child again—it's just wonderful. Well, if you drop the kid a couple of times, the next time you raise the kid up, the child screams, "*YAAAHH!*" But you see that children who are loved and cared for—now, the hands that bear them up will not let them fall!

Yes, he had to have that simple faith of a child who had always been loved, not a child who had been abused. As a child who had been loved, so he could be lowered down from the roof to find healing. We don't know if he had a fear of heights, but he let himself be lowered down, to get down to be healed. Thus, for us to meet God, you and I, we must get down. We must be lowered down—not thrown over a cliff, but have gentle hands lowering us down so we can in all humility meet God, with that simple faith. And it's not easy to do that!

So when he was lowered down, Jesus was amazed at the faith—not just the faith of the man, but the faith of all the friends who had taken this incredible risk. And when he looked at him, Jesus said, "Son, your sins are forgiven!" And, uh…your sins are forgiven? What a strange thing to say! In those days, as well as now, many people who professed to know God, said that physical ailments were a result of our sins. You've heard of that saying: "The sins of your forefathers rest on you from generation to generation."

When I was a child, and I was about seven years old, I met this kid who was a year older than I and his name was Taman. His knees could not bend. They were completely straight. And his hand was this way, bent this way, so he only had one hand to feed himself. When he wanted to turn around, he would drag himself so that this hand was all calloused. And I thought, "Why won't his parents give him a glove or something?" Well, being a kid, I also asked, "Why is Taman this way?" And this is what they told me: "His father thought he would go hunting, but he really wasn't hunting. He shot up at the sky, and the gods, to defend themselves, took the spirit of the pregnant mother's child and used it as a protection, and that's why he's that way." I couldn't understand that. We sat down one day, his leg was stretched out like this because it couldn't bend. I was right beside him. He put his hand like this beside my shoulder and we looked up at the sky and we looked at the birds flying. He smiled; he was so happy. He kept telling me the names of the birds, and I wondered why God would do such a stupid thing. Why would anybody up there need any protection? I felt, "My gosh, this poor kid, for the rest of his life, he's going to think that his father shot at the sky and that's why he is the way he is."

It's probably the same way for that man who was paralyzed. He probably thought he had sinned, or his father had sinned, or somebody had sinned. Some religious folks who come to church may say, "Aha, the way you are now is because you have sinned. You turned away from God; that's why you're sick." So how many times do we tell ourselves, "I've got cancer; maybe it's something I have done. Maybe I haven't been faithful enough. If I had been faithful to God, I wouldn't have cancer." But of course, if you went out and you took drugs and you're higher than a kite and it messes up your brain and you can't think, you may say that's a different matter. I'm talking about the curses we place on each other—the curses we put on each other so that the person will carry them for the rest of their life, feeling like a sinner. And what did Jesus do? He said, "Your sins are forgiven." He said that first, rather than saying, "Hey, let me heal you."

Jesus knew deep down what was the most painful thing in the paralyzed man's life. He was going to make a witness to all those folks that it was not that man's sin that got him into the physical condition. Some people who have been shot and are sitting in a wheelchair hear what others say: "Oh, it's the will of God. Well, at least he's in a wheelchair so he won't sell dope anymore." God doesn't will anything bad for us. God only wants what is best for us, and if anything bad happens it's because we live in this imperfect world. We have to know that God does not want anything that is bad for us.

Because, it says in the Scripture, "Immediately Jesus knew in his spirit that this was what they were thinking in their hearts, and he said to them, 'Why are you thinking these things?'" (Mk. 2:8). It's obvious, isn't it, to him and to everyone else? He said, "Which is easier: to say…, 'Your sins are forgiven,' or to say, "Get up, [and] take your mat and walk'?" (2:9).

Many of us need to get up and take our mats and walk and go on with our lives. We sometimes cannot do that lest we feel forgiven. We have so many sins; we sin every day, but we have to do that. So he said, "But I want you to know that the Son of Man has authority on earth to forgive sins" (v. 10). So the guy got up. Can you imagine that, with him lying down all these years, he probably had little muscle mass, and it was a miracle that he could get up and he could walk. Everyone was amazed. God heals us, but we also must take responsibility in getting well. One of the things we strive to do in living well is to have an authentic relationship with God.

To have an authentic relationship with God takes a lot of work. It is not easy to have an authentic relationship with God. It is not easy, because we have to get through the crowd. Some people would say; "I don't go to church anymore." *Why?* "Well, so and so said this to me," or, "I don't like what the preacher said"; "They sang that song and I can't stand that song, or "She just snubbed me"; "The choir director didn't pick me to sing a solo"; "People just don't care about me"…"I'm not going to go to church anymore."

We associate going to church as a place where we go to worship God, but some people say, "Oh, no, our denominational leaders took a stand for this or for that, which I don't believe in; so, let's pull the church out of that denomination."

It's very difficult to stay faithful. We gather as a community because the person we want to know more about and be like is Jesus. The road to Jesus is not easy, because we have to break down barriers. They had to break open the roof. We have to break things that keep us from opening up to God and community. It's very difficult to do that, because we like to hold on to the roof. We like to hold on to where we are. We are afraid to let someone help us to come down, to have that simple faith inside so we can be open to the healing power of God's love. To have that simple faith is to say I want to meet Jesus; I want to be healed. To be healed, we must break down some things that keep us from going there. It may be vanity, lust, or whatever, and we must find out what that barrier consists of.

It was not easy for them, because they knew it was the roof. The roof is an essential part of the house, which serves as our protection from the elements. We know that we require an intact roof, but we need to break down the roof. We need to break down what makes us comfortable, to get out of that comfortable space, to take the risk of rejection. There is a lot of rejection in it. Peter could have banned them from coming back to his home. Folks could have said, "Oh, those crazy people, we are not going to let them come by. If they want to see Jesus, they'll break down the walls next time."

When we are able to take that risk and we meet Jesus, our souls will be healed. He could seem so far away, but if we are willing to do that, we can get up and walk; we can have hope. And we can care for people all around us: all those who are hurting and in need of healing–so, when we are sitting in our churches, we are not keeping anyone out; we're not so focused over *there,* the front of the sanctuary, that we can't see the needy behind us. How many times have we not welcomed a homeless person to worship because they smell? Or, in what other ways do we keep other people out? "They don't dress right; they're not in the right social status–let's keep them out." We don't even have to be rude. All we have to do is sing and pray and just look forward and pretend those folks don't exist.

We say we love God–so we must open our hearts, open our roofs, and prepare to get down; and, when you are down, God lifts us up. God lifts us up and we can rise and be all that we can be with Jesus in our hearts and continue building a loving relationship with God and experience healing in our souls. Jesus is the healer of our souls.

Let us experience by movement through the song "Healer of My Soul," by John Michael Talbot. I would like you to learn these movements. [Here, Rev. Casey-Allen showed those gathered specific movements.] Whenever the lyrics say, "healer of my soul," please follow along. You may also open your palms like this, during the song, as a symbol of an openness to receive God's grace.

José Francisco Morales

José Francisco Morales Torres (1978–) is Director of Pastoral Formation at Disciples Seminary Foundation in Claremont, California. He is also pursuing his PhD in Comparative Theology and Philosophy at Claremont School of Theology. Rev. Morales holds degrees from Judson University (BA) and McCormick Theological Seminary (MDiv).

José is the son of Puerto Rican pastor-missionaries from the Pentecostal tradition, a tradition that still informs his homiletical approach. A self-described "Pan-American," he has lived in both Americas (North and South). Previously, Rev. Morales served as the Executive Regional Minister of the Central Rocky Mountain Region of the Christian Church (Disciples of Christ) and as Associate Pastor at Iglesia del Pueblo-Hope Center (now named Hope Christian Church), a multicultural Disciples congregation in Hammond, Indiana.

This sermon was preached at the biennial Festival of Preaching Northwest in Seattle, Washington, in 2012. Rev. Morales uses the NRSV. The majority of participants were clergy, mostly from mainline traditions, with a sizable evangelical presence. The message finds common ground for these diverse traditions by focusing on the reality of an increasingly "sideline" presence of the "mainline" church in North America. Linking this condition to the condition of the sidelined church of John's Revelation, Morales then names the hope for church-wide revolution in the work of preaching a countercultural gospel. Morales does not tip-toe around the need for preachers to be bold, something Morales embodies himself.

We sought to preserve the poetic, conversational style of Morales' preaching in the manuscript below.

"Sweet and Sour"

1 John 1:1–4; Revelation 10:1–11

I know where I'm at: I'm in Seattle, the hub of liberal religion and *a*religion, skeptic central and quite possibly (though not for sure) the birthplace of the phrase "spiritual but not religious." I know! I...I know where I'm at. This is the Northwest—arguably the first wave of the sea of cultural change. It's safe to assume that picking the book of Revelation was a poor choice—a risky choice!—on my part. I know I have, without saying a word, started off on the wrong foot. I've dug myself...a hole, a hole so deep that not even my Puerto Rican charm and good looks (and humility) can help me to climb out of it.

Now I know it's not just Seattle. We're mainline—most of us, at least (or, at least, nuanced, *nouveau* evangelicals). And this Revelation craziness is not, stereotypically, in our "canon within the Canon." I mean, it's not like we're running toward, flocking to, the Apocalypse to craft liberal, culturally nuanced sermons. (Let Jenkins and LaHaye have that mess!) *If anything,* we're running the other way; we have apocalyptic allergy. John's visions don't sit well with us. They tend to… *I don't know…*upset our stomachs.

I mean, in this increasingly secular world of ours, we–the seminary-trained Church–we have to protect our intellectual credibility. We wouldn't want folks thinking we're a bunch of pre-modern, backwater, superstitious folks. We're educated, *enlightened.* Visions and images like these–well, they're for those fanatics, holy rollers, and televangelists. John's visions don't sit well with us. They tend, you know, to upset our stomachs.

Revelation 10 may have been a poor choice on my part, and, if so, I apologize; but, then again…

John writes this epistle to a church with no power in the imperial politics, with no financial pull in the state economy, no hand in the shaping of cultural sensibilities. Nothing "mainline" about this early church! At best, they're *side*line, not mainline; at worst: despised, marginalized, persecuted.

The church doesn't own the faith market either. With competing religions, old and new, cultic and imperial, local and ethnic, and with heightening tensions with its scriptural cousins, the Jews, the church has no givens, no automatics, in the marketplace of religion.

Revelation 10 may have been a poor choice on my part…then again…

John's church is seen as the "odd one out," not willing to bend a knee to Caesar, to victorious Rome ever blessed by Nike (the goddess, not the gym shoe). Instead of assimilating, the church, this odd *ekklesia* of...

tongue-speaking Jews,

Ethiopian eunuchs,

fabric vendors,

suicidal jailers,

resurrected seamstresses,

retired fishermen,

bi-vocational tentmakers,

and second-career bishops…

…are proclaiming a conquered, slaughtered "Lamb"–not Caesar–as Savior and Lord.

These aren't movers and shakers in the Chamber of Commerce, shaping community life from their gothic cathedrals. No! These broke peons are gathering in caves, for goodness sake.

Huh! Maybe John's Revelation 10 wasn't such a bad choice after all.

This sounds a lot like the church on U.S. soil today. This is what the church in the U.S. is becoming (or has become). The *main*line has indeed become the *sidd*line. Seriously, who are we kidding, thinking that our general assembly, convention, synod resolutions still have the same sway they did 50 years ago?

Not to mention the growing immigrant churches that may have strong pull in their ethnic enclaves, but not in the predominantly white Congress.

Maybe this apocalyptic madness is exactly what we need to be paying attention to.

There's more! Even if we dare to say that the depletion of power is not accurate, that with a UCC president[1] and the ever-present Religious Right, there's still enough ecclesial power to go around; even if all this is true, there's another dynamic in John's church that he is addressing in his epistle.

You see, it was hard to be countercultural all the time, to always live, in the words of Brian Blount, a life of "active resistance."[2] It's taxing being in the underbelly of history, instead of a maker of history. No power is no fun! The goodies and gadgets offered by the Roman magisterium were too tempting for some Christians. The comfort and safety granted by adhering to the status quo was too juicy to resist. And so, some of these...

tongue-speaking Jews,

Ethiopian eunuchs,

fabric vendors,

suicidal jailers,

resurrected seamstresses,

retired fishermen,

bi-vocational tentmakers,

and second-career bishops...

...left the sideline for the mainline; some got tired of the caves and caved in under pressure to the allure of prestige. As a result, some...

tongue-speaking Jews,

Ethiopian eunuchs,

fabric vendors,

suicidal jailers,

resurrected seamstresses,

retired fishermen,

bi-vocational tentmakers,

and second-career bishops...

...began riding the fence, worshiping the Crucified One over here, and the Empire built on crosses over there. They had forgotten their "first love,"[3] and had fallen in love with power, privilege, and popularity. They assimilated; their saltiness had faded; their light, under a bushel; neither "hot" nor "cold"…"lukewarm."[4] A church that has sold out, that has lost its way, its soul: this is to whom John writes.

A church that serves God *and* Mammon,

A church that's neither hot nor cold, neither here nor there,

A church seeking status instead of service,

A church fighting over the color of carpet while indifferent to the homeless sleeping on cold cement,

A church doing absentee charity instead of incarnational justice,

A church predisposed to be profitable, instead of prophetic,

A church seeking to be in the center, instead of standing in solidarity in the margins,

A church safeguarding its security, consequently sacrificing its soul…

Well, I'll be… Maybe Revelation is what we should be reading, even though *it upsets our stomach!*

Either way, whether the U.S. Church is powerless or power hungry–either way!–it seems that this apocalyptic absurdity is a mirror being held up right in front of our collective face. Fortunately, Revelation, contrary to dispensationalist distortions, is good news: there's hope, there's a way forward,

a way toward renewed holiness,

toward liberating faithfulness,

toward (dare I say) revival.

I just said "revival" in a UCC church building. We should check for structural damage.

And the way forward involves…*you!!!* Yeah, you, the preacher!

You see, this passage of ours, Chapter 10, is oddly placed. In Revelation, we have seven trumpets blown consecutively, without interruption–*except here.* Now this interruption is not an editorial accident, a sloppy redaction; it is deliberate, intentional. You see, chapter 10 (my Latino brothers Justo González and Pablo Richard point out[5]) is the exact middle of the book of Revelation. Print out the entire book (in Greek) on one continuous sheet, then fold that paper in half. The crease: Revelation 10. Meaning, at the middle for this countercultural, radical message intended to challenge and empower a comfortable, lukewarm church; at the center of Revelation, is the preacher's encounter with the word! Verse 8: "Then the voice that I had heard from heaven spoke to me again, saying, 'Go, take the scroll that is open in the hand of the angel...'"

In the middle of this cosmic, transcendent, eschatological movement toward a radical, prophetic church to join God in God's renewal of heaven and earth is the preacher's engagement with the word!

As I see it, Revelation 10 (and its inspiration in Ezekiel[6]) is the only place in the Bible where we get a telling—a description, an enactment—of sermon prep. Revelation 10 is about sermon prep—but not ordinary, blah, status-quo sermon prep. This is church-agitating, faith-instilling, revival-inducing, revolution-stirring sermon prep.

The pivot point of God's great renewal, great reversal, great revolution is...you...the preacher! Preaching is that cosmic! You! (No pressure.)

Now let me tell you, fellow preachers, this ain't no quick, drive-by engagement with the word, business-as-usual reading of the text, no ordinary sermon prep: "So I took the little scroll from the hand of the angel and ate it..." (v. 10a).

John *eats* the word, internalizes it, is forced to slowly digest it (sit with it inside him, upsetting his stomach) before he prophesies to the "nations." This mystical encounter, apparently, was quite the Johannine practice. In our first reading from First John, we see that the preacher is having a similarly transcendent, multi-sensory encounter with the word. The opening line of First John: "We declare to you what was from the beginning, what we have heard, what we have seen with our eyes, what we have looked at and touched with our hands, concerning the word of life..."

The early-Church bishop St. Ignatius of Antioch called for this deepening engagement when he commanded the Church to take "refuge unto the gospel as unto the flesh of Jesus."[7] The process theologian Catherine Keller uses a different image, and asserts that truth is "interaction," or, better yet, "inter-activity."[8]

Interacting and interactive with, taking refuge in, hearing, seeing, touching...eating: central to heating up the lukewarm church is the *humble* preacher's encounter with the *cosmic* word—and nothing less than this will do.

To be the prophetic preachers we need to be, to proclaim the kind of word that will equip the church...

> to ward off the empire's allures of status and security and be countercultural,
>
> to be that "active resistance,"
>
> in order for the church to become drought resistant,

...we need to be pastors unafraid of a little tummy ache, humble yet bold enough to eat some word.

After all, we are called to preach a scandalous word, a revolutionary word—*good* news, not *nice* news. And once we've taken refuge in the word—

heard, seen, touched,...*eaten* the word—then we can preach for real! Then
we can "unveil," "uncover"[9] that scandalous good word about...

a creative God who turns chaos into life,

a liberating God who frees slaves from captivity,

a prophetic Spirit that calls for "justice [to] roll down like waters,
/ and righteousness like an ever-flowing stream,"[10]

an incarnated Word who preached good news to the poor and
liberty to the oppressed,

a risen Christ who conquered death,

a fiery Spirit who is poured with power, shaking upper rooms
everywhere!

We are called to cosmically preach a scandalous word, a revolutionary
word, and that word is a word of hope. Oh, church, let me tell you about
hope! Hope ain't pretty, cuddly or cute. The hope we proclaim is dangerous,
crazy, scandalous. Hope unsettles the stomach. For, this hope dares to
believe that...

Brokenness won't have the last word; healing will!

Sickness won't have the last word; wholeness will!

Sin won't have the last word; redemption will!

This hope dares to believe that...

Injustice won't have the last word; liberation will!

Oppression won't have the last word; justice will!

Demonic "-isms" and "-phobias" won't have the last word;
community will!

Death won't have the last word; life will!

The Devil won't have the last word; God will!

This preaching of dangerous hope, this cosmic preaching, ain't easy;
it's too heavy to bear. Yet if we dare eat the word, it will turn our stomachs
sour—for it is a heavy word, a dangerous word sharper than a two-edged
sword.

And yet...this heavy, dangerous, two-edged word is nonetheless a good
word, a liberating word, the kind of word that makes our joy complete.[11]
And, as such, it does tend to leave the subtlest hint of sweetness on our lips.

Derek Penwell

Derek Penwell was born in 1965 and spent most of his growing up years in Grand Rapids, Michigan. Originally from a family of preachers in the Christian Churches/Churches of Christ, he attended Great Lakes Christian College and Emmanuel School of Religion, where he received a BRE and a MAR. in Church History. Rev. Penwell then sought ministerial standing among the Christian Church (Disciples of Christ), attending Lexington Theological Seminary, where he completed a MDiv and a DMin After leaving seminary, Penwell served churches in Middlesboro, Kentucky, and Louisville, Kentucky, where he is currently pastor of Douglass Boulevard Christian Church. While in Louisville, Penwell completed his PhD in Humanities at the University of Louisville. He is the author of *The Mainliner's Survival Guide to the Post-Denominational World.*[1] Dr. Penwell is European American.

This sermon was preached in worship on the first Sunday after Epiphany, traditionally known as The Baptism of the Lord, in 2011, using the NRSV. The sermon takes as its focus God's determination to break down the barriers that separate us from both God and one another. The radical reordering of reality (spiritual, social, and political) under the reign of God addresses traditional Disciples' concerns about social justice, specifically connected, in this case, to baptism.

"Tearing Open the Heavens"

Mark 1:4–11

Seminary, as you might imagine, has occupied a great deal of my educational life. Heck, if you ask my wife, it's occupied a great deal of my *actual* life. I enjoyed seminary–each of the three different times I went. Seminary, like any other trade school, has certain points of emphasis. They want to teach you to think theologically, for instance–which is to say, they want to train you to view the world through the lens of a theologically informed faith.

When the country goes to war, for instance, they teach you to think of it not first in political terms (What will this mean for the party in power?) or economic terms (What is this going to cost me?) or even in practical terms (What will this mean for me and people I love?), but in theological terms (What does God think of war? How does Jesus view violence?). Sex, money, politics, justice–all of these things are meant, according to seminary, to be passed through the filter of our relationship to God and God's relationship to us as expressed in Christ.

Another biggie they teach you in seminary centers on one word. This word has to do with the minister's relationship to the world—in particular, her relationship to other people. You walk into Pastoral Counseling 101 all ready to learn about how to fix people, and they ruin your day by telling you that fixing people isn't your job.

"What do you mean? I thought fixing people *was* the job. That's why I came! The world's messed up. It needs fixing, and I'm the one for the job, because I know how the world ought to be. I have a *particularly* good idea of how *people* ought to be."

"Sorry, young master Freud, but that's not how it works. One of the most important things we can teach you has nothing to do with fixing anybody; it has to do with *boundaries.*"

"Huh?"

"Boundaries, my friend. We're here to teach you boundaries."

"Why is *that* such a big deal?"

"Well, you can never help anybody if you don't know where you end and other people begin."

Ministry, they teach you in seminary, is about having good boundaries. Otherwise, you get the idea that people have hired you to come in and fix them—or, perhaps, worse, that you're the main point of everything that goes on.

But people, generally speaking, don't want to be *fixed.* And those who *do* want you to fix them,…trust me, you learn very quickly there's not enough Transactional Analysis or Systems Theory in your ministerial tool kit for *those* people.

Boundaries. You've got to know your limits.

Mark, however, completely messes up the whole boundaries thing in our Gospel for this morning. Let me set the stage. The Gospel of Mark, unlike Matthew or Luke's Gospel, opens without any mention of Jesus' birth or early life. In Mark, Jesus shows up on the scene, fully grown and ready for baptism. No history. No background. No polite introductions.

Just John the Baptist—"the voice of one crying out in the wilderness: / 'Prepare the way of the Lord, / make his paths straight'" (Mk. 1:3). In fact, our passage this morning begins abruptly: "John the baptizer appeared in the wilderness, proclaiming a baptism of repentance for the forgiveness of sins." (1:4).

Who is John the baptizer? Where did he come from? No artful segues for Mark.

Then, after we meet John, Mark thrusts Jesus on us: "In those days Jesus came from Nazareth of Galilee and was baptized by John in the Jordan" (v. 9).

The next two verses, however, are the ones Mark's been chomping at the bit to get at: "And just as he was coming up out of the water, he saw the heavens torn apart and the Spirit descending like a dove on him. And a voice came from heaven, 'You are my Son, the Beloved; with you I am well pleased'" (vv. 10–11).

This is the first Sunday after Epiphany, the Sunday traditionally called The Baptism of Our Lord. Mark recounts the story in a straightforward manner. Short. Concise. No extra window-dressing. No flowery language. First, there's John. Then Jesus shows up, and John baptizes him. God identifies Jesus as the Son.

Next.

It would be easy to dismiss Mark's rather spare account of the baptism of Jesus as workmanlike and uninspiring, wouldn't it?

But there's a little nugget hidden in Mark's prosaic rendering of the scene–one that distinguishes it from Matthew's and Luke's telling of the story, setting up this short narrative as a crucial signpost for us. And it's found in one word. When Matthew and Luke tell this story, they use the tamer Greek word, *anoigo*–"to open up"–as in, when Jesus "came up from the water, suddenly the heavens were opened to him."

Anoigo. Open. Nice. Inviting. It's the word Matthew uses when he says, "Ask, and it will be given you; search, and you will find; knock, and the door will be opened for you" (7:7).

Anoigo. Open. It's the same word Luke uses when he says, "For everyone who asks receives, and everyone who searches finds, and for everyone who knocks, the door will be opened." (11:10).

See what I mean? Welcoming. Good liberals like *anoigo*. It's how we like to see ourselves.

Mark uses a different word. Much less polite. Instead of *anoigo*, Mark uses *schizo*. It means to split or tear apart. That's, of course, where we get the word *schizophrenia*–literally, to split or tear the mind in half.

"Okay," you say. "That's interesting, especially for the word nerds. But so what? Mark chooses 'tear open' instead of 'open up nicely.' What difference does *that* make?"

Well, if that were the *only* instance, I'd be just as dubious about its importance as you might be. If it were the case that Mark just used a more violent synonym than Matthew and Luke, it might be worth a mention, but certainly not the belaboring of it I'm doing.

Here's the thing, though. This isn't the only time Mark uses a form of *schizo*. He uses it another time, later in the Gospel. Way in the back, almost at the end. In the 15th chapter, Jesus is on the cross, and verse 37 says, "Then Jesus gave a loud cry and breathed his last." The next verse has this: "And the curtain of the temple was torn in two, from top to bottom."

Of course, the traditional interpretation of this act of the tearing of the temple curtain from top to bottom is that–because it's the curtain that separated the Holy of Holies (God's *true* home on earth) from the rest of the temple—it's a kind of metaphor for God's rending of the veil that separates heaven and earth.

Do you see what Mark has done? In rhetorical terms, it's called an *inclusio,* which is a device in which an author uses a word or phrase twice, as literary bookends. These bookends modify and interpret that which lies between.

All right. Enough with the pointy-headed explanations. Mark opens and closes the ministry of Jesus in spectacular fashion. He announces that in Jesus God has come among us. God has torn the veil that formerly separated humanity from the Divine, and this tearing is no sweet opening of a door. Open doors can be closed again. In Jesus, God has ripped the door off the hinges! God has transgressed the boundaries that separated us from God.

Since Jesus, there's no more, "You stay on your side of the car, and I'll stay on mine. Don't cross the invisible line."

In Jesus, God has announced an intention to barge right into the living room and take a seat in our favorite Barcalounger.

Now, at first blush, being in the presence of God sounds like what we regularly say we want, right? We talk about seeking God's face, standing in God's presence—as if we expect it to be a tranquil encounter: "Come right in. Take a seat. Have a nice cup of cocoa while you wait. God will be with you momentarily."

I'm not so sure. I think this whole God's-tearing-the-heavens-apart-to-get-at-us thing could turn out to be way more than we bargained for.

Don't get me wrong, I like the idea of Jesus' presence ripping a hole in the fabric of reality—to the extent that it proves we serve a God who cares about us, who will stop at nothing to be reconciled to us, who loves us enough to become *like* us; a God who breaks through the theological walls we construct to keep everything neat and orderly and everyone in their place. That's good stuff.

After Jesus, God is no longer an abstraction—"out there." God, in Christ, is "right here."

The problem, though, as I see it, is that "right here" doesn't strike me as a place many folks necessarily want God snooping around. I mean, what with the way things are in the world—children's dying in the night for lack of food and shelter; the elderly having to choose between buying their medicine or paying for heat; young African American men lining the cells in a bloated correctional system, while other young people are imprisoned by a financial system that encouraged them to take on stiflingly large debt to get an education; LGBTQAI folks sent to the back of the very dangerous and punitive social bus; animals factory farmed to make our Big Macs and Chicken McNuggets as cheap as possible; the environment overwhelmed by our ability to engineer machines (the by-products of which are strangling creation); political systems that ensure that the wealthy and the powerful retain their status, while the poor and the powerless are kept...poor and powerless. A God like that might cause some mischief.

I had a guy named John come into the office last week. He was a pretty big guy—leather jacket, beard, big workmen's hands. He just wanted to talk to a pastor. His wife died in July, after a nine-year battle with cancer. He's fighting for custody of his kids, because he's got a prison record. He can't find work. He's losing his house. His life is a mess.

After he finished this awful tale, he looked up at me, tears streaming down his face, and said, "Pastor, I don't know what to do. I keep praying for God to come and show me what I need to do. But I got nothing. Sometimes I wonder if maybe God is for other people—people who aren't like me. I keep waiting, but I haven't seen anything yet."

What could I say? I've taken the class. I've got good boundaries. I prayed with him, then took him to buy some gas.

But it occurs to me that my new friend, John, doesn't need a nice door-opening God; he needs Mark's God, a sky-ripping God—a God who's not satisfied with the way things are.

So here's the thing. If we've got a heavy investment in keeping the world situated the way it is, maybe having God kick down the front door isn't going to be that pleasant an experience for us.

If we think that our biggest responsibility revolves around trying to hang on to what we've got, then maybe having a God who's unconcerned about crossing boundaries is going to sound like *bad news*. The church, for its part, has a history of building walls to mark off its own theological territory. And if God just comes charging in, those theological markers are sure to take a beating; which means we have to contend not only with being in God's presence, but being in the theologically messy presence of one another.

If, however, all the boundaries in your world have been drawn to keep you out, to hold you where you are, to cut you off from life—maybe this transgressive, pushy, boundary-crashing God who tears open the heavens and comes to us in Jesus...is just the news you've been waiting to hear.

Maybe a little holy mischief isn't such a bad thing after all.

Sandhya Jha

In the church of the future, more ministers will resemble Sandhya Jha in their bi-vocationality. Rev. Jha (1976–) is founder and director of the Oakland Peace Center and is an anti-racism/anti-oppression trainer with Reconciliation Ministries for the Christian Church (Disciples of Christ). She is an ordained leader in interfaith and interracial work, shaped first by her Scottish mother and Indian father.

Jha received both a MDiv and Master of Public Policy from the University of Chicago. Her BA is from Johns Hopkins University.

The following was preached at a Presbyterian church after a stunning week in July 2016. National attention was on the shooting of two African American men by police officers in two different parts of the country, followed by the shooting deaths of five police officers by a sniper at a Black Lives Matter vigil in Dallas. In this sermon, you can sense how her role as a voice for reconciliation across racial and denominational lines informs a Church waking up to the already/not yet of post-racial America. Rev. Jha uses the NRSV.

Jha's published works, *Room at the Table*[1] and *Pre-Post-Racial America: Spiritual Stories from the Front Lines*,[2] continue to challenge the church to live more fully into the image of a "Welcome Table." *Publisher's Weekly* listed *Pre-Post-Racial America* as one of the top five books on race and religion in 2015.

"Reluctant Prophets"

Amos 7:12–15

It's a gift to be back with you again this Sunday; I feel like I'm with family whenever I'm here, and that's why Pastor Matt knows I'll say yes whenever he invites me to worship with you when he's on vacation.

I've just come back from a high school youth camp up in the Sierras. I don't know how true this is for you as Presbyterians, but I'm an ordained Disciples minister, and the thing about Disciples is we were shaped by the tent revival movements of the early 1800s. Youth camps are in our blood. They're important to me.

This year I was struck by how many of the youth look forward to that one week of camp each year as the one week of the year they get to be their whole selves; being a youth is so hard today. This is the place where they're not bullied, where they're not judged, where acting hard doesn't actually get them credit–but being vulnerable does. It was a diverse camp: diverse in race and gender identity and class and sexual orientation; and people worked hard to make sure everyone felt embraced and valued. There is something transcendent those youth get to experience for one week, and we try all week to figure out how to help them carry that experience of acceptance and vulnerability and interdependence back down the mountain with them.

Some of the youth wanted to learn about social justice, so I led a workshop with them. I told them that in the model of community organizing I use, faith-rooted organizing, we discern what we're called to organize around based on the question, "What is it that breaks your heart?" and invited them to share around the circle.

Now something you should know is that two guys in the workshop were Jacob, a white teenager from Santa Cruz, and Jeremiah, a black youth from Oakland. They had become tight over the week, and I sometimes sat with them at meals just because they made me laugh so hard.

When we got to Jacob, he said, "So I want to be a police officer," and he looked me in the eye and said "and Jeremiah already knows that," because he already knew the impact that sentence could have on someone from a different race and different community. He continued, "And it makes me so mad that some of these police officers go out there and kill black people for no good reason, because I want to help people, and people's first reaction when I tell them what I want to do is, 'Why would you want to be mixed up with people like that?'"

It's been a painful week. I don't know about you, but things feel insurmountable for me as a justice activist and peace maker right now. I'm not sure I want to bring a message of God caring most about those on the margins. And as an aside, I did say, God cares *MOST* about those on the margins. We often talk about how God loves all of us equally, but, over and over in the Bible, God shows a bias towards, a greater interest in, a greater investment in those who are struggling, who are reviled most. It's what theologian Gustavo Gutierrez calls "God's preferential option for the poor."

Times were hard for Amos too. He did not want to be a prophet. You heard the passage earlier today. Basically, the king says to Amos, "Don't you know where you are? Don't you know who I am? Show some respect!"

And Amos responds, "Listen; I raise cattle. I raise trees. I would not be here if I didn't have to. I'm only here because God made me."

And then he says this, and this is word-for-word from the passage following the one you heard today:

Now therefore hear the word of the LORD.
You say, "Do not prophesy against Israel,
and do not preach against the house of Isaac."
Therefore thus says the LORD:
"Your wife shall become a prostitute in the city,

and your sons and your daughters shall fall by the sword,
and your land shall be parceled out by line;
you yourself shall die in an unclean land,
and Israel shall surely go into exile away from its land." (Am.
7:16–17)

No wonder he didn't want the job.

Who wants to be a prophet?

I want to back up for a moment and ask the question: What is a prophet? My mother used to teach sixth grade Sunday school, and she had a great description. She said, "Prophets aren't people who can magically predict the future. They're more saying that if we don't eat our vegetables and only eat ribs, we're likely to have heart issues."

Someone had to tell Israel what the natural result of injustice would be if we were ever going to live God's dream for us, even though it could be a pretty thankless job.

According to Bible scholar Walter Brueggemann, there's a prophetic arc that shows up everywhere in the Bible: in Moses' prophecies to Pharaoh, in the books of every Hebrew prophet, and in Jesus' own prophetic teachings. The prophetic arc goes like this:

Because you are out of alignment with God's will, here are some horrible things that will happen to you.

God wants you to live into this other way of being, a more faithful one, a more just one, one that honors the dignity of all people. If you live into this other way of being, here is the glorious life you will get to experience.[3]

Amos has something to teach us today. In America, we are living the natural outgrowth of fear and racism. If you don't believe me, look at the current presidential race and the issues that shape it. Immigrants and Muslims and young black men are painted as barely human, objects to be feared, and, as a result, their safety is legitimately at risk. And the thing about fear and racism is that everyone gets hurt.

God needs reluctant prophets today.

Our youth go to camp to get away from what is hard in the world. They did not have access to their cell phones or iPads, to aid in their escape. As the adults heard the news around the country, we wrestled with whether to break into the youth's escape. We were all reluctant prophets that week.

On Tuesday, we told the kids about Philando Castile and Alton Sterling. And we prayed, knowing that could be Jeremiah.

On Thursday, we told them about the shooting of the police in Dallas, knowing that could be Jacob.

It is hard to be hopeful right now.

In this time, my hope lies in a Jesus who forgives my shortcomings and welcomes me to the table.

In this time, my hope lies in youth who want to create a world where Jeremiah and Jacob can live and thrive together and not fear each other.

In this time, my hope lies in this congregation's growing in courage to become the reluctant prophets to end the systemic racism that limits our ability to be in full relationship with each other.

In this time, my hope lies in the fact that Amos did not *want* to speak out but *had* to; and, because he did, the world got better.

When we listen to God's call, when we do not want to speak out but have to, the world will get better.

Thanks be to God.

Contributing Editors

Churches of Christ

- **Dave Bland,** Professor of Homiletics, and Director of the Doctor of Ministry Program, Harding School of Theology

- **David Fleer,** Professor of Homiletics, and Director of the Conference on Preaching, and Chair of the Christian Scholars Conference, Lipscomb University

- **Tim Sensing,** Professor of Ministry and Associate Dean of the Graduate School of Theology, Abilene Christian University

Christian Churches/Churches of Christ

- **Joseph Grana II,** Dean, Pacific Christian College of Ministry, and Professor of Church Ministry, Hope International University

- **Bruce Shields,** Russell F. and Marion J. Blowers Professor of Christian Ministry Emeritus, Emmanuel Christian Seminary at Milligan College.

Christian Church (Disciples of Christ)

- **Ronald Allen,** Professor of Preaching, and Gospels and Letters, Christian Theological Seminary

- **Mary Alice Mulligan,** Minister, Westview Christian Church (Disciples of Christ), Indianapolis, and Affiliate Professor Preaching and Ethics, Christian Theological Seminary

- **Casey Sigmon,** Adjunct Professor, Saint Paul School of Theology

- **Richard W. Voelz,** Assistant Professor of Preaching and Worship, Union Presbyterian Seminary

Notes

Introduction to the Volume: Preaching in the
Stone-Campbell Movement 1968–2018

[1] W. T. Moore, ed., *The Living Pulpit of the Christian Church: A Series of Discourses, Doctrinal and Practical, from Representative Men among the Disciples of Christ* (Cincinnati: R.W. Carroll, 1868), and W. T. Moore, ed., *The New Living Pulpit: A Series of Discourses, Doctrinal and Practical, from Representative Men among the Disciples of Christ* (St. Louis: Christian Board of Publication, 1918).

[2] Hunter Beckelhymer, *The Vital Pulpit of the Christian Church: A Series of Sermons by Representative Men among the Disciples of Christ* (St. Louis: Bethany Press, 1969).

[3] Fred B. Craddock, *As One Without Authority: Essays on Inductive Preaching* (Enid, Okla.: Phillips University Press, 1971; St. Louis: Chalice Press, 4th edition, 2001).

[4] As a quick internet search shows, this phrase was very common, especially among evangelical preachers.

[5] See Lee Sparks & Kathryn Hayes Sparks, eds., *Craddock on the Craft of Preaching* (St. Louis: Chalice Press, 2011), 61.

[6] Craddock, 13–14.

[7] Craddock, 35–37.

[8] Craddock, 50–51.

[9] See Hughes Oliphant Old, *The Reading and Preaching of the Scriptures in the Worship of the Christian Church, Volume 7: Our Own Time* (Grand Rapids, Mich.: William B. Eerdmans Publishing, 2010), 87–172.

[10] Eugene Lowry, *The Homiletical Plot: The Sermon as Narrative Art Form* (Louisville: Westminster John Knox Press, 1980).

[11] Fred B. Craddock, *Preaching* (Nashville: Abingdon Press, 1985), 167.

Fred B. Craddock, "Attending a Baptism"

[1] This sermon first appeared in Fred B. Craddock, *Cherry Log Sermons* (Louisville: Westminster John Knox Press, 2001), 7–12. It appears here with permission.

Section One: Churches of Christ
Orientation to Preaching in the Churches of Christ 1968–2018

[1] Flavil Yeakley, *Good News and Bad News: A Realistic Assessment of Churches of Christ in the United States 2008* (Searcy, Ark.: s.p., 2008; pdf available online), 3.

[2] *Churches of Christ in the United States*, 2015 edition, compiled by Carl Royster (Nashville: 21st Century Christian, 2015), 42.

[3] Lynn Anderson, personal communication, June 2016.

[4] Michael W. Casey, "Preaching," *The Encyclopedia of the Stone Campbell Movement*, ed. Douglas A. Foster, Paul M. Blowers, Anthony L. Dunnavant, and D. Newell Williams (Grand Rapids, Mich.: Eerdmans, 2004), 607.

[5] Tim Sensing, "Finding Practical Theology's Location," *The Effective Practice of Ministry: Essays in Honor of Charles Siburt*, ed. Tim Sensing (Abilene, Tex.: ACU Press, 2013), 33–34.

[6] Charles W. Koller, *Expository Preaching Without Notes plus Sermons Preached Without Notes* (Grand Rapids, Mich.: Baker Book House, 1962). Koller's text was often the textbook for Jones's courses at Harding.

[7] Craig S. Churchill, "Lectureship," *The Encyclopedia of the Stone Campbell Movement*, 468.

[8] Ibid. Other schools followed suit: Harding University, 1924; Freed-Hardeman University, 1937; Pepperdine University, 1943; Lipscomb University, 1947; Oklahoma Christian University, 1950; and Lubbock Christian University, 1957.

[9] Ibid., quoted from William S. Banowsky, *The Mirror of a Movement* (Dallas: Christian Pub. Co, 1965).

[10] Austin Graduate School of Theology Sermon Seminar brochure, 2018.

[11] Richard T. Hughes, *Reviving the Ancient Faith: The Story of Churches of Christ in America* (Grand Rapids, Mich.: Eerdmans, 1996), 368.

[12] Others joined them at their respective schools. Most notably were John York at Lipscomb and Andre Resner, Tim Sensing, Jerry Taylor, Stephen Johnson, and Randy Harris at ACU.

[13] Hughes, *Reviving the Ancient Faith,* 372.

[14] Ron Allen, "Theology Undergirding Narrative Preaching," *What's the Shape of Narrative Preaching?* ed. Mike Graves and David J. Schlafer (St. Louis: Chalice Press, 2008), 27.

[15] Timothy R. Sensing, *Pedagogies of Preaching*, unpublished dissertation, University of North Carolina at Greensboro, 1988, 8–12.

[16] Haddon W. Robinson, *Biblical Preaching: The Development and Delivery of Expository Messages* (Grand Rapids, Mich.: Baker Book House, 1980).

[17] However, *Finding Their Voices: Sermons by Women in the Churches of Christ,* ed. D'Esta Love (Abilene, Tex.: ACU Press, 2015) has published 29 sermons that are mostly narrative, representing the best in biblical studies, homiletics, and, proleptically, pulpits in Churches of Christ.

[18] Phillips Brooks, *Lectures on Preaching* (New York: E. P. Dutton and Company, 1877), 5. We have not changed male specific language for humanity when it occurs in quotations from a previous era.

[19] Ibid., 8.

Batsell Barrett Baxter, "The Beautiful People"

[1] Batsell Barrett Baxter, *The Heart of the Yale Lectures* (New York: Macmillan Co, 1947).

[2] Richard T. Hughes, *Reviving the Ancient Faith: The Story of Churches of Christ in America* (Grand Rapids, Mich.: Eerdmans), 242.

[3] Ibid., 243.

[4] Adam Clarke, *Clarke's Commentary: The Holy Bible Containing the Old and New Testaments with a Commentary and Critical Notes* (Nashville: Abingdon Press, 1977), 1:228.

[5] *The Beautiful Gleaner: A Study in the Principles of Beauteous Character* (Montgomery, Ala: Sound Doctrine, 1945), 22.

[6] In the original preaching, Baxter told Latimer's story in detail. Because of limited space, the editors reduced the story to the reference above.

J.S. Winston, "Beware Covetousness of Authority: A Sin"

[1] Edward J. Robinson, *The Fight Is on in Texas: A History of African American Churches of Christ in the Lone Star State, 1865–2000* (Abilene, Tex.: ACU Press, 2008), 105.

[2] R. E. Hooper, *A Distinct People: A History of the Churches of Christ in the 20th Century* (West Monroe, La.: Howard Publishing, 1993), 276.

[3] Ibid., 269.

Jimmy Allen, "The Great Meeting All Will Attend"

[1] Richard T. Hughes, *Reviving the Ancient Faith: The Story of Churches of Christ in America* (Grand Rapids, Mich.: Eerdmans), 364–65.

[2] The original sermon had several places where space restrictions have required abbreviation. We have inserted ellipses to indicate those. The editors worked hard to retain the meaning and logical flow of the sermon.

Andrew Hairston, "A Divine Requirement: A Faith That Will Stand"

[1] For historical purposes, masculine referents for God have been left as originally preached (ed.).

Jim McGuiggan, "God's Self-imposed Mission"

[1] http://www.history.com/news/history-lists/10-things-you-may-not-know-about-genghis-khan (accessed October 30, 2017). For publication, some websites were recently accessed here and elsewhere in the text to support sermon claims (ed.).

[2] https://www.britannica.com/place/Gulag (accessed October 30, 2017)

[3] https://en.wikipedia.org/wiki/World_War_II_casualties (accessed October 30, 2017)

Lynn Anderson, "Places in the Heart"

[1] Lynn Anderson, *They Smell Like Sheep: Spiritual Leadership for the 21st Century* (West Monroe, La.: Howard Books, 1997).

Rubel Shelly, "Loving Someone Who Isn't 'One of Us'"

[1] Rubel Shelly, *The Lamb and His Enemies* (Nashville: 21st Century Christian, 2013).

Samuel Twumasi-Ankrah, "For God So Loved the World…"

[1] Passages in this sermon that may seem anti-Jewish have been left as originally preached (ed.).

[2] Here, Twumasi quotes the poem "Credo" by John Oxenham. Space restrictions forced us to cut it (ed.).

[3] Story told with permission from Dr. Tommy Drinnen, Knoxville, Tenn.

[4] UNICEF. "Malaria & children: Progress in intervention coverage." United Nations Children's Fund. Accessed 2006, http://www.unicef.org/health/files/MalariaOct6forweb_final.pdf

[5] Nair, Nani, Fraser Wares and Suvanand Sahu. "Tuberculosis in the WHO South-East Asia Region." World Health Organization. Accessed 2006. http://www.ncbi.nlm.nih.gov/pmc/articles/PMC2828794/

[6] "The Worsening Doctor-Patient Ratio…". *The Chronicle*. Accessed 2006. http://thechronicle.com.gh/the-worsening-doctor-patient-ratio/

[7] C. S. Calian, "The Challenge of John 3:16 for Theological Education," *The Christian Century*, Feb. 5-12, 1986.

Mark Frost, "You Can't Handle the Ruth!"

[1] John Burke, *No Perfect People Allowed* (Grand Rapids, Mich.: Zondervan, 2005), 42.

Mike Cope, "Great Is Thy Faithfulness"

[1] Mike Cope, *Megan's Secrets: What My Mentally Disabled Daughter Taught Me about Life* (Abilene, Tex.: Leafwood Publishers, 2011).

Section Two: Christian Churches/Churches of Christ
Orientation to Preaching in the Christian Churches/Churches of Christ, 1968–2018

[1] W. T. Moore, ed., *The Living Pulpit of the Christian Church: A Series of Discourses, Doctrinal and Practical, from Representative Men among the Disciples of Christ* (Cincinnati: R.W. Carroll, 1868), 33.

[2] Ibid., 86

[3] Ibid., 326.

Russell F. Blowers, "The Anatomy of a Preacher's Heart"

[1] Phillips Brooks, *Lectures on Preaching* (New York: E. P. Dutton, 1878), 5.

Marshall Leggett, "Blessing of Christian Baptism"

[1] Norman J. Clayton, "Now I Belong to Jesus," in *The Hymnal for Worship and Celebration* (Waco, Tex.: Word Music, 1986), 511.

Robert Shannon, "The Fox and the Lamb"

[1] Reprinted from *Pulpit Digest,* January/February, 1982.

[2] Cited in Arthur Mee, John Alexander Hammerton, and S.S. McClure, eds., *The World's Greatest Books* (New York: McKinlay, Stone, and Mackenzie, 1910), 14:266.

[3] Cited, for example, in D.A. Carson, *Christ and Culture Revisted* (Grand Rapids: Wm. B. Eerdmans Publishing Co., 2008), 208.

Myron J. Taylor, "The Sacrament of Continuance"

[1] Myron J. Taylor, *Preacher of the Gospel: Myron Jackson Taylor* (Los Angeles, Calif.: Westwood Hills Christian Church, 1999).

[2] Myron Taylor, *Proclaiming the Risen Lord* (Johnson City, Tenn.: Emmanuel School of Religion Press, 2006).

[3] Myron Taylor, *True Faith and Sound Learning* (Johnson City, Tenn.: Emmanuel School of Religion Press, 2007).

[4] Myron Taylor, *Where God Meets Us* (Encino, Calif.: Taylor Publishing, 2008).

[5] Myron Taylor, *One God and Father of Us All* (Encino, Calif.: Taylor Publishing, 2010).

[6] © Myron Taylor, 1997. Used by permission.

[7] N. T. Wright, *For All God's Worth: True Worship and the Calling of the Church* (Grand Rapids, Mich.; Cambridge, UK: Eerdmans, 1997, new ed. 2014), 73.

[8] Paul Tillich, *Systematic Theology* (Chicago: University of Chicago Press, 1951, paperback ed. 1973), 1:123.

[9] P. T. Forsyth, *The Church and the Sacraments* (London: Independent Press, n.d.), 234.

[10] From the *Westminster Larger Catechism* 1647, answer to Q170.

[11] Oscar Cullmann, *Christ and Time: The Primitive Christian Conception of Time and History,* trans. Floyd V. Filson (Philadelphia: The Westminster Press, 1964), 84.

[12] C. H. Dodd, *The Apostolic Preaching and its Development* (New York and Evanston: Harper & Row Publishers, 1964), 94.

Cal Jernigan, "There's More to Life than Me"

[1] http://www.historylearningsite.co.uk/medieval-england/the-black-death-of-1348-to-1350/ (accessed October 30, 2017)

[2] https://en.wikipedia.org/wiki/Black_Death (accessed October 30, 2017).

[3] https://en.wikipedia.org/wiki/1918_flu_pandemic (accessed October 30, 2017)

[4] Shirley MacLaine, quoted in Charles Colson, *Loving God* (Grand Rapids: Zondervan Publishing Co., 1986), 11.

[5] Robert Roberts, *An Essay in Aid of Moral Psychology* (Cambridge: Cambridge University Press, 2003) quoted by Dave Stone, "A Reason for Self-Denial," sermon given at Southeast Christian Church, Louisville.

[6] Dietrich Bonhoeffer, *The Cost of Discipleship* (reprint, New York: Macmillan Company, 1963), 99.

[7] Malcom Muggeridge quoted in Thomas E. Trask and Wayde I. Goodall, *The Fruit of the Spirit: Becoming the Person God Wants You to Be* (Grand Rapids, Mich.: Zondervan Publishing Co., 2000), 56.

Jodi Hickerson, "The Crossing: Life Verse"

[1] Lewis Smedes, *Shame and Grace: Healing the Shame We Don't Deserve* (San Francisco: HarperSanFrancisco, 2009), 9-10

[2] The preacher composed this poem.

Bob Russell, "Why I Love the Church"

[1] Bob Russell, *After 50 Years of Ministry: 7 Things I Would Do Differently and 7 Things I Would Do the Same* (Chicago: Moody Publishers, 2016).

[2] ©2009 Bob Russell Ministries (Louisville).

³ On the growth of the early church: "Spread of Christianity," https://en.wikipedia.org/wiki/History_of_early_Christianity (accessed October 30, 2017)

⁴ John Adams, *The Wisdom of John Adams,* ed. Kees de Moy. (New York: Citadel, 2003), 56.

LeRoy Lawson, "Ebenezer and Me"

¹ Robert Robinson, "Come, Thou Fount of Every Blessing," hymn 16, *The Chalice Hymnal* (St. Louis: Chalice Press, 1995). Words in the public domain.

² George Duffield, "Stand Up, Stand Up for Jesus," hymn 613, *The Chalice Hymnal.* Words in the public domain.

Bob Mink, "This Is Jesus Angry"

¹ Bob Mink, *A Pastor and the People: An Inside Look through Letters* (San Bernardino, Calif.: Amazon Digital Services, 2015).

² Bob Mink, *Questioning Jesus* (San Bernardino, Calif.: Amazon Digital Services, 2016).

Mark Scott, "Kingdom Preaching"

¹ Francis Chan and Danae Yankoski, *Forgotten God: Reversing Our Tragic Neglect of the Holy Spirit* (Colorado Springs: David C. Cook, 2009), 16.

² Ibid., 142.

³ We have been unable to locate a citation for this nursery rhyme, which Boyce Mouton says he memorized from an old phonograph record years ago (ed.).

⁴ Joel Gregory is given credit for the story. From a "Preaching Today" sermon tape on Mark 7 titled "He Could Not Be Hid."

Section Three: Christian Church (Disciples of Christ)
Orientation to Preaching in the Christian Church
(Disciples of Christ) 1968–2018

¹ William G. West, "Toward a Theology of Preaching," in *The Renewal of Church: The Panel of Scholars Report,* Vol. 2, *The Reconstruction of Theology,* ed. Ralph G. Wilburn (St. Louis: Bethany, 1963), 243–44.

² Ibid., 244.

³ Sharon E. Watkins, "Principles of Identity as Articulated by the 21st Century Vision Team," in *Whole: A Call to Unity in Our Fragmented World* (St. Louis: Chalice Press, 2014), 117.

⁴ Joseph E. Faulkner, "What Are They Saying? A Content Analysis of 206 Sermons Preached in the Christian Church (Disciples of Christ) during 1988," in *A Case Study of Mainstream Protestantism: The Disciples Relation to American Culture, 1880-1989,* ed. D. Newell Williams (Grand Rapids, Mich.: Eerdmans, 1991), 438.

⁵ Neal Kentch, "'Vox Populi Vox Dei': Toward a Definition of Preaching," in *Interpreting Disciples: Practical Theology in the Disciples of Christ* (Fort Worth: TCC Press, 1987), 144.

⁶ Joseph R. Jeter Jr., "Preaching Among Disciples of Christ," in *Disciples Theological Digest 7,* no. 1 (1992), 13.

⁷ Ibid., 5–19.

⁸ For a sense of "preaching at the double feast," see also Mary Alice Mulligan, "Teaching Disciples to Preach in the Service of Word and Table," in *Preaching at the Double Feast: Homiletics for Eucharistic Worship,* ed. Michael Monshau, O.P. (Collegeville, Minn.: Liturgical Press, 2006), 46–110.

⁹ This is not to say that we lacked a diversity of preachers during those years, rather that those voices were silenced by the editors at that time. See C.T. Sigmon, "Clara Babcock to Again Occupy the Pulpit: Reclaiming Her Voice as Preacher and Pioneer in Disciples of Christ History," in *Restoration Quarterly* 55:3 (2013). Note that

the previous three volumes in this series (1868, 1918, 1968) did not contain *any* sermons from women preachers.

[10] Ronald J. Allen, *Interpreting the Gospel: An Introduction to Preaching* (St. Louis: Chalice Press, 1998).

Mary Louise Rowand, "Three-Letter Words Can Be Worse"

[1] http://archiver.rootsweb.ancestry.com/th/read/ OBITUARIES/2008-07/1216606299. Accessed September 11, 2016.

[2] The beginning of the sermon is adapted from Fae Malania, *The Quantity of a Hazelnut* (New York: Alfred A. Knopf, 1968), 129–32.

[3] Ibid., 132.

[4] In this quote, we left male specific language for humanity, recognizing that inclusive language would not be the norm for Disciples preachers until a few years after this sermon. Rev. Rowand's sermon manuscript does not give the precise source of the quote; it seems to come from an oral presentation. The editors have been unable to locate it in the Van Harvey corpus.

[5] Alfred Tennyson, "Maud; A Monodrama, Part 1" in *The Works of Alfred Lord Tennyson* (Hertfordshire, Great Britain: Wordsworth Editions Limited, 1994), 388.

[6] Carlyle Marney, "Company of Betrayers," a sermon in his *The Crucible of Redemption: The Meaning of the Cross-Resurrection Event I* (Nashville: Abingdon Press, 1968), 15–21.

[7] Ibid., 19–20.

[8] Medical Mission Sisters, "The Great Banquet," at http://lyrics.wikia.com/wiki/ Medical_Mission_Sisters:Wedding_Banquet. Accessed February 8, 2017.

Norman Reed, "Can We Be One?"

[1] Thomas Campbell, *Declaration and Address of the Christian Association of Washington County, Washington, Pa.* (Washington, Pa.: Brown and Sample, 1809), 1.

[2] John Fawcett, "Blest Be the Tie that Binds," hymn 433, *The Chalice Hymnal* (St. Louis: Chalice Press, 1995). Words in the public domain.

Ronald Osborn, "Faith"

[1] Ronald E. Osborn, *Folly of God: The Rise of Christian Preaching* (St. Louis: Chalice Press, 1999).

[2] Fred B. Craddock, *The Gospels* (Nashville: Abingdon Press, 1981), 20.

Michael Kinnamon, "Bold Humility"

[1] Michael Kinnamon, *The Vision of the Ecumenical Movement and How It Has Been Impoverished by Its Friends* (St. Louis: Chalice Press, 2003).

[2] Michael Kinnamon and Jan Linn, *Disciples: Reclaiming Our Identity, Reforming Our Practice* (St. Louis: Chalice Press, 2009).

[3] Michael Kinnamon, *Can a Renewal Movement Be Renewed? Questions for the Future of Ecumenism* (Grand Rapids, Mich.: Wm. B. Eerdmans, 2014).

[4] Michael Kinnamon, *The Witness of Religion in an Age of Fear* (Louisville: Westminster John Knox, 2017).

Delores Carpenter, "God's Female Activists"

[1] The story of her call, "Acceptance of the Call at a Funeral," is included in William H. Myers, ed., *The Irresistible Urge to Preach* (Atlanta: Aaron Press, 1992), 64–70.

[2] Delores C. Carpenter, *A Time for Honor: A Portrait of African American Clergywomen* (St. Louis: Chalice Press, 2001).

[3] Fanny F. Crosby, "To God be the Glory," hymn 72, *Chalice Hymnal* (St. Louis: Chalice Press, 1995).

Cynthia Hale "Do This in Remembrance of Me!"

[1] Cynthia Hale, *I'm a Piece of Work: Sisters Shaped by God* (Valley Forge, Pa.: Judson Press, 2010).

[2] The editors note there are multiple viewpoints on the relationship of the old and new covenants. Many Disciples today acknowledge the continuing validity of the covenant God made with the people of Israel.

[3] Robert Lowry, "What Can Wash Away My Sins?" http://www.hymnary.org/text/what_can_wash_away_my_sin. Accessed February 9, 2017. Words in the public domain.

Allen Harris, "Palms, Principalities and Powers, and Passion"

[1] Rita Nakashima Brock, *Atonement Theology: The Ideological Root of Christian Terrorism*, http://twofriarsandafool.com/2011/08/atonement-theology-the-ideological-root-of-christian-terrorism/. Accessed February 9, 2017.

[2] Ibid.

[3] Walter Brueggeman, *Mandate to Difference: An Invitation to the Contemporary Church* (Louisville: Westminster John Knox Press, 2007), 16–24.

[4] Marcus Borg and John Dominic Crossan, *The Last Week: What the Gospels Really Teach about Jesus's Final Days in Jerusalem* (New York: HarperCollins, 2006).

[5] "Dr. Marcus J. Borg: On John 3:16," http://day1.org/2897-dr_marcus_j_borg_on_john_316. Accessed February 24, 2017.

José Francisco Morales, "Sweet and Sour"

[1] President Barack Obama, prior to the Presidency, was a member of Trinity United Church of Christ in Chicago.

[2] Brian K. Blount, *Can I Get A Witness? Reading Revelation through African-American Culture* (Louisville: Westminster John Knox Press, 2005), 37.

[3] Cf. Revelation 2:4.

[4] Cf. Revelation 3:15, 16.

[5] Cf. Pablo Richard, *Apocalypse: A People's Commentary on the Book of Revelation* (Maryknoll, N.Y.: Orbis Books, 1995), 77–79; Justo L. González, *For the Healing of the Nations: The Book of Revelation in an Age of Cultural Conflict* (Maryknoll, N.Y.: Orbis Books, 1999), 85–88.

[6] Cf. Ezekiel 3:1–3.

[7] *Letter to the Philadelphians* 5. 2. http://www.earlychristianwritings.com/text/ignatius-philadelphians-hoole.html. Accessed February 9, 2017.

[8] Catherine Keller, *On the Mystery: Discerning Divinity in Process* (Minneapolis: Fortress Press, 2008), 31.

[9] *Apocalypsis* comes from the Greek ἀποκαλύπτω (*apokaluptó*), meaning to uncover, reveal, or unveil.

[10] Amos 5:24.

[11] On joy being made complete, see 1 John 1:4.

Derek Penwell, "Tearing Open the Heavens"

[1] Derek Penwell, *The Mainliner's Survival Guide to the Post-Denominational World* (St. Louis: Chalice Press, 2014).

Sandhya Jha, "Reluctant Prophets"

[1] Sandhya Jha, *Room at the Table: Struggle for Unity and Equality in Disciples History* (St. Louis: Chalice Press, 2009).

[2] Sandhya Jha, *Pre-Post-Racial American: Spiritual Stories from the Front Lines* (St. Louis: Chalice Press, 2015).

[3] Walter Brueggemann, *The Practice of Prophetic Imagination: Preaching an Emancipating Word* (Minneapolis: Fortress, Press, 2012), 1-201.